HORIZONTAL VERTIGO

HORIZONTAL VERTIGO

A City Called Mexico

JUAN VILLORO

Translated from the Spanish
by Alfred MacAdam

PANTHEON BOOKS   NEW YORK

All rights reserved. Published in the United States by Pantheon Books,
a division of Penguin Random House LLC, New York, and distributed
in Canada by Penguin Random House Canada Limited, Toronto.
Originally published in Mexico as *El vértigo horizontal* by
Almadía Ediciones S.A.P.I. de C.V., Mexico City, in 2018.
Copyright © 2018 by Almadía Ediciones and Juan Villoro.
Prologue copyright © 2018 by Néstor García Canclini

Pantheon Books and colophon are registered trademarks
of Penguin Random House LLC.

Library of Congress Cataloging-in-Publication Data
Names: Villoro, Juan, [date] author. MacAdam, Alfred J., [date] translator.
Title: Horizontal vertigo : a city called Mexico / Juan Villoro ;
translated from the Spanish by Alfred MacAdam.
Other titles: Vértigo horizontal. English.
Description: First American edition. New York : Pantheon Books, 2021.
Identifiers: LCCN 2020031282 (print). LCCN 2020031283 (ebook).
ISBN 9781524748883 (hardcover). ISBN 9781524748890 (ebook).
Subjects: LCSH: Mexico City (Mexico)—Civilization—21st century.
Mexico City (Mexico)—Social life and customs—21st century.
Classification: LCC F1386 .V5713 2021 (print) |
LCC F1386 (ebook) | DDC 972/.53—dc23
LC record available at lccn.loc.gov/2020031282
LC ebook record available at lccn.loc.gov/2020031283

www.pantheonbooks.com

Front-of-jacket images: (top) sirtravelalot/Shutterstock;
(middle, Mexico City) Luis Emilio Villegas Amador/EyeEm/Getty Images;
(bottom, Pyramid of Kukulkan, Chichen Itza)
Kofi Adjebeng/EyeEm/Getty Images
Spine-of-jacket image: (El Angel de Independencia, Mexico City)
© fitopardo/Moment/Getty Images

Jacket design by Tyler Comrie

Manufactured in Canada
First American Edition
2 4 6 8 9 7 5 3 1

Regarding these things I artlessly express, which cause astonishment when seen and give so much pleasure, and about which I could say a great deal, well, when I think about them, I'm really shocked, because they bear such a strangeness that even I can't manage to understand what they are.

—JUAN DE LA CUEVA, *Epistle to Master Sánchez de Obregón, First Corregidor of Mexico*

We aren't united by love but by horror.
That's probably why I love it so much.

—JORGE LUIS BORGES, *Buenos Aires*

Contents

Prologue

Making an Agglomeration Look Like a City

Néstor García Canclini

Those of us who inhabit a megalopolis are made uncomfortable by some of the studies carried out by social scientists. Is the order they create to group facts believable? Is their organization of numbers, of kinds of behaviors, of the frequency charts of accidents and thefts over the course of years all that well reasoned for those of us who on a daily basis experiment with less safe streets at different hours of the day or night and try to put up with the traffic and other kinds of chaos all in order to find meaning and relief in the great disorder?

This book is not lacking the statistics or real estate and police accounts we use to explain Mexico City, but to decipher "the surfeit and whimsies of living in this place," where "the figure of the *flâneur* who strolls along intending to get lost on the trail of a surprise was replaced by that of the deported person" (who can't go home again), Juan Villoro gathers together those who narrated the city and discusses things with them. He knows the witnesses who documented Mexico City when it was only the historic center, then he passes through "a tide of low houses" and wonders where we're going when towers 820 feet high spring up. Are we really exaggerating when we believe those heights exceptional?

Our doubts are put to the test by *Horizontal Vertigo* when it compares our megalopolis with facts and stories about Buenos Aires and New York or when it recalls what shocked so many foreigners in other times about the capital of Mexico. He weaves together ethnographies of the Mixcoac neighborhood he lived in as a child with ceremonies in which the Cry of Independence is celebrated or when national heroes (Obregón) and foreign heroes (Hernán Cortés) are honored. As an expert who participated in the group that produced the recent constitution of Mexico City, Villoro notes all the clues as to how it was written and forgotten. He contrasts official excesses with the stories of those who administer daily monotony: office boys, conscripts, wrestlers, "the accidental installation artists" who decorate public parking lots or hang shoes on electric lines.

At times these investigations are dense, like those, as Clifford Geertz says, that anthropologists carry out. For example, the well-documented study of street children. But his gaze is just as incisive in more ludic accounts such as that on the Tepito market, the Chopo market, the bureaucracy of the capital, the holidays, and the theme parks. The pleasure of the text derives from this uninhibited mix of styles and uncertainties.

There is an element of "I'll bet I can do this" in trying to write *one* book about "a city where people live in millions of different ways." Villoro accepts the challenge by taking charge of different generations in a single family, without turning his back on the adventures his own has had. In this palimpsest of memories, of abandoned houses and others where people live as if they were abandoned, of infinite and infinitely varied interior patios, intermediary terraces, storage closets, cafés, and the poems that evoke them, of gas stations right next to the mausoleums of heroes, temples dedicated to lost causes, and simple weather issues, it's almost scandalous, the author says, that so many cities "bear the same name."

"The infinite demands strategies to become something close to us." Making things that are disconcertingly near to us, the thing that reduces distances: that's the chronicler's ingeniousness. But how do you go about setting up a book, a coherent or at least credible interpretation, by means of this "total immersion journalism" that ventures into territories and ruins that are so diverse? There is no interpretation, but there is a book. The book's strategy is to isolate those points where disorder manifests itself in ways that seem urban, behind the trademarks and logos, those "toponymics of No Place," as John Berger calls them.

Shortly after reading Villoro's manuscript, actually, his palimpsest, there appeared a book about another multicultural city, a book that had its orders (never just one): Jorge Carrión's book on Barcelona. That book made Villoro's clearer to me. Why when the various examples of a metropolis are defined by pedestrians, the number of cars, speed, or traffic, does Carrión analyze the Catalan capital using side streets? Because, says Carrión, in each side street "we find the affirmation and negation of the entire city." Those passageways, hyperlinks, connections between places or concepts that are neither roads nor streets, ignore or elude by pausing the vertigo of traffic. Barcelona's side streets are footnotes, tunnels that take us "to what is beneath the page, beneath the urban text."

Villoro and Carrión, heterodox disciples of Walter Benjamin, ferret out metropolitan meanings digging around in the detours through which their respective cities at least become legible if not organized. Their points of reference are closer to the scraps of paper on the streets, what people talk about, their ways of strolling around and inventing side streets than they are in maps without garbage, than the division of Mexico City in administrative zones and other arbitrary notions.

Horizontal Vertigo connects with family patterns, the rites of the inhabitants, their sacred and lay processions, even profane processions, like those told by the street vendors and "Paquita from the Neighborhood." Villoro offers explanations; it's often clear he's studied the sociology and the economy of the Mexican capital. Nevertheless, what he pursues above all is to reconnect our links to the city by means of notes on the things that bind us together, what make us from this place. This book stakes out its territory in an intermediary passage between his celebrated tweets, later published in newspapers and magazines, and his novels, or the novels of so many others determined to decipher the Federal District, which is now Mexico City.

"You are from the place where you gather garbage," he wrote after the September 2017 earthquake, "The one who gives away his medicine because his horror is cured," "The one who went to get his children at school./ The one who thought about people who had children at school./ The one who was left without batteries./ The one who went out onto the street to lend his cell phone./ The one who entered an abandoned shop to steal and repented in a mall." Every one of those verses could be a tweet; poems being another form of writing a chronicle. The descriptions of the city's people after the earthquake can name, one after another, the things this citizen-writer does.

HORIZONTAL VERTIGO

Someone already in Mexico will say, "I'm going to Mexico." Everyone understands that such a person is going to the capital, which in its voracity aspires to absorb the entire nation.

Strange to say, that place exists.

Entry into the Labyrinth

Chaos Is Not Something You Improvise

For almost twenty years I've been writing about Mexico City, a mélange of chronicles, essays, and personal memories. The juxtapositions the cityscape entails—the tire shop opposite the colonial church, the corporate skyscraper next to the taco stand—led me to create a hybrid genre, a natural response to an environment where the present is affected by stimuli from the pre-Hispanic world, the Viceroyalty, modern and postmodern culture. How many different times does Mexico City contain?

The area is so huge you might think it consists of different time zones. And at the outset of 2001, we were actually on the verge of creating more of them. The newly elected president Vicente Fox suggested inaugurating daylight savings time, but the head of the government of the then Federal District, Manuel López Obrador, refused to institute it. Since there are streets where the sidewalk on one side of the street is in Mexico City and the one opposite it is in the State of Mexico, the possibility of gaining or losing an hour by crossing the street became a possibility. The politicians stubbornly stuck to their chronological barriers until, unfortunately, the National Supreme Court declared it absurd to have two time zones. So we lost our chance to walk a few yards and pass from federal time to capital time.

In this valley of passions, space, like time, suffers variations, beginning with nomenclature. For decades, we used the term "Mexico City" to talk about the sixteen neighborhoods that made up the Federal District and the new zones annexed to it from the State of Mexico. The term was a handy shortcut, so linguistic academics advised writing the word city with a lower-case "c." After 2016, the Federal District became Mexico City and acquired the same prerogatives held by the other states in the republic, but its name remained ambiguous because it does not include the entire metropolis (as did the moniker Mexico city) but only a part of it, which previously had been the Federal District. Welcome to the Valley of Anáhuac, where space and time converge!

Syncretism has been our most helpful formula for creating a city. This is true in terms of both building and remembering it. The different generations of a single family turn the city into a palimpsest of memories, where grandmothers reveal hidden mysteries to their granddaughters.

Take, for example, the intersection called Central Axis (formerly San Juan de Letrán) and Madero in the heart of the capital. My paternal grandmother lived opposite the Alameda Central, and her generation's idea of "modern" was the Palace of Fine Arts, that strange deployment of marble evocative of Ottoman fantasies. My generation associated it with a Las Vegas casino. For my mother, the modernity of that zone was embodied in the Lady Baltimore coffee shop, of European inspiration. For me, the outstanding sign of the times is the Latin American Tower, standing on that corner and built in the year I was born, 1956. Finally, for my daughter, the concept of the new is opposite the tower in Frikiplaza, a three-story commercial building dedicated to manga, anime, and other products of Japanese popular culture. So on that corner the "modernities" of four generations in my own family coexist. Instead of a single time and place, we live in the sum and juncture of different times and places, a codex simultaneously physical and one composed of memories of crossed destinies.

Without realizing I was beginning a book, I conceived the first of these texts in 1993, when I visited Berlin to present the German translation of *Argón's Shot*. Since my novel aspired to be a secret map of the Federal District, my publisher suggested I consult an issue of the magazine *Kursbuch* because it contains an essay on Soviet city planning by the

Russian-German philosopher Boris Groys: "The Metro as Utopia." It was a revelation. To my surprise, the Soviet underground's mirror image is our Collective Transport System.

The following year, I spent a semester at Yale University. I was guided by Groys's essay and an anthology titled *Die Unwirklichkeit der Städte* (The Unreality of Cities) compiled by Klaus R. Scherpe, that I found in the labyrinth of Sterling Memorial Library; the book, which tried to understand the city as a unitary discourse, inspired me to write an essay on the Mexican metro system. It was the beginning of a project that grew and changed over the course of years along with its theme and a plan that could accommodate its eventual expansion. Faced with the proliferation of pages, I came to realize that I didn't need an editor so much as an urban planner.

Horizontal Vertigo includes various kinds of testimonial devices. This book combines a multitude of genres, and, in a certain sense, it is various books. Structurally, it follows the criterion of *zapping*. The episodes do not move forward in linear fashion, but, instead, follow the zigzagging of memory or the detours endemic to city traffic.

The reader may follow from beginning to end, or choose, like a *flâneur* or a subway rider, the routes that interest him most: that of the characters, the places, the surprises, the ceremonies, the transitions, the personal stories (they're all personal stories, but the sections gathered under the rubric "City Characters" emphasize that aspect).

A City of Low Buildings

Michael Ondaatje, writing about *Les Misérables,* analyzes one of the many episodes in which Jean Valjean is on the run. Victor Hugo's description of the Paris streets the fugitive follows as he flees the police until they corner him is rigorously realist. How can Hugo save him? The novelist invents a street so that Valjean can escape. I have no idea if Ondaatje is correct in a topographic sense when he says the character flees using a nonexistent street, but he is certainly correct in a literary sense: fiction opens a path for the hero.

That doesn't happen in this book. Even though whenever I ran into numerous bottlenecks I wanted to add an imaginary exit to the myriad streets of the city, I opted for testimonial accounts and for what my memory confirms.

How accurate is what I'm telling? As accurate or false as the image we can have of a city where people live in millions of different ways. It would be inappropriate to rigidly interpret this metropolis that challenges direction signs. Is there a concept that defines it?

When Pierre Eugène Drieu La Rochelle, with all those names in tow, reached Argentina, he wanted to experience the pampa. The French traveler defined those endless grazing lands with unusual accuracy. He said he was standing before a "horizontal vertigo." The Argentine novelist Juan José Saer comments on that remark:

> There is a post-Symbolist residue in that expression which, in my opinion, becomes stronger when pronounced slowly, with eyes slightly shut, perhaps accompanied by a long, self-aware, slightly waving gesture of the right hand raised in front of the speaker, as if the lower edge of the palm were rowing through the air, the arm slightly stretched forward. The effect of that expression would doubtlessly be intense, but the expression itself is false.

This ironic passage from *The River Without Banks (El río sin orillas)* settles the score with the foreigner who left the most celebrated definition of the pampa. Saer discovers enough irregularities and obstacles in the plains to conclude that Drieu's phrase is "a fine poetic figure but an error of perception."

Mexico City has spread out like wildfire. Over the course of seventy years its territory has grown seven hundred times. How can we comprehend such enormity? I'll use Drieu La Rochelle's expression for a reason similar to the one that provoked Saer's irony: "horizontal vertigo" defines our environment, but it's ceasing to be accurate. My first memories of the capital are from 1960, when I was four. Over the course of the half century that followed, the city's expansion was markedly horizontal, a tide of low houses. The Latin American Tower stood as the solitary affirmation that verticality was possible, though hardly advisable in an earthquake-prone territory at an altitude of 7,218 feet to which water must be pumped. "Growth" meant "spread."

The novelist Carlos Gamerro argues with regard to Buenos Aires: "For a city that after four hundred years has still not managed to overcome the oppressive horizontality of pampa and river, any considerable elevation acquires a slightly sacred character, a vantage point against the crushing gravity of the two interminable plains and the enormous sky that weighs down over them"

In Mexico City the symbolic dimension of nature is just the opposite. We are not staring at a river so wide that it seems like a sea, nor are we facing an infinite plain. The city's founders came from a grotto and established themselves among mountains.

According to legend, the Aztlán tribe left Nayarit, on the Pacific coast, and made its way to the central zone, crossing abrupt mountain chains. The Valley of Anáhuac opened before them like an unusual flatland surrounded by volcanoes, with a lake that provided water. The term *highplain* we use for our peculiar geography refers to horizontality at high altitude.

If, as Gamerro asserts, high buildings in Buenos Aires represent a challenge to the pampa and the Río de la Plata, in Mexico, horizontality reminds us that buildings should not compete with mountains.

During the twentieth century, outbreaks of verticality had little luck. In the 1960s, Mario Pani, one of our principal architects, designed Unidad Habitacional Nonoalco-Tlatelolco. Digressing from his practice with other residential structures, he built real skyscrapers. The project had an extraordinary symbolic power because it was part of the Plaza of the Three Cultures, where the foundations of a pre-Hispanic fortress share space with a colonial church and the tower which for years was the home of the Ministry of Foreign Relations, the work of the architect Pedro Ramírez Vázquez, who specialized in buildings dedicated to various expressions of power: the Aztec Stadium, the National Museum of Anthropology, and the new Guadalupe Basilica.

Tlatelolco, a pioneering zone with regard to tall buildings, acquired a tragic reputation in 1968, when the Plaza of the Three Cultures became the sacrificial altar where the student movement was repressed. Seventeen years later, it was one of the places that suffered maximum devastation from the earthquake. A place marked for drama, Tlatelolco seems to suggest that verticality ends badly.

Other attempts to achieve great heights suffered a similar fate. In 1966, the impresario Manuel Suárez y Suárez acquired the tranquil Lama Park in the Naples neighborhood and planned something that seemed (and was) completely irrational: the tallest building in Latin America. By 1978, that monstrosity was six hundred and eighty feet tall, but it was merely a shell. It promised something that was never to be completed: the Hotel Mexico. For years, the building disrupted the cityscape like visible proof that immensity fails in these parts. In the magazine *Vice Versa,* a group of young writers suggested planting vines to turn the building into a vertical garden, a way of compensating for the park lost to that freakish object. Finally, in 1992, yielding to the needs of the moment, it became the World Trade Center. The history of the structure reveals how difficult it is here to build upward.

For two decades, the 1985 earthquake dominated perceptions of the city and produced a moratorium on tall buildings. But forgetting is allied to speculation, and the city began to gain altitude. Even a roadway became an elevated structure—the superhighway and the second level of the Periférico.

The solitary dominance of the Latin American Tower and the "renaissance" the Hotel Mexico as the World Trade Center promised were eclipsed in 1996 by the Arcos Bosques Tower, known as the Pants Building. At sunset, the shadow of the building, designed in Santa Fe by the architect Teodoro González de León, falls in spectacular fashion over a still low-rise city.

Another boastful attempt at verticality came to Paseo de la Reforma with the Torre Mayor, which from 2003 until 2010 was the tallest building in Latin America. Alongside it proliferated other buildings that altered the urban landscape without reaching the gigantism of Panama, where, in 2016, nineteen of the twenty-five tallest buildings in Latin America rose up: fifteen of them built after the Torre Mayor.

Even so, the days of the city's dilated horizontal expansion are numbered. In the Xoco neighborhood, near the house from which I'm writing these lines, an immense hole, which aspires to be the foundation of the tallest building in the city, is opening: Torre, whose sixty-two floors intend to rise to eight hundred and seventy-six feet. The dirt removed during excavation could fill the Aztec Stadium. The project, designed by the Argentine architect César Pelli, author of glittering towers in

Kuala Lumpur, has been opposed by ecologists and is frozen because of problems related to its budget of one hundred million dollars. At this moment it is in presale. It's entirely likely that this marvel will cause not only traffic jams but helicopter jams as well.

The city that was spreading like an ocean wave has now taken on another defining metaphor: the jungle. As the new undergrowth emerges, the territory is becoming a kind of swamp, a stagnant tidal pool dotted with buildings on stilts that grow higher and higher.

This vertical voracity announces another city, one marked by real estate avarice and corporate infernos. Drinking water, which reaches the city from a distance of one hundred eighty-six miles, will still have to travel up the sixty-two stories of the Torre Mítikah. In the well-to-do neighborhood of Santa Fe, buildings have collapsed because they were built on a sandy soil where there used to be mines. Mexico City is dying from real estate "success." "With usura hath no man a house of good stone," wrote Ezra Pound.

The Many Styles of a City

When the Venezuelan writer Adriano González León visited Mexico City, he was shocked when he found this sign:

MATERIALIST TRUCKS:

NO PARKING IN THE ABSOLUTE

It took the author of *Portable Homeland (País portátil)* a while to understand that he'd reached a place where materialism is not a brand of philosophy but a matter of loading and unloading construction vehicles. The reference to the absolute meant that the trucks must not park there even for an instant. That sign was really a prophecy about urban stagnation: these days, materialists have really parked on the absolute.

After writing about the city for twenty years, I searched for a notion of limits, and I found it in the landscape. I'm depicting the last half century of an immense but low city. Every brick that rises announces the end of that place. Besides, the fact that in 2016 it stopped being the Federal District and became Mexico City also represents the end of an era.

Kierkegaard pointed out that life takes place going forward but is understood by looking back. Explanations are always retrospective. According to pre-Hispanic mythology, the first inhabitants of the Valley of Anáhuac were searching for a prophetic image: the eagle devouring a serpent. They caught sight of this symbolic conjunction of air and earth on the shores of Lake Texcoco. The visionary meaning of reaching that place was now fact. Nevertheless, as the archaeologist Eduardo Matos Moctezuma notes, the interesting thing is that story was concocted after the arrival of those pilgrims. Tenochtitlán's founders settled on the shores of the lake, but they had no explanation to justify it.

Upstarts, the Mexica, or Aztecs, lacked a tradition that could glorify them. To supply themselves with a foundation epic, they appropriated the mythic past of *other people,* the Toltecs and the inhabitants of Teoti-huacán. In the fifteenth century, the Mexica invent—a posteriori—the legend of their grandeur. From that moment on, Mexico-Tenochtitlán only acquires logic working backward. Plans are not for us; our task is to decipher a mystery that is already in place.

Horizontal Vertigo is part of that extended tradition, but it derives from a rigorously personal point of view. Martin Scorsese praised Woody Allen's vision of New York because, among other things, it's so different from his own. I'm putting forward an interpretation among millions of possible interpretations.

For Carlos Fuentes, "Mexico City is a phenomenon in which there is room for all imaginations. I'm certain that Moctezuma's city lives, latent, in perpetual conflict and confusion, with the cities of Viceroy Mendoza, Empress Carlota, Uruchurtu, and the 1985 earthquake. How can anyone ask for a single, orthodox version of this urban specter?"

The city varies according to the perception each of its inhabitants has of it. Over the course of sixty years, I've had about twelve different addresses. All of them are south of the Viaduct, and that defines my point of view. I've traced my way through the labyrinth, but only seen it from one angle.

How can anyone represent a city that grew up around the dual temple of the Aztecs and that a few years ago was the *natural* setting for the futuristic, apocalyptic film *Elysium*?

In "The Immortal," Jorge Luis Borges describes a disorienting city that confuses without having a precise goal: "Corridors without exits abound, the high, unreachable window, the elaborate door that opens into a cell or a well, the incredible upside-down stairs, whose steps and balustrades go downward." The reason for this demented construction is the idleness of the immortals, who trifle away time and have no regard for finite purposes. At certain moments, Mexico City causes a similar sort of shock. To write about it means inventing explanations.

Three Decades After the Earthquake

On September 19, 1985, those of us who lived in the capital thought the city's expansion would only stop in the worst way. The earthquake destroyed many buildings, most of them public buildings. For a moment it seemed impossible to go on living here. But the Federal District was saved by its people. For days and days without rest we improvised as rescuers, and the destroyed city found a new face, screwed up and covered with dust, but ours. More than thirty years later, the city still exists.

I've wanted to answer in writing the fears, illusions, utter annoyances, and whims of living in this place. I've also tried to have my book approach the form in which I've decided to live in this city, convinced that being informed is a good thing, but that the facts, often bitter, should not dampen the principal forms of resistance: pleasure and a sense of humor.

My story takes place in density: I write surrounded by millions of people who have another opinion about the same subject. Bewilderment is something we experience in different ways, and no definitive version can be sanctioned. To write about Mexico City is a challenge as elusive as describing vertigo.

Mexico City, June 24, 2018

Living in the City

"If You See Juan . . ."

I came into the world in the Insurgentes Mixcoac neighborhood, a place of small houses, most of them built during the 1930s. It was there my grandfather, a Spanish sheepherder who came to Mexico to "make his American fortune," built a duplex with extremely solid walls, inspired by those of some fortress he'd seen as a child. Directly across, on the other side of the street, lived other Spaniards, the owners of the La Veiga bakery, the most popular shop in the neighborhood, along with the French Dry Cleaners, an enormous establishment on Insurgentes Avenue, a place that revealed the importance removing stains from clothing had in those days.

The house owned by the Fernández family, owners of the La Veiga, had the same square consistency as ours. Apparently that was the sign of immigrants who prospered, even if they went on fearing the roof would fall in on them.

The neighborhood streets were named after Spanish cities. We lived on Santander, at the corner of Valencia. I would spend long hours sitting on a bench waiting for a car to pass, like some unusual spectacle. When we played soccer in the street, using the storm sewer drains as goals, we used an atavistic warning cry to announce the occasional arrival of a vehicle: "Water Coming!"

Back in the days when the viceroys ruled, families would get rid of their urine by tossing it out the window shouting "Water Coming!" A couple of centuries later, we used the same term to say a car was coming. The time out gave us a chance to catch our breath and study the make and model of the automobile. If there was a woman in the car, we would approach the side window to see her legs: the age of the miniskirt was beginning.

It's hard to talk about those years without assuming a nostalgic tone. The city has changed to such an extent that merely describing it as it was seems a criticism of the present. Let me be clear, just to mitigate the struggle between historical moments: I have no desire to reincarnate myself in the boy who grew up in Mixcoac, "the place of serpents." That was the worst time in my life.

I'm not idealizing what has disappeared, but I do have to make note of an unquestionable fact: the city in those days was so different that it's almost shocking that it has the same name.

In the neighborhood I grew up in, all you had to do was open the door if you wanted to socialize. In a generic way, we would talk about "neighborhood friends," even if they were merely people with whom we had a nodding acquaintance. When they went outdoors, everyone spoke to everyone, not always with positive results.

Isolation was for misanthropes. Next door to my house was a tiny building, overwhelmed by a chaotic garden, where the plants grew in the same disorder that swirled the hair of the owner. Only rarely did we see him leave. Besides, he had a telescope, a clue that his turbulence might be astral. His wife's attributes in terms of a wild mane, style of dress, and long nails contributed to her being considered a witch, and that included a cat that followed her with a strange magnetism. That childless couple, isolated in their mini-bastion, confirmed the idea that only the very odd refused to speak with other people.

Even so, the task of socializing wasn't simple for someone six years old, with no links to the area, and with parents who lived there, but were only rarely at home. The child who went out to meet his fellow human beings was confronted by a complex culture of affronts, where it was thought challenging to "stand there staring" at someone (how many seconds of optical insistence counted as an offense?), where diminutives denoted a lack of virility, and where cordiality depended less on warmth than on the fear of being attacked.

Street life was governed by a primitive Darwinism, a peremptory appropriation of space, where a single word out of place could get you into trouble. Territorial prestige was imposed using fists, charisma, or money. I lacked those virtues and needed protection so I wouldn't become the slave of those who decreed the laws.

The great utopia of my childhood was to have an older brother. I wished, invoking an inexplicable charge of luck, a person two or three years older who would appear at the door of the house and demand the rights of primogeniture which I abominated. Being the firstborn obliged me to go out on the street with no instruction manual.

When I was six, I wasn't brave. I lacked both an overpowering personality and the money necessary for getting on the good side of the others by inviting them to have a soda in the corner store La Colonial.

I was accepted into the gang without becoming a subordinate of the lowest rank because my way of talking amused them. I had no ingenuity, no gift for telling jokes, but I said strange things. That came from my miscellaneous cultural influences. My father was born in Barcelona and grew up in Belgium. He would say whirligig instead of top and staff instead of cane. My maternal grandfather was also Spanish. He lived in the ground floor of our duplex and almost never spoke, but when he did he spoke like an angry priest in a movie (in those days, all the priests in Mexican films spoke like Spaniards, and my father had played the part of a priest in *The Shulamite Girl* (*La Sunamita,* 1965), a film directed by Héctor Mendoza based on a story by Inés Arredondo. My grandmother came from Yucatán and told stories in a motley linguistic potpourri. She would say *hallelujah* instead of *super-duper.* We didn't always understand her. Made desperate by our incomprehension, she would say, "I'm killing my turkey," which meant "I give up."

My mother studied psychology, and a few years later went to work in the Psychiatric Hospital for Children. She would come home exhausted after seeing deeply disturbed children, unwilling to deal with my sister, Carmen, and me, mildly disturbed children.

I studied in the Alexander von Humboldt German School. The goddess Fortune is capricious: I fell in with a group of Germans. At the age of six, I knew how to read and write, but only in German.

All that turned me into someone who spoke in an odd way. It wasn't a great virtue, but that singularity saved me from a few beatings and allowed the strongest to protect me, in the same way they would have protected a parrot able to pronounce a few insane words or recite the lineup of the Guadalajara all-stars.

The neighborhood had two areas of mystery: La Colonial and the abandoned houses. The store smelled of chiles preserved in vinegar, wrapping paper, and sweet things. That badly lighted cavity put us in touch with a distant and multifaceted universe—a decidedly modern universe: the world where candy came wrapped in the crackling prodigy called cellophane.

We measured out our lives in pennies: a small Coke cost thirty-five cents; large cost forty-five, and family size ninety; shortbread cookies, fifty; Motitas Chiclets, ten, Kangaroo Chiclets, five cents. My mind was never so attuned to economics as it was then. I cannot for the life of me remember the price of something I bought yesterday in Oxxo, but I cannot forget that the unusual Delaware Punch cost forty cents, five less than a medium Coke.

We gathered in La Colonial, mostly for the purpose of discussing any subject that came along and to long for the junky cakes that were beginning to dominate the market with their fabulous names: Geese *(Gansito)* and Penguins *(Pingüinos)* (later on Mammoths—*Mamut*—would appear). For us, the store was the equivalent of the agora in Athens. The place to think about the city.

The other location of interest was composed of abandoned houses. Real estate life seemed subject to intense personal tragedies that forced people to leave a place without putting up a "For Rent" sign. Plants would invade those homes, and squatters would light fires in the rooms using pieces of furniture. We would hop over the fences whose bars were decorated with fleurs-de-lis to explore those museums of abandonment and misfortune. The empty mansions were usually more luxurious than our houses, which made the mystery of their being given over to mold and mice even greater. What catastrophe could explain the inhabitants' flight? Something really bad would have to happen for someone to abandon those rooms painted pale pink to the tender mercies of the neighborhood children.

I explored the area on my own, but I found my greatest friendship right outside the door. An old maid became enormously fond of me. She lived in an old-fashioned house with wooden floors. There the air smelled of gentian and moist rags, good and vaguely submarine things. She would invite me to have a snack, ask me to tell her about school matters, ask me about the homeless cats, and ask me to baptize them for her.

One afternoon, she prepared a bath for me. I was delighted to enter the room with its white mosaics and archaic furniture—a chipped water pitcher, an armoire with double mirrors, a tub held up by four feline claws: a tub from the time of the Mexican Revolution. I continued the friendship even as I soaked.

Looking back, I'm surprised at my relationship with that woman, whose name I do not remember and whom I called the Lady Friend. There was no rubbing, no signs of early and confusing erotic behavior. She did not want to abuse me. She was simply a solitary person. She seemed made for the abandoned houses in the neighborhood. I enjoyed myself in her discreet company, submerged in a warm nirvana devoid of obligations, until my mother found out about it and reacted the way any intelligent woman who studies psychology would react, that is, like a madwoman. That was the first jealousy scene I'd ever witnessed in my life, and I was the involuntary protagonist of the offense. My mother accused me of preferring the Other Woman.

"If you love her so much, why don't you move in with her?" she asked on the brink of collapse.

Before I could answer, she got out a valise, brought it to my room, and began to pack up my things. She carefully folded shirts and rolled up my socks without my being able to believe that she was really throwing me out of the house. This was my mother, the woman I adored to the point that I believed, with grammatical conviction, that her biography would someday figure in one of my favorite comic strips, *Illustrious Lives,* which narrated in melodramatic form the martyrdoms of the saints.

I saw her put my belongings into the valise we used for trips to Veracruz, hoping against hope that from one minute to another she'd stop performing this absurd task. She didn't stop. Then she went to the kitchen and came back with the steel jar. Every morning, I swallowed a spoonful of that thick syrup which supposedly was helping me to grow.

When the container went into the valise, it was like a magic touch: all of that was really true. If my mother was taking the trouble to pack something as precise as that she could not be playing.

That was the best and most painful literary lesson I ever had in my life. In order that a scene can appear plausible, what's necessary is something that shouldn't be there but is there nevertheless. The fly in the soup. That incredible and at the same time logical presence confers on the event a singularity which can only be believed.

When I saw the jar in the valise, I fell on my knees, begged forgiveness, swore I would never love another woman. I could remain in the house.

I told that anecdote in *The Wild Book* as an homage to my mother's literary teachings and as a late effort to overcome the trauma of not loving her and only her exclusively.

After that incident, I stopped going out on the street. I conceived a negative fantasy. I imagined I was running away and that my parents missed me terribly. For years, I lived in a hollow inside a cypress tree in Chapultepec Park. When they finally found me, I was a mumbling beggar who had forgotten Spanish. Pondering my linguistic defects, caused by suffering and misery—my tough unlearning process in Chapultepec—my parents felt a deep pity for me, but, above all, they felt tremendous guilt. I would imagine, in delightful detail, their repentant faces. My life ideal consisted in ruining myself to make them suffer.

I had no chance to practice that masochism because they changed fate in another way. Both came from separatist traditions—he from Cataluña and she from Yucatán. So it wasn't at all odd that they separated when I was nine.

We left the house on Insurgentes Avenue in Mixcoac and moved to an apartment in the Del Valle neighborhood. The family had shrunk to my mother, my sister, Carmen, two years younger than me, and me. My father lived quite close to us, in the Aule building on the corner of Xola and Insurgentes. He ate with us twice a week, took a siesta, and on Sundays would bring us to the zoo or the movies, and would take me to a soccer match. That superficial normalcy was insufficient in a world where divorce was surrounded by the black halo of failure and scandal. None of my schoolmates had divorced parents, and among my

new neighborhood friends, only the Mondragóns had passed through
that ordeal. That was my first reason for getting to know them.

My life changed forever thanks to my contact with that family. Jorge
was my age, and that facilitated our friendship. The eldest of the sons,
Gustavo, was four or five years older, but he really enjoyed the company
of the younger set. He spent afternoons teaching us new ways to control the soccer ball or introducing new rock groups to us. I understood
that life had meaning because soccer and music existed. Shortly thereafter, the Mondragóns surprised me again. They studied in the Colegio
Tepeyac, in the Lindavista neighborhood in the north of the city, and
one day they invited me to watch Monks, the American football team,
practicing.

Thanks to that trip, I entered the labyrinth. We crossed the Federal
District on buses and streetcars. In an inexpressible but solid way, I felt
as though those streets, plazas, roundabouts, avenues, movie theaters,
shops, neon signs, and unknown parks were mine.

My family had been reduced to a minimum, I was studying in the
German School, where I did not control enough sentences with subordinate clauses to really be a part of things, and I spoke in an odd way. I
was out of place. Nevertheless, the vastness of the territory made me
realize that I could find my own space there. I decided to belong to the
city, as if I didn't before. I decided to love it and despise it in the way you
love and despise something that belongs to you. I decided to understand
it with a mixture of enthusiasm and astonishment. For someone who's
disoriented, the labyrinth is a house.

Right after moving to the Del Valle neighborhood, I started spending
more and more time on the streets around the San Borja cutoff, something that turned out to be convenient for my mother, who would get
home very late from the Psychiatric Hospital for Children. At seven or
eight o'clock in the evening, she would arrive, not having the slightest
idea where I was. That didn't bother her at all. When she didn't find me
in the apartment, she would go down to the street and say to the first
person she knew: "If you see Juan, tell him to come home."

No further searching was necessary. Sooner rather than later, the
messenger would run into me: "Time for you to go home," they'd say.

There was no need to search for people because they were right there.

We were all there, in a self-contained microcosm. Insecurity existed in the mind, not on the streets.

Something of that era has stayed with me forever. I walk through the city going nowhere in particular and without thinking about when I should return, confident that someone I know will tell me soon enough that I should go home.

City Characters

El Chilango

It's easy to define *el chilango* as "numerous." From a demographic point of view, he's surplus.

The most interesting thing about the word *chilango* is its confused etymology. It was a pejorative term which we now use with pride, in the same way we refer to the Distrito Federal, the Federal District, as the Federal Defective.

Following Gabriel Zaid, the origin of the word *chilango* derives from the Mayan word *xilan,* which means "unkempt." It was used first in Veracruz to define criminals sent to the capital to stand trial who would end up in the San Juan de Ulúa prison. So: criminals sentenced in the capital who returned to a province.

Other hypotheses link the name with a bundle of chiles, someone from the provinces, and even a red fish. The fact is that nowadays very few people concern themselves over the original meaning of the term, which does not derive from a geographic designation. Where do the chilangos begin and end? People born in Ecatepec, Atizapán, Ciudad Satélite, and other places in the State of Mexico, have their own regional pride, but they don't take offense if they're assimilated into the multiplicity of delinquents from the Anáhuac Valley (to be regionalists in this immensity reduces the possibilities of participation).

In this city, the only thing that matters is what happens to multi-tudes. People from the capital do not struggle to adapt to overcrowding; they know it is their only possible condition. If someone finds a taco res-taurant with lots of empty tables, they suspect the tacos served there are filled with dog meat. Anything not overflowing is a failure. That explains why the airport is filled up with a compact mass of visitors: a chilango only knows he's arrived if there are ten relatives waiting for him.

For a long time now, our crowds have stopped having any cause. They are not a social but a meteorological phenomenon. This in no way implies that the inhabitants of Chilangopolis are patient. If anything defines them it's their intense desire to be elsewhere. Whenever I visit the tropics I'm surprised by the way I walk. After two blocks I find myself soaked with perspiration. Out of breath, my eyes clouded, I ask myself: Why am I walking like this when there is no one waiting for me any-where? Because I come from Mexico City.

Chilango motion makes us move forward as if we knew where we were going. You find a space and you speed up. Our progress through space is conditioned by the idea of the "escape route." Even if we're in a tranquil café under a leafy bougainvillea, we suddenly move to another table so that someone (invisible as yet) doesn't take possession of the ash-tray. It's a permanent tic, something second nature that makes us rec-ognizable. In places where a dead calm reigns, we evince the frenzy of people who have adapted to desperation.

Too many days spent in traffic jams make us idolize speed. To com-pensate for the incessant loss of direct connections, we believe in alter-nate routes. The two huge works of devastation in favor of transit (the axis throughways and the second level of the Peripheral Ring) engen-dered Magellan Syndrome. The relief both brought was minimal but they did make us believe it's worthwhile taking these grand arteries to create roundabout routes. In search of a path of circumnavigation, driv-ers abandon their chosen path and believe a twisting side road will make things better if only because they keep moving forward.

The chilango views streets as a lottery. Even though anxiety is his usual state, he consoles himself thinking he's only an hour late. A toss of the dice will indeed abolish chance: he'll arrive very, very late, but some people will still be awake.

The old Federal District and its outlying villages (the Great Annexations) boast the most intense exploratory traffic on the planet. More than five million cars take to the road, not in search of a specific course but to see if it's at all possible to move forward. Not even the movements of public transportation are stable. The minibus, the bus, the taxi, and other transportation vehicles make unforeseen detours in search of the miracle that will smash the walls and open a path in the way the Red Sea parted. The search for side roads is embarked upon with the devotion drivers have for Saint Christopher, patron of sailors, or the Virgin of Transit (who in our case should augment her abilities by resolving not only our passage to the great beyond but also our movement here below).

The chilango is no angel, we have to admit as much. It would be futile to consider he might be worse if he put into practice everything that occurred to him going from one place to another. He suffers his own suffering, who doubts it? His life evolves on a checkerboard without defined rules. Suppose he starts playing snakes and ladders and all he finds are snakes until he realizes that the ladders have been privatized and there's only one left, which you can only use if you win a raffle. Strange to say, that consoles him. The archetypal chilango has a bad character, but he believes in luck in the face of all predictions. Dr. Johnson said a second marriage was the triumph of hope over experience. That is the chilango's basic mode of behavior. Negative facts do not undermine his incurable illusions.

Our dealings with reality are really esoteric. Most pharmacies are named after churches, as if the remedies were acts of faith, and there are people who believe that the condoms they buy in the Pharmacy of God or the Pharmacy of Saint Paul render all sins venial.

Even garbage is subject to a system of beliefs. If someone throws his trash onto your street, the only solution is to set up a statue of the Virgin of Guadalupe so he'll throw it elsewhere. The day will come when every street will be so packed with Virgins they'll look like celestial parking meters.

Transcendental convictions even turn up in the most banal places. Photocopy shops usually decorate their walls with prayers for unborn children, litanies on the wholeness of man, and the spiritual value of perennial herbs. Palinodes on love and repentance. Perhaps because they

are crypts dedicated to reproduction indifferent to copyrights, the photocopy shops compensate for the sin of excessive procreation by exhibit-
ing pious slogans so we'll view them as informal chapels.

In this theater of superstition, businesses do not promise honesty or
instantly hand over a receipt. They try to gain prestige in another way—
with a protective crucifix or a pennant honoring the national team. In
that regard, Fabrizio Mejía Madrid writes, "People feel confident about
a fried chicken restaurant only because it contains a picture of the Pope."

To coexist with horror, we memorize disasters and imagine even
worse ones. If the ordinary U.S. citizen is an expert in repairs in the "do
it yourself" sense, the ordinary chilango is an expert in catastrophes he
cannot repair. Our version of the magazine *Popular Mechanics* would have
to be called *Popular Apocalypse* and be dedicated to earthquakes, landslides,
volcanic activity, water shortages, pollution, thefts of cash machines,
pirate taxis, and other tragedies about which we'd like to know a lot—
not to remedy them but because we're convinced that information about
the ills of the world mitigates their effects. Facts, no matter how brutal
they are, do not alarm us. The chilango judges his situation in the same
way a combat pilot judges his mission: turbulence is good news because
it tells us the plane hasn't been shot down.

When we learn just how much lead we carry in our blood, we don't
think we should be sleeping in some radioactive refuge and wearing tita-
nium pajamas. If we learn about it, it's because we've survived, and luck
has enabled us to pass to the other side, to the last-chance playoffs where
zombies with metal in their bloodstream can still compete.

At every urban street corner, it's survival of the fittest, meaning the
person who's craftiest. When you find a great parking space, you also
discover that there's a bucket sitting in it. That means it's been "expropri-
ated" by a car guard, a *franelero*. That word tells you this is not just any
person but someone authorized by urban custom. In his hand he carries
his identification: a rag or a piece of flannel *(franela)*. The only requirement for the bit of cloth is that it be absolutely filthy.

While it seems logical to us that in London, New York, Tokyo, or
Paris there are parking meters in all commercial zones, millions of chilangos simply do not trust that tool for organizing street parking. It's
possible that the first pipes carrying drinking water were viewed with

the same distrust. The fact is that the informal economy of the *franelero* has the full support of people who prefer to fight with him rather than with a machine whose coins could end up in illicit pockets.

But life in this density also possesses compensatory virtues. The first is the ability to be anonymous. Our behavior is only rarely at the level of the most select principles of humanism, but those who watch us pick our noses while we wait for the light to turn green are, fortunately, people we don't know. Another virtue is there are so many of us that it doesn't really matter where we come from. In Chilangopolis, there is no original sin. We all have the right to err in the present moment.

The city may be governed by someone with a coastal accent, even if there is no ocean in sight. That was the case of Andrés Manuel López Obrador, mayor from 2000 to 2005. People belong to the capital for the simple reason that they're here (the problem is getting out). Our only quality control is that we remain here. Since our traditions are daily improvisations, we don't demand that anyone dominate it. We are from the place where we're all squeezed together.

We endure this inevitable proximity in various ways. One of them is suspicion. The chilango coexists, but always on the defensive, always alert to the possibilities his fellow citizens will cheat him or think him ugly. Even if he has no problem accepting that others have come to sink to the bottom here, he suspects that no one will ever give him the right change. Resigned to thriving in a multitude, he's suspicious when he starts analyzing others one by one. If he doesn't communicate his misanthropy, it's because he's heard legends about souls who are apparently unprotected who actually have brothers-in-law who are magistrates.

We put up with a lot out of a need to survive, and we blurt out a lot on the telephone. It would be interesting to know how many crimes are avoided thanks to our healthy mania to blow off steam into an understanding ear. If it hadn't been for Edison, the current proliferation of cell phones, and our sophisticated ability to slander others, we would have succumbed to all kinds of riots and brawls. This is not meant to suggest that we're easygoing. It only indicates we could be terrible.

Out of nowhere, a strange phenomenon moderates our steadfast nature: that day "the volcanoes came out." With no logic, we use the verb "to come out" to refer to mountainous formations, as if the two volcanoes, the Popo and the Izta, decided one day to take a look at us. On those rare, clear days, we're a bit better. I know of romances that were consummated with no other explanation than the good vibe derived from contemplating, just once, the possibility of a horizon. Seeing a sky of an extravagant blue color, how could we not believe that our affections can advance like a *National Geographic* expedition? For the chilango, tenderness is a variation of geography. A native of Milpa Alta cannot allow the expansive waves of his love to reach Ciudad Satélite. If he does, his libido will vanish in the traffic. The Viaduct, the transversal axis of passion, is a border that should only be crossed with caution.

According to Heinrich Böll, a city fills up with meaning "if it can be exaggerated." If that's true, we inhabit a bastion of meaning.

In his novel *Hombre al agua* (Man in Water), Fabrizio Mejía Madrid creates a chilango litany using epigrams:

> That city is one where nothing is either destroyed or created, everything is regulated [. . .] a city where old things are so recycled that a soda can may have originally been a taxi [. . .] a city where household decorations most resemble things that survived a garage sale [. . .] a city where people don't sell you fish but their word of honor that it's fresh [. . .] a city where the morning crowing of roosters was replaced by car alarms [. . .] a city where it's entirely possible that the person threatening you with a knife may either kill you or try to sell it to you.

In essence, what best defines the chilango is his obstinate way of staying here. But he doesn't hold out because of some suicidal drive, like the three hundred martyrs of Thermopylae. His endurance does not depend on the epic but on the imagination: he goes out on the street to carry out fictions, and he joins the tale of a city that overflowed urbanism and installed itself in mythology.

Shocks

How Many of Us Are There?

Is it possible to adapt to something that constantly changes? The chilango's principal "means of adaptation" consists in thinking about moving elsewhere, about evaluating the alternatives, admitting the momentary impossibility of leaving, and then remaining, but with the intention to make a better escape plan.

Over the course of half a century, I've lived for three years in Berlin, three in Barcelona, and two semesters at universities in the United States. Seven years away with some trips added to that. I've thought of moving about a thousand times, but time has transformed me into the only member of my family born in the capital who still lives there. I don't know if that's a matter of will or destiny. The fact is that the city has become a second nature for me. If the Barça team wins the league when I'm in Barcelona, I want to go to the Angel of Independence on Paseo de la Reforma.

In my case, my eagerness to leave heightens toward the end of September, after I've survived two illusions I no longer believe in: national holidays and my birthday. In September, I'm a year older and the nation celebrates itself for no apparent reason, but the worst part is that during that period we've already had four months of rain.

Rain does not fall in this valley: it cascades down as if something had broken in heaven. The avenues recover the current they had when they were rivers. Everything floods, and we confirm the fact that filling in the Aztec lake was a disaster only inferior to the threat that the lake will reappear in our living room. After the third pair of wet shoes wrapped in newspaper to dry, I want to leave forever, knowing full well I won't.

The mere fact of living here is a half-time job, where you're paid with annoyances. But it's hard to give the place up. "You're back from Berlin?" an acquaintance asks. "Thirty years ago." "Ah. Didn't go well, right?"

That dialogue reflects a popular superstition: leaving is a chance for salvation; returning is a defeat. Even so, the majority of those who think that way stay in the city—which grows and in doing so constitutes an ironclad proof that we'd be worse off elsewhere.

"Mexico City, above all, is too many people," declares Carlos Monsiváis in *Rituals of Chaos (Los rituales del caos)*. In *Images at War*, Serge Gurzinski describes the city as a "chaos of doubles."

There are a lot of us, but no one feels superfluous. When Günter Grass visited the city during the 1980s, he wanted to know how many people lived in the Federal District and the adjacent areas. Bewilderment arrived with the answer we usually gave at the time: "Between sixteen and eighteen million." The "margin of error" was the population of West Berlin, where Grass lived. The uncertainty has only grown since then.

Various studies, serious, at least in appearance, contribute disparate numbers of people, and a negative narcissism induces us to believe that the highest is the most correct. I have the feeling that there are fewer of us than we think, but even so there are so, so many of us. Fifteen, seventeen, twenty million? What's interesting, from the point of view of the psychology of the capital, is that the exact number transcends comprehension.

Whenever I bring a German friend somewhere, I make one or two wrong turns, either out of forgetfulness or because some street was closed to celebrate a holiday or a marathon. Seeing hesitation, the friend asks: "Did you get lost?" Germany is a country where people who fail the taxi driver examination three times commit suicide. The test is so demanding that drivers have to know the best routes to take in the city at any time of day, taking into account the end of the school day, religious holidays, and soccer matches. A wrong turn reveals that the test taker does not really know the territory.

It's true that Waze and Google Maps can save us, but with the proliferation of streets with the same name, both apps can take you to the wrong place. The user must also know the name of the neighborhood, but even that is not conclusive. I live in a neighborhood with two official names, Villa Coyoacán and Coyoacán Center. Despite that, the Uber operating system gives it a third name, Santa Catarina. The street is named after one of the strongmen of the Mexican Revolution. That means the name reappears in the furthest outposts of the city. Following the 2017 *Roji Guide,* the metropolitan area contains four hundred and twelve streets, roundabouts, and avenues named Carranza. To get to my house, you have to reject four hundred and eleven options located in other zones and know beforehand the three different names the apps ascribe to my neighborhood.

Besides all that, the Waze programmers are not always up to date on the sudden uses we make of space: after a wave of muggings, the neighbors gather one fed-up Wednesday and put up a gate to keep outsiders from entering their street; but with the same spontaneity on some Thursday or other they organize the Tamarind Feast on the avenue you were foolishly trying to cross.

In a landscape where orientation is almost impossible, a wrong turn constitutes a mere test. Making mistakes gives us confidence (and if you detect it and say "that's not the way," you confirm that the goal actually exists). The territory exceeds us in such a way that it's better to ignore certain things. Not knowing how many of us there are can upset visitors but not us, because we're convinced that the "margin of error" is never completely wrong because it announces the possibility of reaching something that is not an error.

Crossings

Memory Atlas

In the early years of the twentieth century, Walter Benjamin advised intentionally getting lost in the city in the same way a person might get lost in the forest. It required talent, but also an apprenticeship. Urban wandering still contained reference points that precluded getting absolutely lost.

The megalopolises came along to change our notion of space and to decenter their inhabitants. Nowadays, getting around in Tokyo, Calcutta, São Paulo, or Mexico City is an exercise more related to time than space. In terms of movement, the route and the means of transportation are more important than the surroundings: if movement takes place, the physical mass of the city goes from being an obstacle to being a landscape.

In his novel *Mao II,* Don DeLillo points out that New York stands out because no one wants to be in the same place for more than ten minutes. This impetus defines the tense tone of the city.

Getting somewhere is such a severe challenge that quite often public works are conceived of as a metaphor for roadways, not as a real form of travel. In Mexico City, there has never been a lack of unfinished bridges, of streets that flow into dead ends, uneven stairs that are never used, or two-lane streets "widened" by a third, painted lane that replaces the two real ones. At the edge of the Peripheral Ring, near the New Chapultepec

Forest, there is a monument to useless roadways: the bicycle route goes up a ramp so steep that only the winner of the Tour de France could possibly climb it.

Benjamin's idea of getting to know streets by walking them with no particular destination in mind cannot be an original goal for us because it's the ordinary situation in which a pedestrian finds himself.

Ten years ago, a woman friend came by the house to pick up my daughter to bring her to a children's party. I was surprised to see a pillow on the backseat: "It's so she can sleep, we're going far away," she explained. The car becomes a bedroom to make the trip bearable.

Two immense tribes travel on a daily basis, sleepwalkers and insomniacs. Five million sleepy people use the subway, and another five million suffer nervous attacks in their cars.

Under such circumstances, it is impossible to have a comprehensive representation of the city. The idea of order is alien to a place that functions as an assembly of cities. The Santa Fe neighborhood, where big capital is concentrated, could be a suburb of Houston, to the same degree that Ecatepec might be on the outskirts of Islamabad.

You can see the structure of a city in the way a child sees it. My father lived in Barcelona until he was nine. Eighty years later, my daughter spent three years there, from age one to age four. Despite the vast arc of time and the transformations brought about by the Spanish Civil War of 1936–1939 and the urban reordering caused by the Olympic Games of 1992, the image of Barcelona a child from the 1920s might have is not very different from that of a child of the first generation of the twenty-first century. I came to know that thanks to a drawing.

We were at the beach, sharing one of those afternoons where we adults chat at length. My daughter got bored. I suggested she amuse herself drawing, so she asked what she should draw. I came up with a title: "Max in the City." (Max was her favorite stuffed animal.) After a while she came back with the results: I saw Barcelona's Gothic district, the Ciudadela park, the port, the aquarium, the San Juan walkway, Mrs. Miracles' shop, where we bought her toys, the Kiddy Park . . . Except for a few details, the city was identical to the one my father evoked in his exile. The emblematic places in Barcelona seemed to quote one of Salvador Dalí's titles, *The Persistence of Memory*. The Spanish Republic, the dictatorship, the fads of the Generalitat have not taken away the essence of the story the city tells itself.

I wondered if my daughter could have drawn a map, not comprehensive but just approximate of Mexico City. Not a chance: her life was defined by closed spaces and means of transportation.

This fragmented, shattered, discontinuous vision is shared by millions of chilangos. For a long time now, the figure of the *flâneur* who strolls along intending to get lost on the trail of a surprise was replaced by that of the deported person. In Chilangopolis, the Odyssey is a daily adventure. No challenge is greater than returning home.

This journey is made all the more difficult by a lack of natural reference points. Cities usually grow around a defined landscape: a mountain, a lake, a river, a slope between sea and mountains. But Mexico-Tenochtitlán buried its lake, and the smog blotted out the volcanoes. So, no natural sign stands as an orientation point.

The air is crisscrossed by helicopters that report on the challenges to travel. For people in cars, the map is a conjectural landscape transmitted by radio. If Roland Barthes found in Tokyo a de-structured city lacking a center and made of successive shorelines, the inhabitant of Mexico City finds an impassable tide with the radio advising him to take "alternative routes," a name we ascribe to the parallel reality we cannot enter.

The ancient Federal District retains inhabitable zones, almost all of which derive from the Baroque city of the seventeenth and eighteenth centuries. The Aztec *calpulli* or wards distant from the great Tenochtitlán (Tlalpan, San Ángel, Coyoacán) grew in the colonial era under a Renaissance inspiration. They were neighborhoods that flowed into plazas, places meant to be traveled on foot.

What remains of colonial Mexico City (the historic center and the adjacent areas where the conquistadors and religious orders resided) is a city to be walked. The rest requires vehicles. After Independence, it was better to traverse the capital on horseback. In 1878, trams pulled by animals appeared, and by the end of the nineteenth century there were three thousand mules dedicated to passenger travel.

The tidy lines Antonio de Mendoza dreamed of became rare because of traffic. Then diagonal lines and roundabouts were discovered. Rivers—the Consulado, the Magdalena, La Piedad, and Churubusco—

were forced into tunnels, paved over, and became streets that followed
their path. The map of the capital could no longer resemble Piet Mon-
drian's rectilinear adventures and had to accommodate itself to splatter-
ing in the style of Jackson Pollock.

Urban specialists use the term "intermediate city" to refer to the
neighborhoods that separate the center from the periphery. The Roma,
Condesa, Villa de Cortés, Nápoles, Tacubaya, San Pedro de los Pinos,
and Del Valle neighborhoods are part of the second circle surrounding
the center. Then come the ancient Native American communities, followed by the suburbs and by indefinite zones of urbanization whose
boundaries are almost always unknown.

The architect Rem Koolhaas has taken an interest in urban scale.
"Composing a city" depends on a dialogue between space and demography. To pass from size S to XL involves severe changes in social behavior.
What is the size of this space? We inhabit a city size XXL that contains
cities size S.

European urbanization usually dissolves into innocuous peripheries
and industrial parks. These are apparently places that arise precisely not
to be described. Peter Handke has changed that conventional attitude.
My Year in No-Man's Bay chronicles the secret life of a bedroom community on the outskirts of Paris. There, the Austrian writer discovers the
private language of a standardized ecosystem, in appearance devoid of all
singularity. His virtuosity consists in uncovering something unique in a
place where people live according to the logic of Juan Rulfo's imaginary
town, Comala, in *Pedro Páramo,* "as if it didn't exist."

In Mexico City, certain "peripheral" zones are almost in the center.
The airport is surrounded by residential units and scattered little houses
that would merit Handke's description. The strangest thing is not that
these bedroom communities exist in a central area but that the airport is
also located there.

To what sort of property does the inhabitant of Mexico City aspire?
The concept of luxury today is isolation, the gated community, the self-
sufficient and impregnable citadel besieged by barbarians. Insecurity and
simultaneous processes of de-urbanization and re-densification have produced that strange alternative where well-being means being in the margin. Even if the cloistered life is the very antithesis of the city, projects

that attempt to remove themselves from the shared urban experience are more and more frequent.

When I was a boy, the concept of urban order was represented by the aerial map of Paris we had on the wall, a cartography where the buildings appeared as if drawn for the illustration to a fairy tale. In essence, that concept still dominates the life of the French capital. For centuries, literary characters have been using the same Parisian streets: in *The Three Musketeers,* d'Artagnan walks along Rue de la Huchette, the same street that Horacio Oliveira, many years later, walks along in Julio Cortázar's novel *Hopscotch.*

I grew up looking at that map without knowing that time would give me the opportunity to get lost in the City of Light. Perhaps to extoll its virtues as a walkable space, Paris does not always supply taxis at night or at least didn't when this anecdote took place, around 2002. In that Parisian dawn, taxis weren't a service but an anecdote. It was told that someone, at some time, had hailed a providential cab. Perhaps that was the reason why, years later, the event inspired the appearance of a ghost taxi that links different zones of time in Woody Allen's 2011 film *Midnight in Paris.*

But the story I want to tell has nothing to do with problems finding cabs but with the representation of space. I left a gathering at a bad time and failed to get a ride. It was raining, and I had to traverse the historical center of Paris from end to end. I knew the basic coordinates of my route—eastward on the other side of the river—but I had no idea how to cross the myriad boulevards. Besides, I wanted to find the shortest route given the time and the weather. What mechanism did the setting supply me? Outside every subway station there is one map of the neighborhood and another, more detailed, of the surrounding streets. It was no problem at all going from station to station, from one fragmentary map to the next. After an hour and a half, I reached my goal without for a minute feeling I was lost.

That experience leads to the way in which I try to understand my city. Ecocide has devastated not only space but time as well. We remember lots of things that are no longer there but still shape our memory map. To live in a space in incessant deconstruction makes us reconfigure our memories. Depending on each person's biography, the past may be more intense and decisive than the transfigured city we see daily.

Losing a city is a formidable literary tool. At times, a novelist goes far away in order to recover his surroundings with the sharpness only nostalgia can provide. After he abandoned Dublin, James Joyce could travel around it in his writing. On other occasions going far away is forced on us by world history or the avatars of a family. Günter Grass left behind the Free City of Danzig and Salman Rushdie emigrated with his family from Bombay to London. What is certain is that being uprooted demands repayment in the form of stories.

The Polish poet Adam Zagajewski was born in the city of Lviv (Leopolis), which was annexed by the Soviet Union when he was four months old. His family moved to Gliwice, where the solid old furniture was a reminder that the town had belonged to Germany, while the newer items showed the flimsiness with which Polish socialism compensated the "new man."

It may well be that the most significant function of paternity is to remind children of what happened during their first years of life, that escaped time memory cannot access. Zagajewski grew up listening to stories about the beautiful city they'd had to abandon, a city very different from the gray cityscape of Gliwice. For him, that beauty became the lost treasure he longed for from a suburb where the only prominent structure was the empty stands of a soccer stadium.

Something changed when he discovered literature. In a setting that seemed to inspire absolutely nothing, Zagajewski found the elusive glitter of good fortune. "Try to celebrate the mutilated world," he says in one of his poems. In a similar way, Milan Kundera coined the expression "beauty by mistake" to define the aesthetic pleasure he derives from the things that should repudiate him.

In *Two Cities,* his memoir, Zagajewski elaborates this idea. His essential rite of passage consisted in discovering that the blue flower of poetry could blossom in the "wrong" place. "A bicycle, a wicker basket, a stain of light on the wall stopped being 'objects that could be catalogued' and became instead mysteries 'with a thousand secret meanings.'" The streets devoid of charm he'd walked until they acquired the aura that his elders had conferred on Liviv, the *other* city. From that moment on, he understood the poet's mission, to convoke beauty where it doesn't seem to have any right to exist: "There exists a meaning, habitually hidden though graspable in moments of maximum concentration, when our self-awareness loves the world. Capturing this difficult meaning is the same as living a very peculiar happiness, losing it leads to melancholy."

The inhabitant of Mexico City does not have to be deported to lose his native land. The city has metamorphosed to such a degree that it offers two cities: one is composed of the evanescent tales of the collective memory; the other is its devastating, daily expansion.

We live on two simultaneous planes, the present, which we know, and the past, which never stops returning. South Axis 5, once upon a time Eugenia, allows us to travel over the traces left by palm trees, and a new Oxxo, that sells commercial hardware, is being built where there was a mansion from the first years of the twentieth century. What we see now does not completely eliminate what we used to see. Each generation adapts its memory to those transformations.

Zagajewski invites us to celebrate the mutilated world and warns us that not celebrating it "leads to melancholy." In Mexico City, inspiration to celebrate can come from tainted objects we arrogate to ourselves with deep emotion: the shoes hanging from an electric line, a tree covered with multicolored dots that once were chewing gum, a chemically reddened sunset, benches destroyed by tree roots, looking like an ice floe broken up by a battleship. The capital has lost any possibility of offering a harmonic discourse, but people and nature just won't give up; someone will decorate a wall with graffiti and weeds sprout from every crack.

The real city generates another city, one that is impossible to find, one that must be imagined to be loved.

We have to recognize that not all change is negative. There are times when we're thankful for the demolishing work of the pick. Many of the zones devastated over the past five decades were horrible. At the end of *Battles in the Desert,* which captures the Roma neighborhood of the 1950s, José Emilio Pacheco writes "Who can feel nostalgia for that horror?" In a paradoxical way, pointing out that loss and recording it as a memory allows us to survive today's disaster.

In *On the Natural History of Destruction,* W. G. Sebald observes that Germany's World War II defeat brought about a later cultural defeat. The feeling of guilt in the face of the ignominy committed by the Nazis deprived the Germans of recognizing themselves, yes, them as well, as victims of the destruction. Sebald comments that riding on a train in 1946 it was easy to spot foreigners because they were the only ones who dared to look out the windows.

Chilangos feel less guilty about their environment, but they also need compensatory mechanisms to put up with destruction. One of the most effective is memory, which creates a sentimental link with the earlier city, the city submerged in the city of the present. What was lost as tangible space returns as personal evocation. What was once a cityscape is now our autobiography.

Integrating ourselves into this megalopolis by means of memories has been an operation shared by various writers of my generation in Latin America. You don't have to be old to have good nostalgia.

Antonio López Ortega grew up in Potosí, a town in Venezuela flooded when a dam was built. All his childhood memories were submerged. Visitors to that place during droughts, when the water level sinks, can again see the bell tower of the church. For decades, López Ortega has lived in Caracas, a city built following the idea that an oil emporium (Venezuela) should be a paradise for cars. Faced with the incessant transformations of Caracas, the novelist has experienced exactly what he felt in Potosí: an invisible flood has covered what once was there. Evoking his hometown is the same as lowering the water level in his memories so the bell tower can reappear and the bells can ring. The same thing happens in his recovery of the neighborhoods in his changing Caracas, with the difference that this flood is metaphoric.

The writer who tries to recover an expanding urban territory draws the map of what he is looking at and the mental map of what once stood there.

Living in the City

The Child Heroes *(Los Niños Héroes)*

W hat nationalists you are!" a Colombian stewardess said to me as we took off from Mexico City one September 16. The previous night she'd witnessed the ceremony of the Shout *(El Grito)* and was surprised at our ability to express our love of the nation with party horns and clouds of confetti.

The longest avenue in the city bears the name Insurgentes, to commemorate "the heroes who gave us the nation." How necessary was it to found Mexico? Nowadays, we have no grand merits we can use to justify ourselves in the concert of nations. Everyone knows that doing something "Mexican style" means something negative, but we also know, as the song says, of a "Mexico beautiful and beloved." This logic allows us to appreciate those who had the outsized illusion of creating a nation whose greatness is not always perceptible.

In September, the streets are decorated with immense, luminous structures. Those who design with light bulbs reduce a face to essential features. The man with the huge bald head and hair swirled around his temples is Miguel Hidalgo; the woman with the powerful nose and hieratic bun is Josefa Ortiz de Domínguez; the man with the eminent side whiskers is Agustín de Iturbide; the man with the round face, with a kerchief wrapped around it, is José María Morelos.

The city fills up with electric ideograms, but the favorite by far is the bell of the church of Dolores which Father Hidalgo rang on September 16, 1810.

When I was a boy, I was excited by the huge display of flags, the cars with tiny flags on their antennas, the pinwheels frantically spinning. The Comercial Mexicana supermarket held its September sale and set a nationalist price on turkey breast.

Studying in the German School enabled me, above all, to appreciate Spanish. For nine years, I studied every subject in the language of *Sturm und Drang* and *Blitzkrieg,* all except National Language. The school had been the main center of Nazi propaganda and was closed when Mexico sided with the Allies. I entered in 1960, fifteen years after the end of World War II. Most of my teachers had been trained during National Socialism, and some still expressed nostalgia for the Third Reich. Rudy Roth, my fellow student, went to a camp where one teacher ruined a meeting around a campfire. That severe man, who until then evinced an iron self-control, began to sob. There is something especially devastating in the collapse of a person we think imperturbable. The professor was weeping and there was no relief possible. When someone dared to ask him what was wrong, he answered: "Today is the *Führer's* birthday."

The rigid instruction program in the German School enabled me to understand my own language as an elusive free space that I had to treasure at all costs. It also transformed me into someone who was a folkloric patriot, one who longed to fight against foreigners and against the mysterious "Masiosare" about whom our national anthem spoke (in fact the incomprehensible first words of a future subjunctive phrase "mas si osare" or "but if [a foreigner] were to defile your soil with his foot"). It's easy to understand that my favorite heroes were the cadets of the Military College who fell fighting against the United States. While the demands of a military education had to be stronger than those of my school, I idealized those demands with narcissistic masochism. I didn't want to suffer in the name of German declensions: I wanted to suffer for the fatherland.

I was amazed by something Miss Muñiz, our National Language teacher, told us. Every September 13, roll was called at the Military College, and the names of the six cadets who died in 1847 were included.

The professor would say: "Agustín Melgar?" and the infatuated students would answer "He died for the fatherland!"

In class, we memorized one of the most enigmatic poems in history. We didn't understand it, but it made us cry. Amado Nervo, "the poet of ecstasy," wrote:

> Like fresh stems whose tender shoots
> In bloom a gelid wind withers
> So fell the boy heroes
> To the bullets of the invader.

The first line was incomprehensible, the second confusing, the third awe-inspiring, and the fourth beyond judgment because we were already crying. The impenetrable Amado Nervo was a man of irredeemable vulgarity who also happened to be an extraordinary poet of the Modernista school. As Alfonso Reyes suggested, he is one of those poets who only survive in anthologies. The verses I quoted from memory, half a century after learning them, do not belong to the salvageable part of his work but to the poems that gave him exceptional fame.

Before the death of the singer Juan Gabriel in 2016, the most highly attended funeral in Mexico City had been Amado Nervo's. Not even the earlier funeral of yet another singer, Pedro Infante, or those of the comic actors Cantinflas or Chespirito reached that dimension. In 1919, the author of *The Immobile Beloved (La amada inmovil)* closed his eyes after asking that the curtains be opened so he could see the light one last time. He was in Montevideo, and the return by ship of his body became a maritime funeral that lasted six months. He received homages in numerous Latin American ports until being buried in the Rotunda of Illustrious Men (Vicente Fox, president of the democratic alternative that defeated the Institutional Revolutionary Party [*Partido Revolucionario Institucional,* or PRI] which had been in power for seventy-one years, would not carry out his promises to change everything and instead focused on cosmetic modifications: starting in 2003, the Rotunda lost its masculine exclusivity and is now the resting place of Illustrious Persons).

In my living room, Nervo's verses impassioned us, setting aside aesthetic considerations and the fact that we didn't really understand them.

An indecipherable but concrete pain came through that complicated evocation of the boys who died. Because of the U.S. invasion, Mexico was despoiled of half its territory. The occupying army lost fewer than two thousand soldiers in the struggle. "In terms of war, it was like winning the lottery," the journalist Pete Hamill commented.

Learning about all that was one of the central episodes of my childhood. The landscapes we would see in the cowboy films on the *Disneylandia* program had once been ours. In defense of our national soil, six young men sacrificed (a favorite verb among civics teachers) their lives at the Chapultepec Castle, where the Military College was located. At the foot of the hill where that fortification stands, the Boy Heroes *(Los Niños Héroes)* were commemorated with columns crowned with laurel leaves that looked like gigantic asparagus.

I always longed to be able to disappear in spectacular fashion. As I've already said, I wanted to leave my home and be found by my parents years later as a living ruin that would fill them with guilt. Then I imagined myself as a bloodstained cadet who would return every September 15 along with the shout: "He died for the fatherland!" Unlike my friends who wanted to triumph as soccer players, presidents, police chiefs, or rock stars, I was entranced by the contradictory celebrity of lasts because he's no longer there. The Necessary Absence.

The Boy Heroes were ideal for linking sacrifice with pedagogy. They died young, splendidly dressed, defiled by Mexico's historic villain: the United States. We know what they looked like thanks to the fact that one of their fellow students, Santiago Hernández, painted them from memory for a commemoration in 1871. Hernández was one of the principal caricaturists for the magazine *La Orquesta* and had a privileged visual memory. More than twenty years after the events, he captured the young faces we see today on stickers still being sold in stationery shops.

Just to add the perfect finishing touch to the matter: the most dramatic of the Boys had my name. According to the legend, Juan Escutia climbed up to the terrace of the Military College. Mortally wounded, he went to the flag and tried to keep it from falling into the hands of the invaders. In a sublime gesture, he wrapped himself in it and threw himself down the hill. Our great heroes jump. The fate of Cuauhtémoc, the last Aztec emperor, was inscribed in his name: the Eagle who falls. Juan Escutia found his fate on the hillside.

The Boy Heroes entranced me to such an extent that because of them I gave up one of my childhood passions: baseball. In 1965, I became infatuated with the King of Sports because I discovered Sandy Koufax. I've always admired southpaws. All they have to do is write down their names to be original. In 1965, Koufax was the first lefty to pitch a perfect game since 1880.

His ability with his left hand dazzled me. Though my favorite radio sportscaster was Ángel Fernández, I admired the baseball narration of Septién the Magician, who described the game as a "ballet without music" and gave an epic meaning to statistics. There was something bewitching about an activity where those furthest away were called *jardineros* (gardeners or outfielders) and where the batter had to carry out Ulysses' unfathomable task: get home. The pitchers were the great heroes, and they exercised their profession in an enchanted spot: the diamond.

All idolatry includes elements unrelated to the hero's tasks. Sandy Koufax, the great pitcher of my childhood, has extraordinary attributes unrelated to sports. That he was left-handed captivated me from the start, but there was something more. When the first game of the World Series between the L.A. Dodgers and the Minnesota Twins (the name was right out of legend!), Koufax refused to play because it was the same day as the start of Yom Kippur. That's how I found out my idol was Jewish. For someone who'd suffered the rigors of the German School and had seen enough World War II movies to be able to tell the difference between an *Oberstabsfeldwebel* and a *Feldmarschall,* a Jewish pitcher had the rank of Avenger.

I admired Koufax as if he were throwing curveballs against my teachers. From the mound, he fought for us. Oddly enough, the Boy Heroes ruined that fantasy. In around 1967, I learned of their existence, I knew their dramatic fate, and I transformed them into my favorite martyrs. Because of that war, California was "on the other side." Koufax played for Los Angeles, territory stolen from us. He was a Jew and therefore the enemy of my teachers, but he was also a gringo who usurped ancient national territory.

On September 17, 1963, the United States gave back to Mexico a tiny parcel of dry land: el Chamizal. While this was a bonsai-sized recovery, it was celebrated with enough vigor to arouse the interest of a boy who one week later would be seven years old.

I remember the images of President Adolfo López Mateos on black-and-white television. My generation grew up to the rhythm of a festive nationalism. We learned that being Mexican is such a good thing that there's no need to argue the matter. We liked imported products more than the domestic version, and the word "Indian" was only used to insult someone. Even so we knew that "there's only one Mexico and one Mexico only" (and it would never have occurred to us to say "luckily").

Mexican nationalism is not based on demands or on confrontations with other nations but in the awareness, decidedly contradictory, that what we see around us is deficient but magnificent. Knowing about disasters did not put the brakes on idolatry.

The person who shouts "Viva México!" does not raise a triumphal index finger, which in the United States means being "number one." Our national pride does not depend on achievements and implies no other superiority than that of celebrating what we are in an inevitable fashion.

It's easy to take on an identity based on celebrations, and even more so if those celebrations take place during the month you were born, although that too created problems. The candles on my birthday cake were lit as a domestic interlude between the parties honoring our great men. I never considered emulating them, but I paid them devout homage. My father was most certainly an influence in that. He was a philosopher who'd written *The Great Moments of Native American Life in Mexico (Los grandes momentos del indigenismo en México)* and sought out national essences with the intensity of a man born in Spain who wants to find a new belief system in his adopted homeland.

I was never an exemplary patriot, but one September 13, the Boy Heroes destroyed my Sandy Koufax cult. In point of fact I only understood it a long time later, when I read an extraordinary tale by Luis Humberto Crosthwaite: "Where Have You Gone, Juan Escutia?" The story is about a boy from Tijuana who is a fan of the San Diego Padres who one day discovers that the Boy Heroes died fighting against the United States. That's the reason he lives on the poor side of the border:

the nation shrank because of the war, and Tijuana, a place that until then lacked any relevance, stood by chance on the frontier. For that reason, Crosthwaite considers Antonio López de Santa Anna, the big loser in the war, the greatest real estate dealer his city has ever had.

Crosthwaite skillfully links his protagonist's childhood to the broken history of the nation. When I read his tale, I understood my own muddled identity. Years later, I read this aphorism by Canetti: "The enemy of my enemy is not my friend." The lefty from Los Angeles, usurped territory, had no reason to represent me.

From then on, baseball for me became something distant that nevertheless had a mysterious presence in the city. According to legend, Septién the Magician got his nickname on the afternoon he performed the feat of narrating over the radio an invented baseball game. From start to finish. In his articles, Septién would describe the Social Security Sports Park as an infinite coliseum. The game was just about to end: "Bottom of the ninth, two outs, three balls and two strikes on the batter. The last pitch . . . The stadium is about to explode . . . Not a speck of space . . . But people keep on coming!"

For the Magician, the crowd represented an incessant wave that never stopped breaking, even when there was only one pitch left. This vision of the fans as an infinite wave is a metaphor for the entire city, and the dynamics of the game reminds us that the challenge we all face is being safe at home.

The Social Security Sports Park was at the juncture of two highways, Viaducto and Avenida Cuauhtémoc. Even though soccer is a much more popular sport, baseball, for years, had a powerful urban presence thanks to the location of the stadium and to the fact that two teams, the Tigres and the Diablos, had their home field there. Whenever someone knocked one out of the park, Magician Septién would say, "Drivers on Viaducto, there's a meteor heading your way!"

Baseball was the fascinating activity that showered balls over Mexico City. I went to the stadium a couple of times to see unimportant games. The half-empty stands seemed as depressing to me as the pork tacos, which were vastly inferior to those my grandmother, an exemplary Yucatecan, made. No matter, years later I was saddened when the baseball diamond was replaced by a shopping center. Nowadays, that insipid temple of consumerism is a square wall. Memories of epic games were replaced by sales. Center field, where some outfielder made a magnificent catch, is now a tiny island stocked with perfumes.

After a confused patriotism distanced me from baseball, I imagined myself, every September 13, as a Boy Hero, even though I never dared to justify that tragic fame. Three days later, patriotic fervor continued in the military parade. My paternal grandmother had an administrator, Don Pancho Gándara, who every September 16 managed to find us splendid places to witness the display of our armed forces. We would arrive about an hour early. Like Goethe's *Faust,* the pageant had its prologue in heaven before the arrival of the troops: small fighter planes would carry out deafening maneuvers while pumping out tricolored smoke.

Mexico did not possess outstanding military equipment. The audience could recognize tanks and rifles from World War II. It was a secondhand army.

Long-distance telephone calls were becoming fashionable, and people said the United States was so powerful they could defeat us by telephone. That was that. And it was enough for us to give up. In the parade, the modest jeeps of the Mexican Army confirmed the fact that we lacked the warlike arguments to recover any territory except for the Chamizal.

The great moment of September 16 was the arrival of the cadets from the Military College. They marched as if they were floating over the pavement, their arms coordinated in a perfect choreography—the left traced an impeccable diagonal while the right held the rifle as if it weighed nothing. Their uniforms were an impeccable black marked with bright red. To make their image perfect, they included a battalion equipped with hooded hawks. We applauded the cadets with the fervor the Boy Heroes deserved.

The strangest part of the parade came with the arrival of the last contingent, which had no relationship with the army. A delegation of cowboys and cowgirls from Puebla riding spirited sorrels. These civic theatrics suggested that our secret weapon was folklore. "If the bazookas don't impress them, we'll use the rodeo." Our definitive rear guard was made up of ranchers dressed up for the part. The final message was dear to us: we could be defeated but we'd never stop dancing the Mexican hat dance.

When that Colombian stewardess praised our nationalism, images from another time came into my mind. I remembered my passion for the Boy Heroes, my conflictive romance with baseball, and the Mexican Army backed up by a column of cowboys.

What fails as ideology triumphs as nostalgia.

Ceremonies

The Shout *(El Grito)*

Father Hidalgo inaugurated the epic of Independence with an act that would define one of the principal customs of the nation whose creation he was proposing. He rang the church bell at Dolores and began shouting to rouse the people. Not all of my fellow countrymen know that he was proposing that Mexico should continue to be ruled by the king of Spain but with a local government that would be more autonomous. What they do know for sure is that this founder-priest opened his mouth to pronounce the words that today determine our principal national ceremony: The Shout *(El Grito)*.

After celebrating the bicentennial of our independence in 2010, what is the health status of our Identity? When we shout out "Long live Mexico!," we don't think about reconquering Texas or kicking out the Argentines who dominate the fashion world and the national soccer team; we preserve the Mexican custom of being together (and, preferably, packed together like sardines).

Even if the tricolor flags were made in Hong Kong, they constitute talismans of authenticity and serve as a license to set off fireworks, eat *esquites,* take over the plazas: the symbol of the nation is a password that opens all doors. A Mexican waving a flag has the same relationship with normalcy that a Formula 1 driver has with speed limits.

On September 15, public life is interrupted by frenzy. One day later comes the valiant parade, but that night being a patriot means going to the Zócalo, smashing an eggshell filled with confetti on the back of your buddy's neck and having him smile, thankful for that fraternal smack.

The event possesses the soul of one and all, with no importance given to recent news, the value of our gross domestic product, the price of oil, or the conduct of the president. We're not celebrating the nation's status but the joy of shouting its name.

By definition, every nation is founded by amateurs. Ours revolted out of haste. The Querétaro conspiracy was revealed, and Father Hidalgo was forced to open the revolt with modest publicity resources: the church bell, a standard emblazoned with the Virgin Mary, and the power of his throat. As a reminder of that rapture, on September 15 the incumbent president shouts out the names of the heroes of Independence and adds a few with whom he identifies particularly (Benito Juárez and Lázaro Cárdenas are the most frequently mentioned reinforcements).

As happens with so many historic events, the deep meaning of the Shout only appeared in the future. Father Hidalgo wanted to free the nation from the yoke of the viceroy, but not from Fernando VII, and proposed the Catholic faith as the state religion. On September 15, we do not shout for that independence. Nor do we shout for any other independence that might be corrected from the perspective of the present moment. We shout because we like to shout.

Paradoxically, post-Revolutionary Mexico, manifestly ultranationalistic, has never stopped seeking an occult pact with the Virgin of Guadalupe, whose image Hidalgo carried on his standard. "We're not all Catholic, but we're all devotees of the Virgin of Guadalupe," as the saying puts it. The highly disputed bank bailout (known as Fobaproa) which would save Mexican financiers from bankruptcy and leave 95 percent of the banking system in foreign hands was approved in congress in the early hours of December 12, 1999, the day of the Virgin of Guadalupe. The same thing happened in 2013, with the privatization of the oil industry. Two decisions that put national property at the service of foreign capital sought the protective mantle of the Virgin. Father Hidalgo was less contradictory when he sought independence under the protection of the king.

When the president exclaims "Long live the heroes who gave us our nation!" he sounds like an actor performing before an audience that's hard of hearing. This rhetoric devoid of emotion reached its highest point in September of 2013, the first time Enrique Peña Nieto recited the names of the heroes from the presidential balcony. He spoke in the tone of someone reading from a teleprompter.

On the day of the Shout, we all fuse into a fabric articulated by horchata water; seeds held between the index and the thumb; the oilcloth that tries to cover us like a raincoat and which becomes a second skin; the sour smell of the crowds moderated by vapors rich in cilantro and epazote; the exclamations of "Don't push!" followed by "MÉ-XI-CO" (which allows you to push); the blessed pot of tamales and the nautical whistle of the sweet potato vendor; the excessive number of beers; the urgent use of the pavement that allows us to pee in the open air; the unmistakable pressure of a corncob in your ribs; the buzzing tricolored fireworks; the street vendor making offerings: "Get your Trump mask"; the splendor of pirated goods (in the very eye of this human hurricane, someone is selling digital camera batteries or jackets to protect your iPod in the grand bazaar of trinkets and junk, the many objects—all of them provisional—that allow us to recognize ourselves as part of the tribe).

As with the celebratory gatherings at the Angel of Independence, the September 15 flock commandeers the streets, but, in this case, it doesn't do so stirred up by an unforeseen sports victory or a brave draw (the Mexican variant on victory). During the night of the Shout, the nation can be going through one of its worst moments or be in competition with Iraq in numbers of kidnappings and murdered journalists without any of that interfering with the tossing of streamers. We are not celebrating success or unheard-of merit but the norm, that is, being just as we are.

The requirements for September 15 are sentimental: the remote promulgation of a right makes our bilirubin level soar. No one investigates carefully what happened in 1810 or what might have happened if Father Hidalgo had seized the capital when he could have done so or if he'd associated with Spain in some confederated form as he'd wanted. The original motive—the insurgents with their huge sideburns—disappears in the face of the needs of the present, dedicated as they are to dissipation.

To participate in the event no other password is necessary than pronouncing *chiquitibum*—our cheer at sporting events. There's no need to know the words of the national anthem or know just who Pípila (hero of the first Independence uprising in Guanajuato) was. In that moment you're a Mexican with the rude naturalness of someone shaking a rattle or wearing a sombrero a yard in diameter. Lineage in this case does not depend on *ius soli* (being born in Mexico) or *ius sanguinis* (having Mexican parents) but in the right to join the crowd, to be one with the many others.

An essential figure in this Mexican chaos is the gatecrasher. In the festival of the Shout, people not from here abound, but they become domestic products with mouthfuls of tequila and triple-impact howls. Would it really matter if some clueless type shouted "E-cua-dor!" in that vernacular chorus? The truth is, we wouldn't take any notice and would go back to hearing "Mé-xi-co!," the three syllables that constitute the bass drum, the sonorous foundation of the night, the boom you hear in your stomach, the tribal pulse that displaces the reggaeton, the Tex-Mex quebradita, the ponchis ponchis, the hybrid rhythms unable to silence the devout blood that quotes Ramón López Velarde.

With the roar of plastic horns as background music, the talismans bring us together better than the heroes. Aldama, Mina, and Allende are less important than the Aztec feathered headdress, a tricolored Afro hairdo, and a jorongo or poncho made of chiles serranos. A night of disguises and artisanal work, ex-votos, and souvenirs, September 15 follows the model of carnival but without carnival's religious or esoteric implications. People know one another and stop knowing one another; they paint their cheeks green, white, and red; give in to Dionysian raptures; and reach the catharsis of fireworks for no official reason other than a passion for the republic. Isn't it strange to be in a frenzy in the name of the law? The same nation that turns its back on the constitution and regulations transforms a juridical principle, an act of sovereignty, into a moment of wild partying.

Unlike many national ceremonies that combine Christianity with pagan sensuality, the Shout does not ask myths for their support. It includes no ritual other than repeating the names of the heroes. The rest is a spree sanctioned by what we judge to be our own, the natural resources that run from punch to the song of "The Mad Mariachi."

The sensorial intensity of dawn brings with it the unifying gestures of rapid romance and pig feet, the foot stomping and risk, a caress warmed up by the jug of atole, the neighboring shoulder we use to wipe off the water that fell from heaven or perhaps from a kidney.

What sort of identity takes shape there? The plazas fill up with Mexicans—tattooed, twisted, blond (some bleached), with piercings, Mexican pirates, wasted Mexicans, Texas Mexicans, space alien Mexicans, express Mexicans, commonplace Mexicans, export Mexicans, typical Mexicans, odd Mexicans, calendar Mexicans, Mexicans fed up with being Mexicans, comic book Mexicans, Mexicans as unique as Mexico itself, the many ways we have of configuring La Raza, the mob that only allows one statistic: "There's a shitload of us, and there will be more!"

La Independencia, S.A. de C.V.

The nations of Latin America, who just over two hundred years ago decided to live their own lives, constitute a theater of paradoxes. With Bolivarian spirit, the region's soccer teams united to form the Liberators League. Even so, as a function of the times we live in, the project received patronage from a Spanish bank and was rebaptized as the Santander Liberators League. Perhaps in the future other projects will appeal simultaneously to independence and dependence. Will we live to see a Museum of the Nation named after the Spanish department store chain Corte Inglés?

That Latin American soccer should depend on a Spanish bank may be an insignificant detail. Unfortunately, it's the perfect metaphor for countries that celebrate their independence and where some of the most profitable businesses are named Repsol, Gas Natural, Endesa, Telefónica, Iberia, Caja Madrid, or Mapfre. The most important publishing houses in the region are Spanish, and the main newspaper is Spanish. The Bicentennial Tower, which was just on the verge of being built in Mexico City, with support from the Spanish company Inditex, which owns Zara and Massimo Dutti, would have added yet another irony to the celebration. Is it their virtue or our fault?

As Spain was becoming a prosperous, middle-class country, Mexico was revealing a very different face. According to the 2015 statistics of the National Council for the Evaluation of Social Development Policy, we are a nation with 53.3 million people living in poverty: 45.4 percent of the populace.

Two hundred years after the end of the colonial era, it's cheaper to buy a tourist package for the Mayan Riviera in Spain than in Mexico. A telephone call from Madrid to Mexico City costs the same as the value added tax—just the tax—for a call in the opposite direction. What happened?

The city is draped with tricolor wreaths, people hang flags on their balconies, and the celebratory spirit does not diminish, even if we know that the country has been mortgaged. The streets of independent Mexico are places where one, two, three Starbucks are prospering. Will we reach the utopia that appears in an episode of *The Simpsons,* where an entire street is occupied by Starbucks?

Corn, the origin of humanity in pre-Hispanic cosmogonies, is the national plant. Of course, we import our corn from the United States, where it's used to make ethanol (maybe that's why Speedy Gonzales is so speedy) and where our countrymen live, our fellow Mexicans whose remittances keep our economy afloat.

Just how independent is a nation where the money circulating derives in the main from drug trafficking, from the earth, which, sooner or later, will stop supplying oil, and from émigrés? It's not only our economic self-sufficiency that's in question but our very sovereignty as well.

Mexico's most "typical" cities (Zacatecas, Oaxaca, Guanajuato, or Morelia) have a colonial-Spanish shell, and the name most commonly found is not Ilhuicamina but Juan Hernández. Even so, in our schools Independence is taught as a strange return to origins: we were pure Mexicans, we ceased to be that during the Conquest, and we became pure Mexicans again when the Dolores church bell rang out.

This ultrapatriotic vision of our origin has had the ideological function of rationalizing our failure. NASA is not in Mexico because the conquistador Pedro de Alvarado slit the throats of the native astronomers. In official discourse, the Conquest serves as a pretext for justifying our bogged-down present.

Accepting the mixtures out of which we are made belongs to the same intellectual operation as criticizing the colonial era. In *The Labyrinth of Solitude,* Octavio Paz challenged us to recognize our identity in order to overcome complexes, to define what we are as a prerequisite for confronting that which is alien to us. This exercise can lead to a simplification, to exclude too much and to idealize a condition which is complex and even contradictory. There is no absolute Mexican, identical to others, in the way genetically modified kernels of corn can be identical. As a result, Paz nuanced his focus in *Post Script (Posdata):* "The Mexican is not an essence but a history." Open to time, he subjects himself to new realities. In *The Cage of Melancholy,* Roger Bartra liquidated the theme of identity taken as something that cannot be modified. We're a mix, and we're not all mixed the same way.

In *Screaming Place,* the French playwright Guy Foissy suggests the creation of a space where people can blow off steam by howling. It wouldn't be a bad idea to have an urban screaming place where we could purge our discontent. No one would listen to us, but it would be therapeutic. For the time being, we do possess an incontrovertible date when we can join together in venting and transfigure our unfulfilled desires into partying and hedonism. It's an enthusiasm that requires no more reason for taking place than the calendar.

On that day, in the city plazas, we melt into a collectivity without individual faces. Assimilated into the herd, we are all like those ghostly heroes that entranced me as a boy: the Necessary Absent Ones.

The next day, we buy *mole* in Walmart and pay with our BBVA card.

Places

The Back Patio *(La Zotehuela)*

Mexico City is secretly determined by a space, slightly on the margin of houses, a kind of back patio or intermediary terrace, a refuge between one floor and another: we call it the *zotehuela*.

Normally, the water heater is located there. In earlier times, the boiler would be there, fueled by sawdust. It usually includes a sink, sometimes a propane gas tank, some odds and ends, perhaps a pet too bothersome to be allowed in the house. It is not the main terrace where the water burbles in the tanks.

Out on its many peripheries, Chilangopolis opens out into inhabitable units and little houses of "social interest" crowned with water towers. It's possible that the guilt complex we endure for having dried out the lake has led us to accept this anodyne, precarious architecture built in series, whose distinctive mark is the tank. We haven't even been able to improve on those towers: there are no signed tanks. Indifferent to design, they are the protagonists of an architecture that renounced the adventures of form.

The *zotehuela* is too small to hold water tanks. Which confirms its tranquil character. Its equivalent in churches is the alcove dedicated to the Virgin or the confessional. A place out of the mainstream, perfect for prayer or quick confessions.

A bastion for solitude, it's also a bastion for furtive meetings, especially among women who wash clothes while they sing, smoke a cigarette without their husbands seeing them, converse with their friends about "their things." They talk about pressing, personal matters, perhaps terrible things, which can only be spoken about in a free zone, a place separate from the house but still part of it.

The *zotehuela* is the enclave for blowing off steam in a machista society. The expression "laundry room" is a synonym for gossip. It alludes to this emblematic place where women can be together without arousing suspicion: after all, they're washing the stains out of the men's T-shirts. The *zotehuela* is, perhaps, the only place where a woman wearing an apron and with wet hands can be sincere to the point of rage, where she can say everything about herself.

It didn't take a psychological genius to invent that space. The *zotehuela* is a time-out from geometry, a pause that could not be filled in any other way. In a society that imagines them subaltern, it was women who gave it meaning. Who would dare express anything personal at the dinner table, where the "head of the table" is destined for the "owner of the house"?

Mexican cinema has used that open-air space well. When the mother has to speak with her firstborn daughter without being heard by men, the screenwriter locates her in the *zotehuela:* "I must tell you something, my daughter" (the expression "my daughter," spoken more often on the screen than in reality, guarantees melodrama).

Since, in essence, it belongs to the feminine world, the *zotehuela* is ideal for the unexpected entrance of the ardent suitor or the jealous husband. If the man appears there, it's because, for the first time in a long while, he's got something to say.

The *zotehuela* is ugly: a space devoid of decoration where no one would hang a mirror. It's the place where things that cannot be stored elsewhere end up, things that if they rust it doesn't matter. They have no good views because they face other *zotehuelas,* or a wall, or the rear of a property.

No matter: it's there that women sing. For three years I lived above *zotehuelas.* Sometimes I would open the window and hear mysteries like these:

"I was taken by a delightful sadness: you can't imagine how beautifully I cried last night."

"I'm really conceited, my friend: if I'm not understanding I don't bother to understand."

"A wasp stung me, and my arm swelled up like that. And then my other arm swelled up, I think out of pure sympathy."

"When I wash clothes, it's like I'm washing my pride."

I wrote those sentences down in a notebook I lost and then found again years later. The involuntary aphorisms of the *zotehuelas* transmit the wisdom of women whose hands are reddened from so much washing.

If the city goes on living, it's because of the rumors that circulate there, the wailings, the whispers, the conjectures that ease the tension; stories destined to disappear like the water in the tub, things said to clean a soul the way you'd clean a shirt.

Living in the City

Oblivion

When I was ten or twelve years old, my knowledge of the streets suddenly expanded. Baudelaire's *invitation au voyage* came in the form of a milk truck.

Every morning, the Del Valle neighborhood awakened to find white bottles at the door. The milkman would leave them there according to each family's order. The deliveries fell into groups, like packs of puppies. The bottles with the metallic, purple tops contained whole milk, the ones with the red cap contained skim milk.

In those days, there were few varieties, so milk without lactose, slim, or low-fat milk didn't exist. The bottles were glass and had to be returned. They entered the house as loans, something that reinforced the certainty, which existed then, that either there were few thieves or that the thieves had no interest in milk.

The milkmen would come twice to each house. They would leave full bottles before breakfast, never knocking at the door, and then begin a slow tour to pick up the empties.

I don't know if that system was practical, but it was the reason why all milkmen had a reputation. It was easy to look fondly on them in a milk-consuming community that had fewer allergies than exist now. Carrying a basket from door to door filled with clinking bottles was popular, but the real prestige of the profession was erotic.

Whenever a child didn't resemble his father, people would say—in a tranquil, natural tone: "He's the milkman's son." No one had more possibilities for entering houses at odd hours.

It was the milkman's second tour that fomented the lubricious legend. By then, the family had already had breakfast; the father was at work and the children at school. That was the moment for picking up empties and settling accounts with the lady of the house.

According to the myth, milkmen had an honor code that kept them from rejecting the advances of a woman. Like construction workers, they had the obligation, a bylaw of their guild, to be hot, but unlike the construction men, they could not settle for coveting women with their gaze or flirting with them. They had to go all the way. We viewed them with the admiring respect reserved for a dangerous profession: test pilot, emergency room doctor, the fireman surrounded by flames.

The collective fantasy assigned them an exhausting route of fornication. But that alone did not define their fame. The decisive fact is that they ceaselessly procreated.

As I mentioned earlier, there has always been a disturbing lacuna in population estimates for Mexico City. The ghostly citizens who mark the difference between one set of statistics and another, may well be the children of the milkmen.

A town in the State of Mexico bears the name Dairy Land. I imagined it as the point of departure for men who before noon had fornicated far from home. The fact that they had children everywhere led me to associate them with one of the principal avenues in the city: Niño Perdido (lost child). That avenue once metamorphosed into San Juan de Letrán, but nowadays they constitute the Lázaro Cárdenas Central Axis.

Milk and semen are linked in myriad jokes. Maybe the erotic legend surrounding milkmen derives from that initial association. Mammals evolve, but not too much.

It's worthy of note that in the devout society of that era the promoters of lust enjoyed respect. All communities, no matter how ill conceived, require exceptions and escape valves. Milk reached homes like a gift, and the bearers of these gifts were regarded as a tolerated danger.

I never heard of anyone complaining about them. If they did seduce some lady, they did it without scandal or offense. Maybe they didn't act out of their own will and were slaves of someone else's ardor. Unlike construction workers, they made no obscene comments and never bragged about their fiery legend. Silent, perhaps indifferent to the desire that they nevertheless obeyed, they would enter a house and from time to time take a while to leave. That was all.

In the several neighborhoods I lived in as a boy (Mixcoac, Del Valle, Coyoacán) no one ever discovered them in a compromising situation. And I never heard of any wife abandoning her husband to jump onto the milk truck. We simply ascribed to them an invisible sexuality, which was only carried out and insinuated through them. Despite everything, life in those small houses could actually possess some mystery.

Before supermarkets and the Tetra Pak cartons retired them forever, milkmen bore the fantasies of others with rare dignity. They followed their routes knowing that we attributed multiple coituses to them, an unbridled libertine life, the long-suffering obligation of discharge. In a certain sense, they were home-delivered martyrs.

Shaped by the beliefs of others, they made a limited world seem complex and suspicious. They were the repositories of a faith: they accepted the weight of pretending that in a world devoid of significant events they had adventures.

The reputation of these libertines in motion interested me less than the essential fact that they delivered my favorite drink. One milk truck that belonged to a small company was destined to remain in my memory forever: its name was Oblivion. That name, appropriate for a small dairy farm, has disappeared from the market, and I never managed to taste its products (my family bought milk from a different company), so for me Oblivion represented a means of transportation. I was intrigued by the truck's small size, more like a van, from which a man descended carrying baskets. When he did, a friend and I climbed on and hid behind the bottles.

Along the way, the bottles filled with milk disappeared and were replaced by empties, which, because they were clear, made hiding difficult. At some moment, the driver would discover us and kick us out. Suddenly we found ourselves anywhere in the city. The game consisted in getting home hanging on to a streetcar or as stowaways on a bus, because of course we had no money. Although we never ended up at the distant town of Dairy Land, at times it would take us two hours to get home.

I knew the city of that time in a disconnected way. The way out was a blind path and the return was a variable detour. When we were expelled from the truck, we had to figure out just how far away we were and mobilize our knowledge to find a return route.

In *Peeling the Onion,* Günter Grass observes, "Memory, like children, enjoys playing hide and seek." Often, what we look for in the strange land of childhood must be boldly deduced, investigated, and pursued.

Yes, memory plays hide and seek. Hiding out in the Oblivion milk truck trained me for the exercise I would practice later on—the search for memories that also had the habit of hiding. It also determined my relationship with a city I will never know completely. That fragmented way of articulating the territory resembles the structure of this book.

Ceremonies

Coffee with the Poets

Alejandro Rossi liked to remind himself that the Semitic peoples who settled on both shores of the Mediterranean stopped producing, when adults, the enzyme that helps the human body digest milk. From that perspective, maturing means abandoning milk. That has increased in the allergic condition of the modern world.

Ever since my daughter, Inés, was born seventeen years ago, I've been finding children whose bodies reject all sorts of environmental stimulants. In an emblematic way, their favorite toys are allergic. Contemporary reality makes everyone sneeze.

In such a context, cafés are not, as they are in other parts of the world, places where you can escape from snow but places where you combat haste and can breathe in a different way. Some coffee shops have a system known as "washed air," but the most traditional do not and don't need it: they compensate for the vapors generated by the Italian coffee machine with a fan that at the same time lightens the air. The best climate in Mexico City is to be found in a café.

In his fascinating conversations with Adolfo Bioy Casares, Jorge Luis Borges laments that while literature deals with wine, heroin, opium, and absinthe, it completely ignores café con leche. Despite its tonic effects, the mixture lacks the glamour that would justify an alternative vision of the universe.

When I was a teenager, people would talk about "café intellectuals," not with the respect granted to a sect that transmits ideas sitting at the confined space of a table but with the contempt shown for people who turn their backs on reality and take refuge in vain speculation. Which in no way prevents the elusive cafés of Mexico City from being singular refuges where the real was reinvented by means of words.

In my childhood, there was only one Vips, which opened in 1964. Shortly after, a Denny's arrived. Years later, Sanborns began to scatter branches in various neighborhoods, but franchises were not yet ubiquitous. Those of us who were beginning to read sought out quiet cafés where we could have discussions that looked like conspiracies, not for what we said, but for the lack of participants and the fanaticism we assumed.

When I was in high school, milk no longer had the erotic prestige of yesteryear, even if the members of my generation talked about "hermanos de leche" (brothers suckled at the same breast) to refer to two men who'd slept with the same woman.

From the nomadic space of the Oblivion milk truck I passed to the sedentary life of the café. There were never very many in the city. With the exception of the places opened by Cubans and Spaniards in the center of town, the café has never had among us the preeminent place it's had in other major cities. Besides, little by little, U.S.-inspired chains replaced the small establishments where the owner would be smoking on the other side of the bar, next to a dog who had his comfortable cushion there. Those cafés were unique, unrepeatable, grottoes for initiates.

The most well-known in the capital is Sanborns, located in the House of Tiles, built by a revengeful Spaniard who wanted to get even with his authoritarian father, who predicted: "You'll never be able to build even a house of tiles," by which he meant dominoes.

This seigniorial building has a mural by José Clemente Orozco on its stairway. On the upper level, there is a bar with a small flower-shaped window that provides one of the best views of the historic center of the city, a vista dominated by cupolas and bell towers.

The Zapatistas had breakfast in that Sanborns when they captured the capital in 1914, and they left the indelible picture of common people for the first time receiving the bounteous gift of *pan dulce*.

That structure of indisputable lineage was the first in a chain that today is the property of Carlos Slim, one of the richest men in the world. Carlos Monsiváis liked to pose the question, "What percentage of you belongs to Carlos Slim?" As with boxers, who are owned by various investors, the owner of Sanborns controls a part of the life of every Mexican. The House of Tiles is merely the point of departure for an emporium of ubiquitous businesses. In 1990, President Carlos Salinas de Gortari privatized the Mexican Telephone Company. Slim owned the enterprise as an absolute monopoly for six years and as a partial monopoly for ten. Without that impulse, outside free competition, which derives from a traffic in governmental favors, he would not be the magnate he is today. The coffee served at Sanborns is terrible, but it tastes even worse when you know the details of its owner's career.

Until the 1980s, Italian coffee machines were highly specialized devices that emitted their aromatic vapors in the Tupinamba Café, where Cristino Lorenzo, now blind, would report soccer matches on the radio, or Gino's in the southern part of Mexico City, where the cakes competed in complexity with the hairdos of the female customers.

The Sanborns became so popular that the political class and the many fringes of the leisure set found in them their favorite space. For two years, I worked on a project for founding a new newspaper, to be directed by Fernando Benítez. On one occasion, we were discussing the possibility of hiring a certain collaborator, and Benítez rejected him with this sentence: "He spends his time having breakfast in Sanborns!"

The sanctuary of idleness, the coffee shop reinforced the bad reputation of "café intellectuals" and brought about the creation of an annoying nickname: the *Homo Sanborns,* meaning a useless, enormously pedantic individual.

In his short story workshop, Augusto Monterroso would always warn us about the sterile bohemia that took shape in cafés and would tell us anecdotes about an acquaintance he referred to as *Iguandadon sanbornicus* because of his antediluvian looks and his café-going lifestyle.

Sanborns' regrettable success was imitated by franchises where they serve weak, burned coffee and prosper under onomatopoeic names: Vips, Toks . . . The proliferation of those places with their plastic armchairs gave the real cafés an almost secret air. Places for a sect to which you belong for not always definable merits.

Thanks to the broadcasts made from the Tupinamba, I associate the culture of that café with radio. That impression was reinforced when I walked Ayuntamiento Street, downtown, where station XEW is located, a station that for decades was the most important in the country. Just across the street there was a restaurant with the appropriate name: Hope. It was there those who aspired to be announcers killed time and stirred up their hopes. On the next corner, the San José café restored those who'd been rejected and improved their voices (just one sip of the powerful espresso was sufficient for anyone to acquire the tone of a soap opera villain).

Cafés are places where you can talk. The mythology of the radio announcers was replaced in my mind by the mythology of writers, especially poets. When I was in my twenties, I would make my pilgrimage along Bucareli heading for the La Habana café, where, to use Roberto Bolaño's phrase, the "poets of iron" gathered.

In one of my first incursions there, I discovered that if you seek coffee you find poems. One afternoon, Jorge Arturo Ojeda, a writer proud of his athletic torso who wore basketball jerseys made of translucent mesh and who tossed his mane back over his head in a studied Byronic gesture, approached our table. I'd read his book, *Letters from Germany (Cartas alemanas)*.

"The cover of your book is reddish," I said, just to add something to the conversation.

"It's magenta," he corrected me.

Then he expressed an interest in knowing if I was publishing anything. I told him my book *Navigable Night* was in the pipeline at Joaquín Mortiz Editions. He recalled Gerardo Diego's poem and recited it:

> You and your naked dream. You don't know it.
> You're asleep. No. You don't know it. I sleepless,
> And you, innocent, sleep under the skies.
> You cross your dreams and the ships cross the seas.
> . . . .
> What islander's horrifying slavery,
> I, insomniac, mad, on the cliffs,
> The ships cross the seas, and you cross your dreams.

I never saw Ojeda again but I'll always remember the poem random café life allowed me to associate with my first book.

In the Superleche Café on San Juan de Letrán, I got to know the most antisocial poet in Mexico, Francisco Cervantes. "You have to talk to him about Fernando Pessoa because every other poet annoys him," Monterroso warned me.

Cervantes lived in the Hotel Cosmos, above San Juan de Letrán, and was in the habit of having his evening snack in the Superleche, which collapsed in the 1985 earthquake.

You didn't have to see him at night to know why he was called the Vampire. On several occasions we'd run into each other at the Fondo de Cultura Económica publishing house where we both did translations, and he accepted my friendship because I quoted a poem by Francisco Luis Bernárdez he liked a lot, "The City Without Laura." I was in my twenties at the time and admired, with all the romanticism of someone who really knew nothing about such suffering, the idea that a city might be defined by love for someone no longer there:

> In the silent, lonely city my voice arouses a deep resonance
> . . . .
> To populate this desert all I need is a single word.
> The sweet name I speak to populate this desert is Laura's.

As is usually the case with people who are encased in angry armor, Cervantes was secretly sentimental. However, there were things he hated obstinately, obsessively, against all reason. When I was editing *The Weekly Roundup,* I published one of his poems. In my introduction, I mentioned his exceptional titles. Few authors have Francisco Cervantes's gift for naming their books: *Memorable Men, Alternating Wounds, Pilgrim Bones* . . . Unfortunately, in my praise-laden introduction, I used a term he hated: "poetic output" *(poemario).*

"It's one of the three expressions I most detest!" said the Vampire, a man whose hatreds were nicely classified.

"What are the others?" I inquired.

"The second is *Latin America.*" Then he fell silent, stared at the ceiling with sublime satiety and said, "You don't deserve to know the third."

A week later, we were drinking in the Negresco, an infamous bar on Balderas someone with a sublime sense of irony had baptized with the name of a sumptuous hotel in Nice.

The bar was just up the street from *The Weekly Roundup*. That was the only reason for being there, though Francisco was amused by the waitresses, whose thighs were thicker than Spanish hams. They would come over to our table with fearsome coquetry, pick up the shaker of whatever we were drinking with fingers whose nails were brilliantly polished, and say, with sibylline sweetness, "Want me to shake up for you, daddy?"

Francisco always wanted them to do just that.

We went to the Superleche in a good mood and to the Negresco to let bygones be bygones. The poet preferred Negrita rum and anisette or anise, which won him the alternate nickname of Saint Francis of Anise.

On one occasion, he emerged from the Negresco more than a bit worse for wear. He didn't care that he'd lost a false tooth under the table, and he came back to the office with me. A few minutes later, there was a commotion on the street below.

The *Roundup,* the principal informative organ of the left, was quite near the Government Secretariat, and demonstrations were in the habit of pausing at our door so we would take notice of their struggles. Emboldened, Cervantes the poet opened the window, walked out onto the balcony, and faced the crowd below with an extemporaneous shout worthy of his friend, the Colombian writer Álvaro Mutis: "Long live the King! Return the nation to Spain!" The crowd couldn't hear a word, but they cheered him enthusiastically thinking he'd said something else.

Cervantes was the extraordinary translator of Gaspar Simões's biography of Fernando Pessoa. Among the many lessons he learned from the Portuguese poet, one transcended writing: the Vampire admired Pessoa's art of living free in a café.

The owner of the Hotel Cosmos was a man from Galicia in Spain who loved Portugal, the *saudade* or nostalgic longing of Portuguese songs, and poetry. He adopted the great poet, as did so many others in bars and cafés where he recited, got angry, wanted to end the world, was removed, and recited again.

In one of his luminous nights, the Vampire portrayed himself better than anyone else:

Rage, silence,
Their high masts
Gave you this winter.
But listen in your tongue:
perhaps Spanish
is uncertain.
. . . .

Love? Let's say you understood and let's say moreover
that such tenderness was given you
But neither then nor even less now
did the understanding you did not seek matter to you
and of course you don't have it.
It's certainly true that it's not only you who lacks it.
Anger, insult
the low feelings
gave you this song.

In the La Habana café I'd meet up with another poet of harsh character. Mario Santiago Papasquiaro. We met around 1973, in Miguel Donoso Pareja's short story workshop, on the tenth floor of the Tower of the
Rectory.

The offices of Cultural Diffusion were located there. Toward seven
in the evening, the place would empty out, and only one ceiling light
remained on, the one over the desk where Donoso edited manuscripts.
The huge windows opened onto the campus, itself dominated by the setting sun. On the horizon, we could see the shadow of the Ajusco volcano
south of the city and closer to us the stadium of University City, like a
scarab flipped over on its back.

We were listening attentively in a semicircle of chairs. Among those
present were Luis Felipe Rodríguez, who wrote notable science fiction
tales and who years later would be one of Mexico's principal astronomers; Carlos Chimal, who would publish stories, novels, and numerous
popular science books; Xavier Cara, who would soon opt for medicine
and die standing guard at the General Hospital during the 1985 earthquake; Jaime Avilés, future reporter on medical abuses and other forms
of corruption.

Donoso Pareja had been a sailor and had suffered jail time as well as exile. It was his charisma that attracted those of us who aspired to be short story authors, but also those who wanted to find a good place to argue. One of the latter, without any doubt the most eloquent, was Mario Santiago, who at that time used the name José Alfredo Zendejas. He only wrote poems but loved to debate about narrative. His critical sense was ferocious, but he tempered his fire with jokes he himself celebrated with raucous guffaws. He'd read more than we had, knew all about the avant-garde, had fought alongside Roberto Bolaño and other rebels involved in Infrarealism, and planned an epic trip to Europe.

His poem "September 19, 1985" recovers the impact of the earthquake with the same force as a broken mirror:

> The families who lived right across the street no longer exist
> Metaphor fell off its scaffolding
> from yesterday to today blood became other
> outside of sleep sleep is raw
> children, parents, the lovers of priests
> there is black dust: flowers or ire I chew and chew

During the 1990s, that poet with burning eyes and tousled hair was already a diminished man who walked with a cane because he'd been run over. A forty-year-old with thin hair and bad teeth. People dealing with him adopted an air of annoyed suspicion. When he came to see me at *The Weekly Roundup,* the receptionist, accustomed to dealing with all kinds of bizarre people, telephoned me to ask if I really wanted to let Mario in.

I much preferred seeing him in the La Habana café, where he would order a beer at ten a.m. as we talked about Donoso's workshop and about the 1960s, the time when Bolaño would become famous for *The Savage Detectives,* where Mario appears under the name Ulises Lima.

In and around 1996, we would meet in the café with Samuel Noyola, a poet from Monterrey who lived in my house for six months in 1986. Immersion in the depths of the Federal District would be even more intense in Samuel's case. Throughout his entire life, Mario was an irregular, a brave man ready, like Kid Azteca, to box against wind and destiny. His fall was that of a warrior on the battle front he invented for himself. Samuel's case was completely different. A solar poet, the Kid Marvel who conquered the capital, worked with Octavio Paz, had an extraordinary girlfriend, and suddenly went into eclipse. After going through various purgatories, he would live on the street, first in La Condesa, then in Coyoacán, he would go to jail and would finally disappear, chasing an uncertain flame or simply fleeing his ghosts.

I introduced these street poets in the La Habana café. Samuel greeted Mario in his northern Mexico accent and proudly showed off the cowboy boots he was wearing for the first time. It was about noon, and the Infrarealism chief baptized him as the Midday Cowboy.

Mario Santiago felt closest to the radical avant-gardes of Latin America (Zero Hour, Nadaism, the Mandrágora, the Roof of the Whale) than to the tradition of Mexican poets, which he judged to be made up of courtiers, more interested in grants and jobs than in their work.

His poetry is willfully uneven in the sense that he takes it to be a truth that every poem is the result of an accident that should not be silenced. He accepted and abandoned his poems as the chance events of destiny. In the style of Allen Ginsberg, he firmly believed the text to be the child of chance; he understood the poet to be an intercessor and nothing more. A good number of the verses of this savage detective were written on paper napkins and ended up in the café trash bins.

He would telephone my house at dawn and improvise poems until he used up all the memory on the answering machine. Faithful to his condition as vagabond poet, he wandered the streets until he was run over in 1996, this time fatally. The warrior fell without anyone's really knowing his battles. He'd published a few *plaquettes,* but it was only with the posthumous release of his book *Mug of a Saint* that his work became known.

A poet diametrically opposed to Mario Santiago, Tomás Segovia nevertheless shared with him the conviction that all writing transcends the author's intentions and lives on its own. The author of *Anagnórisis* did not have a shamanic vision of poetry but he did consider that, once consummated, the poetic act breathes on its own and should not be denied. "For some reason it happened," he would declare in a voice that seemed scraped by the harsh wind to which he dedicated so many verses.

Segovia understood poetry as a natural outpouring. What right did he have to cancel that existence? He did not presume to be receiving a

divine order but thought each poem to be evidence of a linguistic possibility that he must not hurt.

At Christmas in 2008, he sent this poem to his friends, wishing them
happiness, "as odd as that seems":

> There were probably few of us who at this dawn
> from the thick depth
> of the city still barely awake
> can have seen there on the white altitude
> the delicate flight of wild ducks
> haughtily focused
> on their impeccable, blindly locked law
> our law is different
> other laws work other layers of world
> but this silent flight floats
> almost there in the heights forever intact
> where sovereign laws
> make love among themselves.

In café gatherings, Tomás would talk about his passion for repairing
houses. He was a consummate artisan extremely fond of carpentry and
even of installing electric wiring. That *bricoleur* aspect contrasted with
his respect for the manuscript that was never to be modified. For him,
language required less maintenance than a house.

A Spaniard translated to Mexico, Segovia habitually wrote in the
Chiandoni ice cream parlor, always aspiring, without always achieving
it, to the European condition of being left in peace.

His disciple, Fabio Morábito, a poet of my generation, was born in
Alexandria in a Milanese family. He was an adolescent when he reached
Mexico. He learned to love and to write in our language, but he retained
some elements of the immigrant who hasn't managed to accommo-
date himself anywhere. He pronounces our double "r" in the slippery
tone of a northern Italian and feels comfortable in places far from home.
He reads, writes, and sees people in cafés. For years he had no telephone.
The only way to find him was to visit him at his café gatherings.

Perhaps because he prefers not to acclimate himself completely and in
order to preserve, at least sentimentally, his status as a foreigner, he rejects

cafés of the "intellectual" sort and favors cake shops with complicated pastries, where even the décor has too much sugar in it, places where perfumed ladies raise their voice to drown out the clink of teaspoons. In this noisy setting, the poet concentrates in order to say: "Noise is our caffeine."

One of his best poems evokes urban space as a void. Can we preserve at home the emptiness that made it possible? A rare nostalgia emanates from Morábito's poems. It's no accident that he's written about moving house, the traces previous inhabitants leave in a house, or the loss of decisive spaces, like the Italian Club, where foreigners had a refuge (closing the club forced them to recognize that, indeed, they were living in Mexico).

Standing in front of a house, Morábito recognizes the empty lot that made it possible. The most valuable thing is to be the owner of that naked space, the void necessary for a home to be imbued with meaning:

> I'm going to look over this property
> slowly, to trace it with my eyes
> and feet
> before building the first wall,
> like a virgin landscape
> full of density
> and dangers,
> because I want to remember it
> when the house hides it from me,
> I don't want to confuse myself
> with the house,
> I'm not going to forget
> this landscape
> or the way I am now
> owner
> of an amplitude,
> of everything I have.

While he may write novels, stories, and essays, Fabio is above all a poet who can work between cappuccinos.

The rhythm of the café lends itself to the reworking of verses that move forward in the same way cigarette smoke did before. But you can't write novels in cafés. The pressures of journalism and a need for isolation took me away from those places where I began to think myself superfluous. I wasn't a poet, and I was wasting time. That's what my puritanical conscience, well trained in the German School, told me.

Sometimes I get out of the rain in a café or even kill time between one chore and another, but cafés have stopped being goals in my life. I admire the people who do gather there, with the bemused distance of someone who's spent thirty years missing something. All cities have parallel societies: bettors, beggars, drug traffickers, and addicts usually associate with one another in a clandestine way in order to fraternize on the fringe of the norm. For me, cafés have become something similar, almost forbidden. Is there any reason for this renunciation? It's possible that it all has to do with the way we administer the future. For years I sat down with poets to talk about the future. I had no intention to write poems, but like the characters in Kerouac's *On the Road* or Bolaño's *Savage Detectives,* I aspired to live poetically. The café was the site of violent conjecture, where we could conceive strange, perhaps unattainable hopes. Little by little, the horizon stopped being imaginable and became a certainty left behind.

But sometimes, the spurt of milk in a café cortado hits me like a telegram from another era: I remember the aimless wandering, when I was hidden in the Oblivion milk truck and the teachings of the poets who scanned verses tapping their teaspoons against the cup.

In *Poetics of the Café,* Antoni Martí Monterde analyzes an Edgar Allan Poe story "The Man of the Crowd," about the depersonalization of modern man. The plot begins and ends in a café, a privileged observation post in the ebb and flow of the streets.

The history of cities is the history of cafés, where life mixes with culture. The Spanish author Ramón Gómez de la Serna set up his observatory in the El Pombo in Madrid; for Claudio Magris, it's the San Marco in Trieste; for Karl Kraus, it was the Central in Vienna. Jean-Paul Sartre used the Deux Magots in Paris; Fernando Pessoa, the Martinho da Arcada in Lisbon; Juan Rulfo the Agora in Mexico City.

Is there a better way to get to know the city in sedentary style? If the stroller deciphers the territory using what he sees, the café man understands his era using what he hears.

When I was a boy, milk represented wandering, getting lost, a shy eroticism. During adolescence, the café for me was a voyage through words and ideas.

Every city is crisscrossed with nomadic and sedentary tensions: taxi drivers and barbers, those who are seen and those who see, the passersby, and the tranquil witnesses.

Café cortado mixes both systems: the dark liquid of the person fixed at a table, affected by what comes from far off, the milky cloud with the scent of the countryside.

I discovered the aesthetics of the fragment on a milk truck. Cafés sanction another exercise: being in the city without being absorbed by it, seeing others in the instant when they withdraw from their codified, habitual conduct. The urban usage most turned to in that limited space is conversation, whose method knows no conclusions and only aspires to prolong itself.

The infinite demands strategies to become something close to us. Mexico City is infinite in a provisional way, like a cup of café cortado.

City Characters

El Merenguero

One major player in the nomad food business works so good luck can exist. The croupier who deals cards in a casino, the jockey who spurs on a horse, or the man who trains fighting dogs all belong to the same species because they stimulate the superstitious ambitions of others. Nevertheless, the strangest profession linked to luck is that of the merengue man. When I was a boy, I was overjoyed whenever this man came to my neighborhood. He'd be holding up a wooden board covered with a sheet of clear plastic that protected it from flies and allowed us to see the pinkish and white glow of the candies. He was usually followed by bees, with which he had a friendly relationship.

I never knew anyone who really longed for merengues. It's a sweet that cloys all too soon. Even though there are high-class merengues that dissolve on your tongue and taste like a subtle air encapsulated in a crackling shell, the ones sold on the street have the chewy consistency of something made carelessly, hastily. Their pale color does not stand out in a nation that loves visual vertigo, where even the seeds form a chromatic fan, as if they were posing for Rufino Tamayo, and the combination of commercial bread making and cartoons produced the short-lived but unforgettable Tuinky Dálmata.

What separates merengue selling from other city trades is that the seller has to raffle his merengues. "How much for a merengue?" That does not mean that the customer is going to buy it. He wants to know how much the customer will bet with a flip of the coin.

The same can't be done with sellers of gelatin or *elotes* with cream. And the bread man never jumps off his bicycle to raffle the *conchas* that decorate his basket. Only merengues are priced according to chance.

How did this tradition arise? It's possible that it came about because these candies are not very attractive when they enter the market to compete with the virtuosity of coconut sweets with their burnt fringes, milk fudge, or anise candies. Not even their defects are supreme. For someone really hungry for sticky stuff, the merengue is too neat. How much more delightful is the sticky bun, which impregnates the fingers, the gums, the very conscience!

Even industrial candies have found ways to be original. The Pelón Pelo Rico (Baldy with the Delicious Curl), a little gentleman with sweetened tamarind or chili hair, shows what madness can do in favor of sweets. What sweet shop Salvador Dalí invented this creature?

The merengue is tedious, but it has a surprising fate. Its life is that of a bureaucrat who ends up as an adventurer in the raffles of fate. In a country where laws are not carried out, the humble merengue vendors respect the harsh contract they never signed.

One hard-to-forget afternoon, I witnessed a terrible drama. Carlos Induráin, a guy we called the Onion because on cold days he would wear three shirts, was a child devoid of charm until we discovered he was also a gambler. He won three tosses from the merengue man, and his eyes were glittering, animated by an unknown power. He wanted to go on tossing the coin. Faithful to his ethical code, the vendor accepted.

One by one, the sweets passed to Carlos. There was a moment when we begged him to stop the torture, but the merengue man said that this was his job. His soft, measured voice contained so much dignity that it silenced us instantly. This complete stranger accepted bad luck as if it did not affect him. Meanwhile, the Onion celebrated his triumph like an idiot. He jumped up and down waving his fists, convinced that luck is a personal merit. We should have stopped him, told him he had no right to be so presumptuous, that he was nothing more than a maniac who wore three shirts. But the integrity of the merengue man held us back.

He'd appeared before us to provide an example. His moral superiority paralyzed our twelve-year-old consciences. We watched him the way you'd watch a saint or a hero, or someone perhaps more mysterious: a merengue man.

When his board was empty, that man with extremely black hair obsessively combed straight back went his way. He took a few steps, then stopped, and came back toward Carlos. We feared a fight was about to start, but we learned another lesson. The merengue man had forgotten to return the coin, which belonged to his adversary.

Perhaps without knowing it, the merengue gamblers constitute a sect scattered over Mexico City. They walk the streets to allow mutable chance to mix with luck. Their profound meaning is this: they accept losing as a mere possibility of the soul, and they reveal those who think themselves deserving of good fortune.

In an era of competition, when winning is a celebrated imposture and few even recognize defeat, the merengue men offer their lesson. Wise, silent, they preach through example and show that no one owns luck.

Shocks

Street Children

The Child and the Tree

When I was thirteen, I longed to live like an untouchable. I'd abandon my clothes and toys, I'd sleep in a ravine, and I'd forget language. That last detail now seems strange to me: you can be homeless without losing the ability to speak. I added that blot thinking about the soap opera moment when my parents would find me only to discover that it was just too late, because I could no longer talk to them.

I dreamed about that flight from reality until I met a boy who in fact had lived in a tree.

Jorge Portilla, a philosopher friend of my father, also lived in the Del Valle neighborhood. One afternoon, his children found a child at the top of a tree, and the author of *The Phenomenology of Disorder (Fenomenología del relajo)* decided to adopt him. Many years later, Jorge, the oldest child in the family, would compare the boy with Kaspar Hauser. Suddenly, he was there, with no antecedents whatsoever.

The street boy only grew a little and found work as a jockey in the Americas Hippodrome. Then he moved to the United States, where he won various derbies. Every Christmas, he would send the family who'd raised him a photograph of his wife and children. As far as I know, he never came back to Mexico. His destiny was made for leaving, winning races, chasing a goal with eyes half closed against the wind.

Knowing that a boy lived on the street confirmed the fact that I could have had the same fate. I savored that possibility as if I were tasting an innocuous dose of poison. Deep down, I knew I was incapable of putting it into practice, and for that very reason, I liked it. It was an *idea*. For the son of a philosopher it was the equivalent of having a weapon.

Ever since then, whenever I see a child wandering the streets, I feel a mix of guilt, nostalgia, and shame. The tragic fantasy of a boy who in truth has no serious problems is a rather luxurious caprice. I never had to face a real danger.

Faced with a child who lives his destiny on his own, I remember what I didn't dare to be and I understand, with the feeling that I'm doing it too late, that my tediously common life saved me from disgrace.

The Temple of Lost Causes

The Church of San Hipólito stands just a few meters from the Central Alameda, where Avenida Hidalgo meets Paseo de la Reforma. To one side of the church, at two o'clock in the morning, a melancholy accordion splits the night. Leaning against a metal screen, a musician tries to get the people leaving bars to give him a few coins.

Nearby, a cargo truck waits for dawn to pull out. On its bumper sticker: "My love is portable." Under the truck there are some shadowy shapes: children napping, taking advantage of the heat given off by the motor. The fantasies I had about living in a tree and my contact with the boy who came down from the branches to become a jockey are fairy tales compared with the brutal reality of street children.

The Guerrero neighborhood has enough night life to stimulate odd activities at odd hours. Agustín Lara, the legendary "poet-musician," sang in many of the local cabarets and lived in some buildings here. In this zone of dancing and vaudeville you'll find the Salón México, the Blanquita Theater, and the joint where Paquita from the Hood, high priestess of the bolero, vindicates the freedom of all women in order to cuckold her husband.

This part of the city has not given in to gentrification, nor to the real estate raids that "modernize" the space by expelling its longtime residents. Cantinas abound along with hotels where rooms are rented by the hour, a place where night owls are the favorite targets of the street children who beg, who sell flowers stolen from some market, and deal drugs on a small scale.

Just by chance, all this takes place in a locale with historical resonance. The fall of Tenochtitlán took place on August 13, 1521, Saint Hippolytus Day. And Hippolytus became the city's patron saint.

He was a polemical bishop. In 217, he was called "antipope" because he defended the rights of the excommunicated. In an almost miraculous way, he managed to reconcile with Rome, and on August 13, 236, his remains came back to the city along with those of other exiles. A saint of inclusivity, Hippolytus is not well-known. A supporting actor in a religion replete with major actors. Chance caused him to become the patron saint of Mexico, but even among us he has no relevance. In 1982, the church that bears his name received an altar dedicated to Saint Judas Thaddeus, Jude the Apostle, patron saint of lost causes. Ever since, the church is associated more with him than with Hippolytus, perfectly explicable in a country that's lost its way.

Opposite the church of San Hipólito or Jude the Apostle the most recent manifestation of the Virgin of Guadalupe took place. In 1997, she appeared at the Hidalgo subway stop. During the rainy season, a trinket seller discovered that the moisture had traced the shape of the Virgin of Guadalupe in an entryway, exactly where the wall met the floor, creating an accidental niche.

The Hidalgo stop, where the 2 and 3 lines meet, is one of the enclaves with the most subterranean traffic. The miracle made the stop an instant point of interest, and the name of the station contributed to the prodigy (primary education depends on the stellar moment when Miguel Hidalgo began the struggle of independence raising a standard bearing the image of the Virgin).

Street children take refuge in that station without knowing they're sleeping next to the church of lost causes, without knowing that only a few years ago the Virgin appeared under the surface of the earth. Fond of symbols, fate has placed them on a corner where hopes mix.

In the twentieth century, the capital of Mexico became a bastion for street children. Many come from the provinces (especially from the southern states) or from Central America. Others come from the neighborhoods, towns, and peripheral areas that make up this macro-metropolis, the most densely populated in the New World.

I sat down with José Ángel Fernández to discuss the issue. The notorious number 217 of Mexico City is one of the most active defenders of street children. Ex-student of the Marists and of the University of Mexico Law School, he can tell the exact moment that defined his social vocation: September 19, 1985, at 7:18 in the morning. The earthquake that devastated the city forced him to do something for the place where he lived. He took part in rescue brigades and understood that he had to take on an even more profound and long-term task, seeing to the needs of the most vulnerable victims of the tragedy: the children.

The March sun floods a small terrace next to his office. Fernández is smoking and recalling the creation of Pro Children, twenty years ago, an institution that in 2017 had one thousand seven hundred patrons:

> There are more than 17,000 street children; 5,000 live there, and 12,000 live there part-time: they have the possibility of going to a house but they don't remain there for long. Another 200,000 spend periods of three or four days on the street. Only 10 percent are girls; it's almost impossible for them to survive under those circumstances; they are immediately pressed into prostitution.
>
> There are also second-generation children, offspring of people who've lived there; they know no other life and are shocked by the sight of a spoon or a shower. In twenty-three years, we've managed to get about a thousand children to leave the street; a lot but not enough.

From time to time, a doorman comes to the table where we're chatting. The notary rapidly signs the forms; the transactions involving the sale of property move forward, protected by his name as he talks about a different city, one where a spoon may be a threat to a child who has only eaten with his hands:

> The earthquake created new spaces for street children. For years they were the principal inhabitants of the Center. They lived in what

is today Solidarity Park, next to the Alameda. As the Center was rebuilt, they scattered. Before they lived in large groups, now in groups of three or four. Many were in the United States and were deported without adults, a violation of international agreements. You suddenly find a nine-year-old boy walking hand in hand with a three-year-old; they're not always brothers, and sometimes from two different countries, but they joined together on the road. The less evil part of the story takes place in Mexico City, while elsewhere anything can happen to them. They can't escape human trafficking networks or people who kill them and harvest their organs. There are children who have worked with gangs in Central America who can kill you with a pen.

After saying that, Fernández pointed to my ballpoint. Objects change meaning because of fear or violence. I go on taking notes and think about the spoon that can be a threat for a child who's never been in a kitchen. Even the tool I use for work can become something else. To what point must life degrade for my ballpoint to become a murder weapon?

Families: The Fingers on a Hand

If there were no family problems there would be no street children. They all come from a background marked by violence, poverty, and addiction. In the Pro Children home, I spoke with Alejandro. He is a tall, good-looking boy with melancholy eyes. I spent some time with a group of boys who live there and with others who are visiting. Almost immediately, he came over to tell his story.

When he was seven, he began to wander the streets. He was born in the Doctores neighborhood and at an early age got to know the downtown. His mother had three children from earlier relationships. He hasn't seen her for four years. He hasn't known a thing about his father for even longer. He remembers the beatings his father gave his mother when she was pregnant with his sister, who was born deaf and dumb. One of his half-brothers, still a minor, was arrested for armed robbery.

Alejandro has managed to overcome that broken horizon and believes he can still salvage something. On February 22, 2016, he turned twenty-one. He works in an office and wants to study administration. He gave up trying to come to some understanding with his mother ("When it comes to thinking, she falls apart"), but he wants to keep his sister from suffering. "I'm afraid she's going to cut herself, hurt herself. She can't communicate with anyone and is locked inside herself."

Alejandro pauses, looks out of the corner of his eye toward his comrades who are playing basketball in the patio adjacent to the hall where we're chatting. Then he looks me in the eye, raises his hand, and says: "Each of my siblings is a finger: I'm this one," he points to his index finger. His sister's name is Karina, she can't talk, and she has had no help. The illusion of the boy who survived the street is to rescue her. Her fate pains him, as if she were a part of his body. Karina is in his hand: she's his pinky.

Alejandro's heartrending desire to recover something of his devastated family stands in sharp contrast to the pride with which those whose principal merit is having inherited a fortune speak. Mexico is a pyramidal nation where a handful of names dominate all the branches of the economy. In the summer of 2015, I flew in one of the helicopters owned by Aeromar, the country's "executive" line. In the magazine on board, an article expressed high praise for the principal national conglomerates and pointed out that most of them are family businesses. The economy was viewed as a branch of tradition and good customs. The article went on to praise the fact that the businesses were administered by relatives and not by professionals outside the clan. In an involuntary way, the article alluded to a fundamental fact: in Mexico the family is a luxury.

Poor people endure workdays that almost always exceed eight hours and deal with commutes that are, on average, two hours each way. According to the Organization for Economic Cooperation and Development, when it compared thirty-four countries, Mexico had the highest number of work hours (2,237 per year).

Day care is insufficient and public schools do not keep the children for the whole day. Given those conditions, who can take care of their children? For some, the family is the transmission of power, which sanctions the administration of businesses created by ancestors (entrepreneurial success depends on inheritance); for others, it is a vertigo in which you try to save yourself from indigence or jail.

I also met Leonardo in the Pro Children Day Center, located in the Buenavista neighborhood, near Tlatelolco. Children who are almost living on the street come to this space, but they don't live here full-time. Sometimes they go home, but here they can change clothes and eat well. The Day Center offers them an option other than the street, a place where they can recover interest in study and work. "The street is a party," says José Ángel Fernández. "It's not possible to tell kids to stop living on the street. They have to convince themselves. That's why we created the Day Center, a temporary space where they can come for a while, eat, and wash without having to stay there. They have to leave their drugs at the entrance, but they can pick them up when they leave."

While there I played foosball with Leonardo, who scored on me: "It was a real pleasure to play with you," he commented ironically. He was the first person ever to beat me. He was wearing a Dallas cap and seemed timid, but little by little he became eloquent, carefully choosing his words.

Because of an accident, he has a droopy eyelid. He speaks scratching his forearm as he stares at the floor. Sometimes he smiles in an oblique way, pauses, then goes on with his story:

I never saw my father: my mother is single and had children with other men. I mistreated the youngest without even realizing I was doing it. She drank a lot because she'd come home tired out from her job as a guard in a private security company. She had twenty-four-hours-on, twenty-four-hours-off schedules. Her knees ached from being on her feet so long. I was a good student, I was even on the school color guard! But my mom had no money to get me a uniform, so they threw me out; then I entered vocational school, but I had no money for books. Once I made copies of some books and was scolded for it. My mom had to support her children and my grandmother, she had no money for anything.

When his mother, drunk, fell asleep, Leonardo would drink up her leftovers. He started going to parties, tried drugs (marijuana first, then solvent), dropped out of school without his mother finding out or even noticing his not being home for two or three days. She guarded businesses on an exhausting schedule without being able to guard her own child.

Leonardo was born in Ecatepec, north of Mexico City, the area with the highest population density and the highest crime rate. But the place doesn't seem violent to him. This may be because of habit, the strange acclimatization to the area that kept him from knowing he mistreated his half-brother. Little by little, he learned to get along with people who find themselves in situations worse than his.

There are boys who have never had a roof over their heads and who reach Pro Children with more serious problems. It's not easy to better yourself when you're in the company of people who've suffered worse wrongs. At first, it was hard for Leonardo to endure the time he spent with boys so hurt that they made him feel he was in a place of degradation. Little by little, he began to understand them and realized he was in a position to help them. Now it's hard for him to be indifferent to the problems of others: "I'd like to be a psychologist, because at times I hear so much from people who start to cry."

At seventeen, Leonardo worked as a waiter in the Roma neighborhood. His bosses were on the verge of firing him because an Argentine customer ordered a Coca-Cola and a coffee and he brought both at the same time. "He didn't explain that he wanted the cold drink first and then the hot one."

Mexican luxury depends on poverty. A building guard who cannot supervise her son protects a business for twenty-four hours straight without rest, and a minor with no money for his school uniform has to satisfy the demands for cold and hot in a restaurant.

Nowadays, Leonardo is studying electricity and intends to finish high school online. He makes enormous efforts not to be distracted by other internet temptations: "My conscience tells me I'm wrong to be watching videos." At Pro Children, he's met German volunteers who aroused his interest in their country: "I want everything, but I have to go step by step. Sometimes I catch the Germans saying silly things in Spanish and I think I could learn German, at least so I could say silly things to them." He smiles.

He forms a pistol with his fingers, squints at me, and lets fly an imaginary shot.

The Outdoor Temptation

"Eighty percent of Mexicans do not take part in public activities because they confuse them with political activities," observes José Ángel Fernández as we make the long trip from his notary office to the southern part of the city, the home of Pro Children in Tlatelolco:

> The Church nurtured a culture of charity by impeding the organization of civil society, and the government has had an assistance attitude which does not include citizen volunteers. We don't do this simply out of charity: it's not a pastoral mission. It's very important to help without taking risks. I'm terrible when it comes to jumping into the sewer, but I can do other things.

There is no way to understand the phenomenon of street children without understanding that living rough is something very attractive for those who choose that kind of life. The tragedy begins as an idyll of fun and indolence.

Mexico City is a perfect scenario for all that. In a place unable to tell the number of its inhabitants, nothing is easier than preserving one's anonymity. Children can run away without being looked for, and the climate is sufficiently benevolent for them to survive. But the decisive factor is the treatment they get from their fellow citizens.

Tense situations and suspicion abound in the city, and only rarely does the community organize itself to deal with social tasks at the margin of the government's control. You might say we live under the aegis of indifference. Even so, in an intermittent and spontaneous way, millions of chilangos help others. They don't follow any program: they help according to their feelings and hunches.

Who are the people who care most for others? In 2016, I interviewed Daniel Goñi Díaz, director of the Mexican Red Cross, and he told me that in their annual call for contributions, the greatest amounts come from the poor.

It often happens that when a beggar approaches a taxi, the driver gives him a coin while the passenger, who usually has a larger income, does nothing. A centavo economy circulates in the same city where the stock market sets its prices in dollars. It's no accident that the Mexican word for someone down-and-out, the equivalent of the French *clochard,* the person who takes up begging as an existential condition, is *teporocho:* "te-por-ocho, tea for eight." The word refers to the centavo economy: a tea made from orange or cinnamon with alcohol that used to cost eight centavos.

A lot is given away little by little in the city. There are no civic associations, but there are more than enough spontaneous impulses to give clothing, food, and centavos. A secondary effect of this custom is that the children can survive on the street. This is not a solution but a palliative: instead of offering alternatives to begging, we allow it to take place under better conditions.

In his novel *Earthly Powers,* Anthony Burgess observes that the English have a noteworthy ability to armor plate themselves against all emotions, except those aroused by pets. In Mexico, animals are usually mistreated terribly. The final emotional reserve covers children. Few countries tolerate the noises, caprices, and disrespect with the kind of resignation we exercise. Among us, a hotel or restaurant that excludes children seems a fascist enclave.

Street children are given more clothing and toys than they need. This is the fundamental reason for understanding why Mexico City is a haven for minors with no home, no family. The reasons why they live rough are terrible, but the illusions that life creates are powerful. A life without schoolwork, without the need to be clean, all reminiscent of what we all longed for when we read Jules Verne's *Two Years' Vacation.*

The 1985 earthquake gave a new impetus to street life. Many buildings in the area most affected, running from the Center to the Roma neighborhood, were abandoned. Those ruins became a ghost city for children. In his documentary *Night and Fog,* Alain Resnais traverses the German cities bombed during World War II. The only thing that gives life to the landscape is the sight of children playing in the wreckage as if it were a strange sort of amusement park.

Something similar happened after the earthquake: those who'd been living in sewers came back to the surface and occupied whole neighborhoods and vice-regal palaces. As the process of reconstruction or restoration progressed, they were forced to yield ground, but they are still concentrated in the Center.

Charity helps the children survive outdoors, but it also contributes to their being victims of later abuses. Very few girls escape prostitution. The advance of organized crime also transformed street kids into targets for drugs: "Twenty years ago, sixty percent of the children could choose between taking drugs or not. Today you see that 95 percent have to undergo an extreme detox program to recover," Fernández points out. "Also, the nature of drug consumption changed. Before they used thinner, turpentine, or glue, all very dangerous but less addictive. Organized crime pushed them toward other drugs (marijuana, crack) and discovered that children are ideal for drug trafficking."

Until just a few years ago, in the area around Saint Hippolytus, you would hear people whistling at all hours of the night. It was a communication system far more efficient than social media. But everything has its historical moment; the art of making contact through whistles has been disappearing and only survives as the patrimony of those irregular forces that have to gather in emergencies.

From time to time, outside the church of lost causes, children, fortunately, still whistle.

Sleeping Under the Earth

"Ninety percent of all street children have a parallel identity. On the street, recognition replaces identity. When they finally reveal their names, it's because they want to change their lives." After a quarter century dedicated to fighting the problem, José Ángel Fernández sums up the fate of these children in an aphorism: "The worst aggression for the individual is growing up." I'm thinking of Peter Pan's motto "Never grow up!" While they're still children, the inhabitants of the street can be tolerated and receive support. When they become adults, only prison or degradation await them.

Just by chance, opposite the headquarters of Pro Children, at Zaragoza 277 in the Buenavista neighborhood, is a police academy. Each sidewalk represents a variation of the country: on one side, child outlaws; on the other, those who serve the law.

Laura Alvarado Castellanos, head of Pro Children, is an expert when it comes to delinquent behavior, to family poverty, and to the lack of hope that threatens the city's poor. In a revelatory way, she points out:

"The most intelligent ones leave the streets." You need initiative, a strong will, and an ability to adapt to survive there. But all that is changing:

> Thirty years ago, the street facilitated the creation of a support network that included newsboys, trinket sellers, taxi drivers. Now organized crime considers children ideal for transporting drugs. Besides, no one is looking for these children, no one is going to claim them. They've already disappeared, and the criminal life trains them to become even more invisible. Many don't look indigent: they have places where they can bathe, they can sleep in hotels, they can camouflage themselves to go on living on the street and selling drugs. Another change we've noted is that they've become big consumers. You may think they have nothing, but that's not true: they earn money carrying drugs, but they also use drugs. They buy cell phones, clothes, and they follow all the stereotypes they see in soap operas or on the internet. For five years now, we've been having more problems in trying to establish relationships with them. Before they were more isolated, but now the people who've recruited them for crime keep an eye on us and threaten us. They even kidnapped one of our female volunteers.

Trained as a psychologist at the Iberoamerican University, Laura Alvarado Castellanos has charted the patterns of life on the street. Many boys have been abused, and during adolescence they assume a homosexual identity because it seems less denigrating to them to have been raped if that was their sexual preference anyway. In a complicated way, they accuse themselves of the crimes they've suffered. Before introducing me to the boys at the Pro Children Day Center, she warns me that they usually change stories if they think it will benefit them.

For years, Laura worked as a volunteer at the Tutoring Council for Minors. There were children no one visited because they had no relatives, and she looked after those solitary cases. There she learned that domestic violence contributes to the problem, but that the worst thing is exclusion and lack of alternatives. The smarter children look for a more challenging and amusing fate: the street, where all personal histories are possible.

Once again, I recall my illusions about getting lost in Chapultepec Park. So I too felt that temptation, and now I share yet another: I also exchange stories for benefits.

Laura continues. "Along with the Historical Center, the children depend on bastions like the Taxqueña subway station, surrounded by ample parking lots that serve as meeting places. Not all of them sleep rough." At any hour of the day, there are children asleep on the subway. They travel in no particular direction. They simply board the subway to rest in the artificial night underground, lulled by the swaying of the cars. They work at night and find a provisional dwelling place in the subway. At some moment or other, they wake up and discover they're in the south, the north, the east, or the west. If it's already nighttime, they take one last trip with their eyes open.

On March 31, 2016, I interviewed Christian in another space at the Pro Children Foundation, the House of Transition to Independent Life in the Santa María la Ribera neighborhood, where these young people can live for up to two years, during which time they learn to make a living. For several years, he slept on the subway during the day and worked as a prostitute at night. It's hard to imagine anyone's having had worse experiences. Nevertheless, at the age of seventeen, he talks about his damage with a sense of humor. He smiles, makes jokes, tugs at his mane of curly hair which falls to the left, gives a mischievous glance before returning to some dramatic moment in his life. His emotional wounds have not completely healed, and he considers himself more vulnerable than most, but he shows an ability to resist that is superior to that of his comrades at the House of Transition.

Christian talks a lot about strength, but he doesn't exercise it in a physical way. His fortitude comes from humor. Like Leonardo, he was born in Ecatepec. His background is identical to that of other street children: "Once I saw my dad, but I don't remember his face." His father disappeared, and his mother had another child with a different man that died at birth. Then she had a third child with a third man and gave it up for adoption. Drugs kept her from taking care of her children. Christian grew up with an older woman, who was affectionate with him even though he continuously got into mischief. "I'm a big joker, I like to make trouble. When I was a little kid I got up to all kinds of stuff. I liked to break things, jump out the window; I was a real handful. Now I make comments that may seem offensive, but only to have fun."

His adoptive mother put up with the dishes broken by this boy, who had a strange school record. In the first trimester, he got C, in the second B, and in the third A, as if his ability to study depended on how soon vacation would begin. Everything changed soon: he flunked third grade in primary school, then fourth, and stopped studying in fifth.

The woman who'd taken charge of him died when he was ten, and he was sent to live with his grandmother, who shortly thereafter went back to her hometown. Christian stayed with an aunt. She was the fourth person in whose custody he lived—and the worst. She pulled him out of school and forced him to sell sweets in the subway. She didn't even share his meager earnings with him. At the slightest protest, she beat him. The aunt had five children she treated well. She vented all her rage on the stepson: "If it rained, it was my fault and she beat the crap out of me."

After a while, she sent him out to sell pirated compact discs. She had him go every day to pick up blanks in the Tepito neighborhood and then gave him copies to sell on the metro.

Until that time, he had no friends. "I've always been very solitary," he observes with ease. "I can talk a lot, but not just with anyone." Suddenly a girl broke the boundary of his loneliness. Her name was Norlendi, and she was two years older than he and also lived in Ecatepec. "We liked to play hand games," says Christian, making gestures in the air, pretending to touch other palms, "and we told each other our secrets. For the first time, I learned I could communicate with another person."

Christian visited Norlendi's home and was shocked to learn that a family could live without beating one another up. "For me, slaps were normal. All my uncles beat up their wives. I didn't think there could be another kind of life." He spent more and more time at this girlfriend's house until his aunt came looking for him and beat him until he left. Norlendi's brothers tried to stop it, and even said they'd call the police, a threat that in Mexico lacks all reality and only made the aunt laugh.

He was forbidden to enter Norlendi's house, under the pretext that the family sold drugs. "That was a lie. It was just because they had a better house that they said that."

While he worked all day selling pirated merchandise, his cousins dropped out of school without that being a problem for his aunt. And no one made them work. As Laura Alvarado Costellanos points out, discriminatory treatment can be worse than physical violence.

One day, Christian dropped off a pirated disc with a man who gave him three hundred pesos. Suddenly it seemed absurd to him to go back to his aunt's house. He never forgets a date that seems important to him: "It was December 14, 2012." On that day, when he was thirteen, he started living on the street:

> I was cold, but I didn't feel all alone. The first night a ton of things happened to me: I met a drugged person, then someone else who tried to mug me (luckily, I'd hidden my money in my shoe), then someone I knew drove me back to my aunt's house where I pretended to ring the buzzer and instead ran off to Aztec City. I didn't sleep all night. Morning came, and the first thing I did was buy Shakira's *Where Are the Thieves?* It cost ninety-nine pesos. Then I bought coffee and a roll. I went down to the subway and fell asleep tossing and turning.

Two weeks before deciding to run away from his aunt's house, he met Erick, who was ten years older. They liked each other, and since he didn't know where to go, Christian decided to talk to him. He called him all day long, wasting his money on public telephones ("One swallowed a five-peso coin") until he finally got an answer. Erick promised to help him, met him at his house, and from there brought him to a hotel:

> I asked for help and suddenly I had a boyfriend. Slowly but surely, I fell in love with him. No one had ever loved me the way Erick did. Everything was fine until my birthday, which is January 18. He asked me to help him download some documents from the internet, but the computer was very slow, and when he came back, I had nothing. He accused me of chatting with other men, got very jealous and beat me up. I felt guilty and told him he was right. From then on, he'd beat me up every two weeks, and I felt it was my fault because I didn't do things properly. He lost his job and said it was because he spent so much time with me. I felt that was true. Then the beatings

became the least of my problems. He wouldn't let me go out, and took away my internet connection. I was locked up. Before, my aunt would beat me, but at least I could go out. Now I was getting hit and couldn't leave. I went on telling him he was right about everything until he started bringing boys home so we could screw them. I told him it was wrong, but he threatened me, and I had to go along. He never used condoms. Every time he beat me up he got excited and wanted to screw me. More than anything, I felt violated, but if I didn't let him use me, he could bring in other boys. I thought, "Those kids leave, but I stay, so I'm better." That's how I consoled myself. He would take them to the movies or buy them ice cream, but I lived in the house.

I ask him if there weren't any good moments that would justify his living there. "Sure, but they were few and far between. All that lasted a year and a half, then, as happened with my aunt, the Lord illuminated me, and I ran away after another beating." He went back to Norlendi's house, where he stayed for three months. Then he went back to Erick. He couldn't leave the person who abused him, but who was also the person who gave him the affection he still hoped to recover. Finally, he decided to break the vicious circle, but he fell into another: a friend connected him with a prostitution ring.

"I felt that my only purpose in life was to be fucked," he explains. He started working at night in one of the places in the heart of the city, the corporate and hotel enclave on Paseo de la Reforma, between Diana the Huntress and the Angel of Independence. Mexico City is an inverted Eden where a minor can buy solvents to drug himself and accompany an adult to a hotel where the rooms are rented by the hour, prostitute himself next to transvestites on the city's main avenue. Christian spent the night wide awake and slept in the subway by day.

In my case, the clients were pretty much alike. There were some little blond boys who attracted handsome guys, but all I ever got were drunken or drugged-up geezers, beyond disagreeable. There was one friendly man who only talked to me and gave me a thousand pesos. I still have contact with a little client who only did things with my feet. He put me on Facebook a little while back. But there were others who were disgusting. One liked to stick dildos inside me. "If I have to choose between that and you, I'll take that." That guy got obsessed and would send me phone messages every once in a while.

Some clients would ask him to take drugs. He tried not to, but sometimes had to use poppers or crack even though he didn't like it:

I wanted to try cocaine out of sheer curiosity, but my hands shook, and I scattered it everywhere. I never stole, I just couldn't do it, though I had many opportunities, but I think I'm too good. I made some night friends, another guy named Christian and a kid named Jair. We played hand games, and sometimes all three of us or two of us would get contracted. Then the two of them left to live together, and I again felt very alone. The whole scene was depressing. So I went back to Erick, my only love, and he started beating me again. I started to fall apart and even thought about killing myself. I started sleeping in a Banamex ATM on Paseo de la Reforma, I was garbage, I almost didn't eat, I drank water out of the faucet in Sanborns. That's how I was when I met a kid from Honduras who told me about Pro Children. I thought it was some kind of reform school where I'd be locked up and mistreated. When I finally decided to go to the hostel, all I could think about was eating and sleeping. But of course I brought my Shakira discs with me, I always had them on me.

With the support of Pro Children, he began to get a perspective on his past and learned to talk about his life with the fluidity he enjoys now. He had one year to go in primary school and took the exams in five days. In six months, he finished secondary school, his only preparation being the study guides. He has an alert intelligence, but he complains that he can't concentrate. "Reading a book is really hard for me, I've only read the comic book *Rubius,* which I have in my room." Now he's enrolled in the open upper school, has taken English classes, swimming, theater, guitar. I ask him how he sees himself five years from now: "In front of a camera or lots of people, saying important things."

Does he still see Norlendi? "She likes the fact that I'm well, but she doesn't like the way I am now. I'm more extroverted, but less of a joker. I like to laugh at the things that used to hurt me. I've got an acid sense of humor. I had syphilis and got cured, it was like being pregnant, and now I can laugh about it."

I ask him what he dreams about, and he says he can't remember. He thinks a while, blows out some air to push aside a curly lock of hair, and says: "When I was on the street, prostituting myself, I would imagine myself singing in an auditorium and feel as if everyone loved me. Recently I have dreamed. I see the Christian my aunt used to beat up, but it's as if today's Christian instantly joins him and stops her."

He watches movies in their original language with English subtitles so he can learn the language, and he'd like to visit Spain and England. He'd also like to have a little dog, maybe a Chihuahua.

I ask him if he's ever thought about getting a tattoo. "Yes, when I can't give blood any more—if I get hepatitis . . . What would it be? Shakira's logo! No, wait, that would be too dumb. I'd rather something else." He pauses. I don't have to push him on this matter; he thinks, he's entirely focused, on what he'd like on his skin: "I'd get a wolf tattoo," he says proudly. "Wolves are aggressive and they survive."

His character is like music. "My personality is like a sponge; with Shakira, I'm sweet (when I met Erick, everything was love, and everything was Shakira), with Gloria Trevi, I'm daring and haughty, with Miley Cyrus I'm obscene and argumentative. I like combining the three of them in my personality, but each one has her place: at a funeral I can't be Miley Cyrus!"

Does Erick look for him? "He just did. I'm in therapy so I don't hook up with him again. I know it's not good for me." Sometimes, because he's repeated his story so often, he talks about himself in the third person, not with the vanity of a soccer star but as if he were really talking about someone else: "Christian is timid and quiet; it's hard for him to make friends." That's how he talks about the past: the first person belongs to the present. "I like being listened to, especially by a large group. I want to give a sex education course."

When the interview is over, I walk through the Santa María la Ribera neighborhood to the San Cosme subway station. I take a train to

Hidalgo, the station where a miracle took place opposite the church of lost causes.

Before I get there, I see a little boy deeply asleep. He's sleeping the only way you can do it if you know that this is your only home, in Mexico City's false night.

The Orphan Who Saved the President

The writer and liberal politician Guillermo Prieto was born in 1818, in Molino del Rey, near Chapultepec, when the nation was fighting for its independence. In *Memories of My Times,* he reconstructs his country childhood. In his day, Molino del Rey was not yet part of Mexico City. Prieto would go to the lake, passing through the forest with its millennial ahuehuete cypresses.

As a child, he lacked for nothing. He grew up in an environment of affection and sensorial stimuli, many of them related to food, which he always enjoyed. When his grandfather died, the family had enough money to move to a downtown area of Mexico City. That arcadia fell apart when his father died suddenly. He was thirty-three, and the consequences were dramatic: "My mother went insane. Strangers took the many objects we had in the house," Prieto writes in his memoirs. At the age of thirteen, he went to live with some seamstresses who'd worked for his family and got used to having holes in his shoes.

From time to time, he'd visit his mother. He found her submerged in a mental fog: a thirty-year-old woman with a calm, sweet appearance, unable to connect with those around her. She didn't always recognize him, but enjoyed the sweets he gave her. Prieto would leave bathed in tears, never losing the hope that she would recover her sanity.

He had no money for books, but he discovered literature in a public park. In the Alameda Central, poets would compete, showing their ability by hanging up sonnets in wooden frames. From reading them again and again, Prieto learned rhetoric: "The Alameda was my great poetic academy."

One night, he heard the seamstresses talking about their poverty: they starved so he could eat. A short time later, a cholera epidemic decimated the city, and his brother almost died.

At the age of fifteen, Prieto had to do something to salvage his life. Enraged by his fate, he decided to visit the minister of justice, Andrés Quintana Roo. In 1833, Mexico was an experimental nation that had yet to define itself. In that territory where hopes exceed realities, a boy could knock at a minister's door. Quintana Roo wept when he heard the story told by the boy, who was almost the same age as the country itself. He got him a job that allowed him to support his mother, help his seamstress benefactors, and continue his studies.

Four years later, Prieto read a poem before the president, Anastasio Bustamante. Impressed, the president asked Prieto to visit him in his office. This short meeting was all it took to unite their destinies. Bustamante had a bed for the young poet installed in the Government Palace and made him editor of the *Official Newspaper*.

In his biography of Prieto, Malcolm McLean writes about this: "The poor orphan boy, by his own efforts, won a position that required the full confidence of the president and a respectable place in the presidential mansion."

Prieto evolved, becoming one of the principal liberal writers and politicians of nineteenth-century Mexico. This resident of the National Palace was the most loyal defender of the republic. Benito Juárez named Prieto minister of finance, and he saved Juárez's life. In Guadalajara, President Juárez was ambushed by enemies. Prieto was with him. Facing the rifles aimed at them, the writer who learned to read in a public park blurted out: "Brave men do not commit murder." The statement caused his executioners to relent.

Prieto was an exceptional witness to the various incarnations of Mexico City, from the struggle for independence until the U.S. invasion of 1847, experiencing the famines, the epidemics, and the continuous changes of government. His fate was as precarious as the Mexican nineteenth century. Between the ages of thirteen and nineteen, his life could have been that of any street child today, but he received support from a nation as unsure of itself as he, a nation that had barely begun to consolidate itself. The minister of justice opened his door to him, and the president offered him a bed in his house.

Prieto placed his confidence in a nation in its infancy. Vicente Quirarte accurately defines his career: "The nation as a profession."

So, there was a time when a boy could knock at the door of justice and be received.

Reality is different in 2017. Tonight, in San Hipólito, next to the Alameda where Guillermo Prieto learned poetry, children will sleep under a bus or in a sewer.

Places

The Mausoleums of the Heroes

When a city has an authentic life, people know where to go to celebrate without having to agree beforehand. In the capital, that place is the Angel of Independence. The curious thing is that the place is a mausoleum. The tribe celebrates sports glories in the presence of those who offered up their bones to the nation, an involuntary proof of the fact that our trophies are so dramatic that they are part of funerary art.

Inaugurated in 1910 by Porfirio Díaz to commemorate the centennial of our Independence, the Angel after 1925 became the crypt of the deluded founders of the nation.

Up until that date, the remains of our national heroes were interred in the cathedral. The man responsible for their disinterment was Plutarco Elías Calles, who governed Mexico between 1924 and 1928 with an anticlerical fury that went beyond the necessary separation of church and state to become an indiscriminate persecution. Graham Greene left two memorable portraits, one a nonfiction account, *The Lawless Roads* (1939), and the other a novel, *The Power and the Glory* (1940). This is not the place to recall the uprising of loyal Catholics against a repression that forbade prayer and turned churches into movie theaters or stables, a matter Jean Meyer studied fully in *La Cristiada: The Mexican People's War for Religious Liberty* (1973). Suffice it to say that such a furious Jacobin could not allow the remains of the insurgents to remain in a church. The issue acquired special importance because the greatest actors in the war for independence, Hidalgo and Morelos, were priests.

Before the transfer of their remains to the Angel, the tomb of the insurgents was the Altar of the Kings, designed for the cathedral in 1659 by the Spanish artist Enrique Verona. His son ran off to escape a fire started by his wife's ex-lover, and that event gave rise to the legend of the lost child, the *niño perdido*. As I said elsewhere in this book, that was the unforgettable name of a stretch of what is today the Central Axis. The story of our heroes could bear a similar name: "lost bones."

Without making much of a fuss, Calles removed the illustrious bones from their religious resting place, transformed the Angel into a civic pantheon, and rewarded himself by placing his visiting card with the remains of Hidalgo, a gesture he perhaps intended as a means to getting an institutional favor from the beyond.

Other national heroes followed later on. There were supposed to be fourteen, thirteen men and one woman (Leona Vicario), but Mexico is a fanciful territory, where unknown things are stored. Let's see what happened to those remains.

In 2010, during the celebrations for the Bicentennial of Independence promoted by Felipe Calderón, the remains of the heroes were analyzed and then exhibited throughout the nation. The funeral cortege constituted an involuntary metaphor for the policies of a president who pulled the army out of its barracks to initiate a fruitless "war on narco trafficking," which yielded one hundred thousand dead and thirty thousand missing. Under orders from Calderón, the remains were brought to the Chapultepec Castle, ancient seat of the presidency, where experts discovered the carelessness with which the nation treats its heroes: the remains of Mariano Matamoros were not in the Angel; on the other hand, deer bones and the skeleton of a little girl, perhaps the daughter of Leona Vicario, were there.

In his essay "Necro-Corrido," Fabrizio Mejía Madrid explains this funerary confusion:

When Plutarco Elías Calles decides to deprive the Church of possession of the bones of our heroes and put them in a place that even though it was created by the tyrant Porfirio Díaz was at least secular—the Column of Independence—Morelos' only presence was a skull with an "M" painted on its forehead. There was no body. And that unleashed the theory that in fact the skull belongs to Matamoros or Pedro Moreno. So many names beginning with the same letter that it makes you wonder why the gravediggers didn't come up with another method to identify the skulls.

So where did José María Morelos y Pavón end up? According to some rumors, Juan Nepomuceno, the hero's son, took the remains out of the cathedral and brought them to France. In 1991, President Carlos Salinas de Gortari managed to have Juan Nepomuceno's grave in the Père-Lachaise cemetery in Paris (where the most visited grave site is Jim Morrison's) opened. Everyone expected to find his father's remains there as well, but all that was found was the mummified body of the son. The studies carried out in 2010 confirmed that the skull with the "M" on it did not belong to Matamoros, so it may actually belong to a minor insurgent, Pedro Moreno.

With simplified optimism, tourist guides declare that the heroes are in the Angel. The true history, more complex and macabre, will probably never be ascertained.

The Biggest Gas Station in Mexico

The real adventures of the heroes who ended up in the Monument to the Revolution were no less perilous than their posthumous actions. And that space was not conceived with funerary aims. It was going to be the seat of congress when Porfirio Díaz ruled Mexico, but the Revolution interrupted the project just when the cupola designed for the state's capital was ready.

As with so many projects of the Porfirio Díaz period, the design for the seat of congress was assigned to a French architect, Émile Bénard. Bernardo Ortiz de Montellano, a member of the Contemporáneos literary group, writes about the era when our city aspired to be Paris. At the outset of the twentieth century: "Mexican culture stretched, in an ideal line, from Chapultepec Forest to the Bois de Boulogne, the Paseo de la Reforma to the boulevards of Paris."

The project for the legislative palace reached Mexico like yet another

French illusion, but only the cupola was finished. It was intended to cover the Hall of Lost Steps. That suggestive name derives from a long architectural tradition: a luxurious transitional space that emphasized the importance of great mansions and palaces. It was not a place where people were to remain but a place for passing through the building, a passageway inhabited by footsteps. Several parliamentary buildings have an interior plaza where the experience of passing through it confirms the meaning of power: beyond that parenthetical space stand things that are stable and long lasting. The people take the pilgrim's road to law.

A symbol of legislative power, the cupola served another symbolic purpose. In 1938, the architect Carlos Obregón Santacilia, who also designed the Bank of Mexico, used it to create a roof for the Monument to the Revolution, a strange building without walls, held up by columns in Art Deco style. In my childhood, people called it "the biggest gas station in the world" (which gives you an idea of what the gas stations of the 1950s were like).

Our history is presented in round numbers—the war of Independence in 1810, the Revolution in 1910—but what you learn from all that is usually chaotic. The knights of the Revolution passed through a funerary plot as irregular as that of the insurgents. So, in the monument you find the remains of Madero, Calles, Cárdenas, Villa, and Carranza. That in itself is conflictive: our official history reconciles—posthumously—rebels who conspired against one another. Villa became disillusioned with Madero, Carranza tried to annihilate Villa, Cárdenas severed relations with Calles. They're all together in the Plaza de la República. The real heroism of a Mexican warlord is to share his final resting place with his enemies.

In this case as well, the national heroes did not reach the grave in one piece. Pancho Villa was buried in Parral in 1923, but his grave was violated in 1926, and no one knows where his skull is. It was supposedly carried off to the United States, where someone offered $50,000 for the head of the Centaur of the North. The legend includes several different conclusions: a millionaire who hated Villa kept the skull in his cabinet of curiosities . . . or, it was shown as a delightful horror for the masses in the Ringling Brothers circus . . . or, it was auctioned off with other famous mummies in Sotheby's . . .

The strange thing is that the rest of the body was also not allowed to rest in peace. In his titanic biography of Villa, Paco Ignacio Taibo II tells us that one of his widows, who answered to the fabulous name Austreberta Rentería, removed the bones left in grave 632 in the Parral cemetery to avoid another violation and gave them a new home in grave 10, where she herself would be buried five years later. Taibo has a copy of the 1931 receipt in the amount of twelve pesos the lady paid for her own burial along with "the remains of General Francisco Villa in grave 10 of the Dolores Cemetery." The only proof that the Centaur moved house posthumously.

According to the same version, the coffin was left empty, but not for long. To avoid suspicion, Austreberta substituted another cadaver for her husband's. About this, Taibo says, "Local historians give credence to the story according to which, in March of 1931, a young woman on her way to the United States to be cured of cancer, died in the Juárez Hospital in Parral." The woman died without being identified. She was destined for potter's field, but she ended up in grave 632, taking the place of the leader of the Northern Division.

In 1976, the presumed remains of Villa were exhumed to be brought to the Monument of the Revolution. Found in the grave were tortoise-shell buttons, a rosary, and lace, items difficult to associate with the general who commanded the Northern Division. René Armedároz, a gynecologist and director of the Parral hospital, examined the remains and declared that the sacrum seemed to be that of a young woman.

In national politics, symbols are more important than realities. In the face of the possibility that a forensic study would disrupt the recovery of the warlord who still fights in corridos, the bones were accepted as authentic, with no further study. With or without buttons, they were taken to the capital.

Born as Doroteo Arango, the unforgettable Pancho Villa began his working life as a wagon master. But inventive history has supplied him with an even more dramatic change of identity. It's possible the remains that represent him in the mausoleum of heroes are those of a girl.

Intended as the crown of the Hall of Lost Steps, the cupola of the Monument to the Revolution, like the Angel of Independence, houses "lost bones."

Apropos of these mystifications, Fabrizio Mejía Madrid writes:

The bones buried in structures built to honor them as part of a single war, even though they fought one another—*the* War of Independence and *the* Revolution—and although those bones are not those of the body of the hero when he was alive, are in fact really the true bones because that is what power says they are, no matter that forensic anthropologists contradict it—they finish up their labors in the kingdom of this world and rise to the Heaven of We Lay Persons: history. It's a retirement from their efforts. The two central monuments—the Angel and the Monument—are like the publication of someone's complete works or the payment of pension funds by their widows. All you have to do is repeat throughout eternity: "Fatherland first." The central monuments of Mexican heroes are a winged woman who now serves as a celebration point for the only possible patriotism: a tie match with Honduras in soccer. The other is a cupola with nothing to cupolate. The abstinence of cold bones.

In its basement, the Monument is the appropriate seat of another catacomb: the Museum of the Revolution, the Revolution being a feat comprehensible only in official discourse.

On top, there is a widow's walk. One of the best landscapes in Mexican painting was achieved from that viewpoint. I'm referring to *Mexico City Landscape* (1949) by Juan O'Gorman. Why did he choose that place? Perhaps for the same reason Guy de Maupassant frequented the Eiffel Tower. The author was one of the many intellectuals who opposed the building of that fantasy in iron. When what is currently the symbol of Paris was completed, a friend was surprised to find Maupassant in the restaurant on top of the building. How was it possible that a declared enemy of the tower was there? Maupassant's response was irrefutable: "It's the only place where you can't see the Eiffel Tower."

Perhaps O'Gorman painted the city from that perspective so he wouldn't see the Monument to the Revolution.

Obregón's Arm

In San Ángel, where the La Bombilla park was, stands the monument to the warlord from Sonora who brought the Mexican Revolution to

closure. Although Ignacio Asúnsol's sculptures on the exterior and interior of the building suggest civil ideals like work and justice, a row of
cypresses reveal that this cement rectangle is a mausoleum. The door has
the solidity of a bank vault.

In 1935, it was there that the remains of Álvaro Obregón were laid
to rest. He was assassinated in La Bombilla in 1928, at a banquet in his
honor to support his reelection as president. Death between plates of
mole and music would be the scene depicted in the drama *The Attack,* in
which Jorge Ibargüengoitia arranges things so that the last words of the
protagonist are not a message to the nation but instead a message to a
waiter, "more beans." Ibargüengoitia's farce desacralizes the general that
the governments which came about because of the Revolution tried to
make into a martyr by surrounding him with all the symbols of early
Christianity.

Murdered by the Catholic José de León Toral, the Jacobin Obregón
would have a posterity clouded over by religious superstitions. The place
where he died became a holy sepulcher, with the word *here* incised by
some mystical chisel. Also, one part of his body was exhibited as a sacred
relic.

In 1935, the governor of the Federal District was Aarón Sáenz, from
Sonora, as was Obregón. He pushed for the construction of that vertical
crypt, horrifying on the outside and terrifying on the inside.

In 1915, the general lost an arm fighting the troops of Pancho Villa.
Gifted with a good sense of humor, he would say that his amputated
member was found thanks to his passion for money: one of his assis-
tants tossed a coin onto the battlefield and, despite the chaos of bodies, the arm revived to catch it. When the Spanish author Ramón del
Valle-Inclán visited Mexico, Obregón invited him to share his box at
Bellas Artes. Since each was missing a hand, they each supplied one to
applaud.

But the arm had a destiny far different from the black humor that
characterized its owner. Several generations of Mexican children were
terrorized in the name of the fatherland when they visited the resting
place of the general. The arm could be seen in a vessel filled with form-
aldehyde, where it became, over time, softer and more yellow. I recall
two details when as a child I visited that dark pit, that strange aquarium

of death: the general's nicely cut fingernails and the long lifeline on his palm. Although that last detail is ironic (Obregón was forty-eight when he died), I couldn't see it that way.

A strange pedagogy of horror allowed the arm to be considered edifying. If religious museums had scabrous examples of Christ's nails or the tongue of some martyr, the Mexican Revolution, no less intense, could exhibit that arm in its progressive deterioration. That fragment gave a terrible image of the revolution it truly resembled, and in 1989 it was removed from the vitrine and placed in the coffin.

If the utterly fantastic Antonio López de Santa Anna, president of Mexico eleven times, hosted a state funeral for his own leg, in 1989, thanks to the gravediggers, Álvaro Obregón became physically what he could never be morally: a complete man.

The Jesus Hospital

One of the most beautiful buildings in the capital stands on the place where Moctezuma II met Hernán Cortés. Inaugurated in 1524, the Jesus Hospital was the first building of this type on the American continent. Its patios embellished with orange trees recall the ancient fable of the immigrants. It takes seven years for an orange tree to produce oranges. Someone coming from far away plants an orange tree like a clock to measure his adaptation: when the first oranges appear on the branches, he can see he is now from this place.

Most colonial buildings have patios containing orange trees, which suggests the Spaniards came intending to stay. "They were madmen, my friend," the poet Álvaro Mutis told me one afternoon, "they had no knowledge of the country, but they set about constructing buildings they would need thirty years to finish. Those crazies really wanted to be here."

The Jesus Hospital, scene of "the meeting of two worlds" and of the first autopsy performed on this continent, is the proper place to house the conquistador from Extremadura. With him began the mixing of races that defines us today and which we still have a hard time accepting.

"Being courteous [cortés] takes nothing away from bravery" is the old saying which in Mexico is rewritten thus: "Being courteous [Cortés] takes nothing away from Cuauhtémoc." None of this means that we consider ourselves descendants of the one or the other. As I mentioned in the chapter on the Shout, in our peculiar mythology we define the Aztecs as Mexicans, so the Conquest interrupted that saga of splendor, and Independence restored our identity.

To face up to the mix of cultures that shapes us with greater sensitivity, Jaime Torres Bodet, poet and functionary, had a motto inscribed at the National Museum of Anthropology: "Here took place a struggle in which there were neither conquerors nor conquistadors; only the painful birth of a nation: Mexicans."

This complex birth has yet to be accepted. Hernán Cortés's *Letters to Charles V* confirm how intense was his interest in New Spain, and, in his testament, he asked that his remains be returned to the land he sacked and transformed forever, bequeathing the language in which I'm writing these words.

Cortés died in 1547, but his posthumous life was as hectic as his military campaigns. He undertook nine expeditions, and, as a posthumous mirror, his remains have had nine resting places. The beyond for heroes is usually an ascending road: relics are brought to more and more luxurious places. That's not the case with Cortés. Mexico City has given him no monuments, and his posthumous movements have been those of someone in need. After occupying several provisional graves, he was sent, in 1794, to the church annexed to the Jesus Hospital. During the twentieth century, at the high point of mural painting, José Clemente Orozco painted the cupola there. He could have chosen as his theme the difficult reconciliation of Mexicans (one of his best works is, precisely, Cortés alongside La Malinche), but instead he chose another subject which perhaps lends itself better to our sense of identity: the apocalypse.

Ever since he was placed in that church, the conquistador has been more hidden than buried. In 1823, shortly after we achieved Independence, the statue that marked his tomb was destroyed. To avoid a profanation, his remains were secretly moved to another place in the same church. He remained in that unmarked grave for more than a century. Finally, in 1947, it was revealed in which corner he was buried, and he was granted a discreet plaque indicating the dates of his birth and death.

When I pointed out the extraordinary ear the poet Francisco Cervantes had for titles, I mentioned one which in this chapter acquires special meaning. It defines the wandering trajectory heroes follow in Mexico City after their death: *Pilgrim Bones*.

City Characters

The Manager

Mexico has produced a social function I would dare to say cannot be exported: the position of "manager." This is not a boss and even less a specialist. It's someone who appears behind a counter to represent the vaguest form of authority: he complicates life without being responsible for anything.

A small business in the capital is a place where three employees stare at the floor and two eat pumpkin seeds. Although overpopulation is one of our specialties, we have an abundance of stores where there are few customers and an excessive number of workers. It doesn't matter that they all carry badges or wear uniforms: only one is *the* manager. If you ask the nearest employee about some product, he nods (rarely does he point a finger) toward a man wearing a fish-belly-colored suit and emits the fatal declaration: "Speak to the manager."

When you approach the figure who pulls the secret strings in the place, he affirms his importance with offensive courtesy: "I'll take care of you from where you are," he says, so you know you've intruded into the space where he is.

Thus begins a commercial fiction in which it is considered professional to set up obstacles. You are standing before a creature who neither gives nor obeys orders, but he does have authority: he represents a limit beyond which you cannot go on your own. The dizzying high and low points of commercial society find an anchor in this man. Will he have what you're looking for? A hasty question. Before you enter the complex world of merchandise, of the price of objects, and of the strange fetishism those prices provoke, there is a protocol. You may talk about the Mexican economy in many ways, but the manager reveals that it has an order. Only he can tell you that something simply doesn't exist or that it does exist, only he can ask someone else to take care of you.

None of this takes place quickly. The process would lack importance if it weren't difficult. You stand before a person who believes that noises are superior to people. All business is interrupted if the telephone rings. The manager will only return to your face marked with urgency after saying the same thing three times to someone who seems to be taking down dictation with a chisel on the other end of the line. The situation is common and annoying, but in the world's balance there is no way to get even for these insults. Your option: either put up with it or put up with it.

Once I went into a mega-stationery store in search of a fountain pen. When I asked an employee, she answered: "The manager will be right with you." Even though this woman was wearing the regulation blue vest, she could not deal with this matter. Twenty minutes later, a woman authorized to do just that did it with great serenity: "We don't sell fountain pens."

There are people born with the temerity to deactivate bombs and people born to resolve social situations. I have not the slightest doubt that the attributes of the manager are innate. It would be impossible to learn that sense of indifference.

An emblematic phrase emitted by this person destined to stop destiny in order to imbue it with transcendence: "You could have told me that before." All complications are the fault of the person who requests something. The manager lives in a state of purity of soul. Within his personal code, recognizing a mistake is worse than committing one: therefore, he never learns about his own deficiencies. One of these is his use of technology, which means he uses it as much as he can. If he's operating a photocopy machine, he does it as if he were drowning a child in a tub. If he sits down at a computer, he only stands up after he's had enough time to reconfigure the operating system. Immune to all pressure, he acts with the aplomb of a stone deity. Then he hands you the article you did not ask to be copied or the bill without the tax factored in (the mantra returns: "You could have told me that before"). By then, the only thing you can do is get out of the store; you accept the incomplete nature of the exchange just to keep it from going on any further.

The manager is a final potentate, a Chinese emperor in his Forbidden City. Mind you, I'm not saying that shops don't have owners or managing directors. Those individuals exist even if we don't see them. Our essential contacts take place with this singular personage who makes mistakes in such a complicated way and with such disinterest that all protest is stifled. To complain about the event would imply reproducing it, and that is what we least desire.

The mirror twin of the rogue, the manager does not steal or complain about his style: "They pretend to pay me, and I pretend to work." That's his motto.

What is the relationship between this manager and the other employees? You walk into a juice bar and ask for a mix of beetroot and celery. The man to whom you make your request is wearing a triangular cap and seems to be the right man for the job. You're wrong: he is not the manager. He pouts in the direction of another man reading the sepia and white pages of the sporting news *Esto* spread out over a watermelon. In that moment, you experience the atavistic Mexican tradition we nowadays call "forwarding": you repeat your order, and the man reading repeats it to the man with the cap to whom you first spoke. In that instant, your request becomes official. A man begins to squeeze the vegetables, but only because the manager asked him to do so.

If they hand you an aloe juice instead of the celery with beetroot or if half an hour goes by without your receiving anything, the manager never changes expression. A protest can lead to a denouement like this: the manager's tutelary eyes lose the apathetic glaze that followed the goals in *Esto* and stare at you with a commiseration superior to contempt. Then comes the worst part: the manager folds his newspaper. He's going into action. He immediately warns you that beetroot is a substance that can clog the machine. He summons another employee. Immediately you notice that your juice is prepared with the mechanic opening up the device. They strain the juice to remove the screws, and do so carefully so their fingers sticky with oil don't mix with the juice. In the face of all this, the manager says not a word: he looks out on the world as if staring at nothing, his eyes at half-mast.

In the Mexican style of production, the manager functions as a gloomy intercessor: he makes sure that everything functions halfway and invalidates all criticism. The minutes you spend in his presence reveal that you will never touch his soul and will only recover your own when you leave.

Incompetent to the point of proselytism, he convinces you that there is only one thing worse than problems: trying to solve them.

Crossings

From Eye Candy to Moctezuma's Revenge

What would we be like if we could travel through this incalculable Mexico City with no problems? Our character would be so stupendous that it's hard to imagine just how stupendous it would be.

We live trying to get somewhere, and that has modified our dining habits, something significant in a country where the preparation time of traditional cooking competes with eternity. If someone invites you to break bread, it is forbidden to be in a hurry: a festive, successful luncheon should last at least five hours.

Up until just a few years ago, turkeys were kept in cages on the terraces people used for hanging up wash. Those rooftop farms announced a dish that would be on the table at Christmas. Nowadays, you can forget about keeping turkeys: we don't even have the time to pluck them.

Recipes have had to accelerate in an era that has abandoned the custom of playing dominoes to aid digestion. The chilango in transit demands another kind of food; he doesn't eat when he's hungry but when he's released from traffic.

When it takes you two hours to get to work and another two to get home, you have no right to complain: your statistics are much too common to make a point of them. That's how things are, so we ought to turn the trip into an opportunity to have a nice bite. Everything begins with the "taco de ojo," which in Mexico can be something to eat but which we use to refer to visual pleasures—eye candy.

Seeing is a prologue to appetite. Our sense of smell works in close proximity with our eyes, but we use it only infrequently, on streets where we don't always have time to approach the aromatic pot of tamales. The food-on-the-run client has to have a good eye.

Fast food restaurants are too static for the traveler who eats on the fly. The passenger in a van has only one privileged instant to spot the snack that will relieve his hunger and not force him to get out of the bus. When he gets it, a rapid safari ensues: the hunter who caught sight of a chile-seasoned mango a hundred yards away takes advantage of the fact that the bus pauses for a few seconds, pokes his head out of the window, and gives the lady selling the fruit exact change.

Traffic defines our way of eating to such an extent that an automotive treat has appeared. Outside the cars stalled in traffic, a sign announces "gorditas de nata," doughy cornmeal biscuits made with clotted cream. Normally, a gordita is a spongy mass with no personality. No one orders them at a stand or expects to eat them at the house of friends. Nevertheless, faced with the desperation of a traffic jam, that insipid food becomes a perfect tranquilizer. At the moment you realize that you're going to arrive extremely late and that the "alternative routes" are as impossible to find as Thomas More's Utopia, chewing that dough mitigates neurosis. Its consistency, its taste irrelevant in this case, is a calming sedative. Perhaps a part of the brain separated from taste but not from sensations allows us to associate gorditas with the mush of our childhood. As with tequila or cognac, this is a product with a defined origin. If spaghetti with ragout sauce is from Bologna, the gordita is from traffic jams, the dish of those being held without being arrested.

Juan José Arreola would laugh recalling that in Zapotlán el Grande, snacks were called "tranquilizers." That is exactly the function of the treat that allows us to survive traffic and which in variations of gourmet inspiration are advertised as "Gorditas D'Nata."

Taste and the Nation

Public events in Mexico only acquire meaning if there are too many people present. It's not enough that the stadium be full: it's essential that many be standing outside. In this bastion of masses, concerts, soccer matches, or demonstrations in the Zócalo only flirt with glory if those present are packed in like sardines.

"Chewing gum, popsicles, caramels!" announces one of the ubiquitous vendors. Also, there are pumpkin seeds.

Only rarely do we feel the spontaneous desire to eat those seeds. We don't go to the market to select them, we don't talk about homemade seeds, or which seeds are in season. Even so, in this nation of more than one hundred and fifty million inhabitants, without them there can be no social struggles, no minor league soccer, no massive concerts.

Our capacity for eating seeds has a long history. The amaranth yielded some vaguely sweet rectangles which our mania for exaggeration calls *alegrías* or joys. In pre-Hispanic times, the amaranth gods were worshipped to the point of being eaten and digested. During the Conquest, that fact facilitated the acceptance of Christian communion. People who'd chewed a Tezcatlipoca made of seeds accepted tasting the body of Christ. Perhaps for that reason *alegrías* are sold alongside *pepitorias* or gourd seeds, our cake shop host, whose seeds, arranged in a semicircle, recall the pyx that holds the holy sacrament.

Alegrías were born to be ambulatory. You rarely find them at food stands. To sell them, you've got to travel, and they've traveled so much that they became the first Mexican contribution to spatial cuisine. In 1985, the astronaut Rodolfo Neri Vela took advantage of his time in the stratosphere to carry out amaranth experiments. That moment marked the union of the last word in technology with an atavistic tradition. Tenochtitlán was founded by migrants who left their pots in the seven caves of origins and then made gods out of amaranth in the Anáhuac Valley. In the solitude of outer space, Neri Vela paid homage to the portable food that saved the founders of Mexico-Tenochtitlán from hunger.

Meanwhile, back here on earth, in the place occupied by Mexico City, food moves around in various ways. Bread-carrying bicyclists put on a circus show: they pedal carrying an enormous basket of bread on their heads. Sweet potato vendors are less agile. Their fortunes depend on the wagon they push, which is quite heavy because it's an oven. In the country where André Breton discovered that Surrealism was a part of everyday life, we enjoy a product sold by sound. The sweet potato wagon livens up city nights with its whistle. Suddenly the air is split by a sound that recalls the old-time trains we never rode and of which there only remains a whisper that seems to say: "I'm riding the train of absence/ and I don't have a round-trip ticket."

The sweet potato is a tuber too dry to be tasty. Compared to the sweet potato the yucca is filet mignon. The sweet potato has nothing to recommend it. Strictly speaking, the whistle announces itself: we buy sweet potatoes so that the wagons made of tin with their fiery stomachs never stop echoing through the city.

Let's pass on to another example of sonorous food. For centuries, Oaxaca tamales have been magnificent, but nowadays they arrive accompanied by a voice. The delivery bicycle carries a recorder with the most listened-to announcer in Mexico: "Tamales here! Oaxaca Tamales! Hot Tamales!" The best part of these treats is the message they transmit. We all have twisted days when everything goes straight to hell and we feel a crown of thorns wrapping our temples, a pain no aspirin can alleviate. Then a sign of hope appears: life is a disaster, but the Oaxaca tamales are nice and hot.

"Don't eat street food," say moms, incapable of understanding that pork rinds, jícamas, hot cakes with jam, and candy cotton only taste good outdoors. And just how healthy is what we buy on any corner? On this planet, there is life thanks to water. In Mexico, drinking water can cost you your life. Which has led to inventions of the highest levels of ingenuity. Can we be certain of the jelly we eat on the street? It's a waste of time asking the vendor if it was made with boiled water. A jelly complies with the sanitary norm if it's in glass. Even if it's really uncomfortable walking through town carrying small glass boxes, that delicate recipient guarantees the quality of the tremulous treat.

Our relationship with health is merely visual. We're not convinced by what we know but by what we're looking at. Which is why cones of scraped ice exist. All you have to do is look at the sweaty block of ice about to be scraped to remember that bacteria don't stop existing just because they're invisible. But the color of the syrups immediately calms us down. The red is so intense it suggests a transfusion, and the green alludes to chlorophyll so enthusiastically that you can't imagine it will make you sick, but that instead it will enable you to carry out photosynthesis. My favorite is blue. Gastronomy has produced very few blue items. A cone of scraped ice colored ultramarine seems the product of a laboratory. If you get sick eating it, it's because the paper cone was dirty.

Mexico City is crisscrossed by transients who try to eat without stopping and ambulatory suppliers who try to sell them something. The territory is so vast that these migratory tribes run the risk of never meeting. Which is why there exist aid stations in specific places, stations that come apart at night and reassemble by day.

On a corner stands a van with four flat tires. It hasn't moved in years because it is no longer connected with movement: it's a shop where juices and fried foods are sold. Like refuge centers up in the Alps, vans transformed into snack bars can save your life, but they aren't always nearby. The diner in need therefore requires other kinds of first aid.

Jorge Ibargüengoitia defined the *taco sudado* or sweaty taco as the Volkswagen of tacos. It isn't the best model but the most practical. Light and economical, it gets everywhere on a bicycle that holds a basket filled with rags that have a thermal purpose. According to the author of *Instructions for Living in Mexico (Instrucciones para vivir en México),* requesting, eating, and paying for the *taco sudado* should not take longer than five minutes.

By comparison, the *torta compuesta,* or stuffed bun, seems a sports model. Artemio de Valle Arizpe praised its preparation, which begins with the removal of the interior of the roll and moves from there in careful stages. José Emilio Pacheco challenged those who consider the invention of the sandwich the invention of the millennium to try a *torta compuesta,* which can contain the twenty-five elements chosen by the master *torta compuesta* maker Armando, a man with encyclopedic culinary knowledge, also immortalized in a newspaper article by Ibargüengoitia.

Your Mouth in Flames

Just how delicious is what we bite into either here or elsewhere? Some dishes are born tasty, while others require outside help. When the taco man standing next to the vertical, revolving spit holding marinated pork asks, "With everything?," he's referring to various food groups, including fruit. The *gringa,* a taco made with white flour, cheese, and marinated pork, extends this variety to milk products and confirms our cosmopolitan relationship with cheese. If the *enchiladas* are not spicy but are sprinkled with grated cheese they deserve to be "Swiss." Our cuisine is so complex that within its repertory cheese represents Swiss neutrality.

The principal remedy for hopeless food is *picante,* hot sauce, fiery symbol of identity; food gets better if it burns your mouth. This applies to the entire catalogue of vernacular food, from tamarind with *chile piquín* to pork rinds daubed with Buffalo sauce and passing through the thick intensity of *mole.*

The *chile* makes our dishes so interesting that we forget the source of the raw material. It's no accident that some stupendous taco stands are located along grand avenues or at exits from highways. Most citizens of Mexico City have eaten run-over dog, but we don't know we're doing it because the sauces transform the meat into a secondary character. I wouldn't like to cause any alarm by saying that in addition to being dog-eaters we're also cannibals. All you need to know is that our sauces burn to such a degree that we don't ask where the meat comes from or where our neighbor, whom we haven't seen for a while, might be.

Charles de Gaulle said it was impossible to govern a nation with 246 kinds of cheese. In Mexico, statistics are a form of conjecture: we simply do not know how many *chiles* there are. We do know there are a hell of a lot. It goes without saying that the Mexican who confesses that something is too hot has yet to be born. If you ask someone about it, he'll say "Not a bit" or "Only to give it some taste." To consume *chiles* is a matter of patriotism. The good chilango will put up with sweat pouring off his brow or the fact that his tears are flowing and still praise just how tasty this torture is.

According to popular belief, *chiles* are like Mexican politicians: we keep discovering they have new properties. Even so, there are still no *chiles* good for ulcers. Delicate or new stomachs have little luck in our ovens. This has led to mixing a sense of belonging with scatology. If some dish has a bad effect on you, you're not from these parts. "Moctezuma's revenge" places your affinity with the nation in doubt. The problem is not that you've eaten two sweaty tacos, three *nenepil* (uterus) tacos, and one *buche* (stomach) taco but that you aren't sufficiently acclimated. Suffering diarrhea is antipatriotic.

One of the most outlandish effects of this belief was the Pepto-Bismol mariachi, which in the ad campaign of 2009–2010 promoted this stomach medicine singing (to the tune of "La Cucaracha"): "The lovely teaspoon, the lovely teaspoon." The musicians were dressed as outrageous emblems of the gastric system, wearing *charro* costumes in *rosa* mexicano (pink)—appropriate because that's the color of Pepto-Bismol.

In a complementary way, there are those who think that because they've eaten in the least hygienic places they're immune to all danger. Daredevils abound who associate their stomach strength with a very precise corner of the capital: "Are you kidding? How could that hurt me when I have breakfast every day in the Vaqueritos roundabout?"

Mexico City is different from other macropoli because of the wealth of its itinerant food. There's no way to keep those temptations from coming our way, something you can confirm when you find a corn cob in your girlfriend's purse.

Like the breadcrumbs in Hansel and Gretel's enchanted forest, the food of the nomads reveals that wandering around doesn't mean losing your sense of direction but losing treats.

When the apocalypse threatens to let its mantle fall, the chilango focuses harder. In the distance, the air vibrates like a mirage in the desert, not because of the temperature but because of the promising presence of boiling oil. A stimulating aroma reaches the nose of the pilgrim, and the city transforms into an ungraspable territory where the oasis smells like cilantro.

Ceremonies

"Do Good Without Staring at the Blonde": Wrestling Movies

Mexico City has made a singular contribution to mass culture: wrestling films. The environment of the pankration, as the labors of the masked men within the twelve ropes, intrudes in the most varied ways in our urban life.

In 2006, just before the World Soccer Cup matches held in Germany, Ángel Fernández died. He was the greatest commentator on Mexican soccer, erudite in billiard matters and baseball, and, occasionally, a commentator on wrestling. His narrative style was based on his vibrant voice and his exceptional ability to mix anecdotes with what was going on in the game. Equipped with encyclopedic knowledge, both of classical and popular culture, he would pass from quoting Greek tragedies to *corrido* lyrics. His natural setting was the epic; not in vain did he say that the audience represented his "formidable chorus."

The funeral of a man who turned excess into a narrative merit could not be linked to discretion. Enrique *the Dog* Bermúdez approached the coffin and wept for the loss of his teacher. Others of us mentally reviewed the nicknames and metaphors that filled our childhood. The man who saw the conflagration at Parque Asturias, the old stadium of Mexico City, understood in that moment that the true cause of sport is not on the playing field but in the reaction of the crowd. That incomparable reporter was gone. Was it fitting to honor him in silence? It was then that among all those bodies wearing black appeared the silvery mask of the Son of the Saint.

His turning up was unforeseen but not strange. I remembered the connection between Ángel Fernández and Doménico the Daring, another chameleon of popular culture: when he retired from wrestling, he founded a tropical music group. When the greatest television announcer was excluded from the principal channels, Doménico proposed (or Ángel himself was the one who conceived that attractive excess) he narrate the dances whose music was supplied by the Daring Group. The announcer who had shouted in Brazil's Maracanã stadium traveled to dance halls with no sound system to invent a new artistic genre. In the breaks between songs, he would comment on what was happening in the dance hall. By doing so, the neighborhood dancers became the heroes in a Homeric epic. With the same passion he deployed to describe a goal made with "exceptional courage," Ángel detailed the miracles of patent leather shoes. Standing inside the orchestra, Doménico watched his friend weave phrases with the same passion he had when he wrestled in the ring.

The great oral narrator of Mexico deserved a farewell of his own dimensions, and several masked celebrities showed up to deliver it to him.

Chance—or the god of epics—decreed that at the moment when Mass was being said, exactly at the moment when the priest was saying "Santo, santo es el Señor" (Holy, holy is the Lord), the wrestler known as Hijo del Santo walked in. It was then we saw the silver mask. No greater homage could be paid to Ángel Fernández than that mix of religiosity, humor, and popular idolatry, similar to the headline with which a newspaper honored the death of the most famous wrestler in our history: "The Saint's in Heaven!"

There are few settings as disproportionate as the one occupied by those who beat each other up in an elaborate gesticulation of offenses. From the instant he enters the ring, the wrestler reveals his character. As an assiduous visitor to the Arena Coliseo and the Arena México during the 1970s, I recall Adorable Ruby, who confirmed his narcissism by putting on perfume before the bout. Another figure who comes into my memory is the Hippy Viking, whose threatening appearance revealed that certain cultural mixtures should not take place. Curiously, when I was doing research for this book, I found the Hippy and the Viking, but not a gladiator who combined them. In memory, as in biology, bizarre combinations have more of a chance to survive.

The repertory of holds follows codes equivalent to those in bullfighting or kabuki theater, a sign system that attracted the attention of Roland Barthes. In *Mythologies,* he observes: "The function of the wrestler . . . does not consist in winning but in carrying out precisely the gestures expected of him. . . . What the audience demands is the image of passion, not passion itself."

If boxing is a competitive activity, and if a boxer can perfect its techniques, wrestling is just the opposite. Any and all aggression is allowed as long as it forms part of the libretto. In wrestling, quality does not depend on athletic superiority or on any strategy but on the repetition of shared values, gestures that incarnate good and evil.

The outlaw wrestler lives for traps, for breaking the rules, the treacherous elbow jab, the lemon in the eyes of the innocent adversary. His wages are outrage; his bonus, booing. The good guy is shielded by his goodness. He uses terrible holds: he dominates the backbreaker, the pin, and the surfboard, but just when his opponent is flat on his back on the canvas and the crowd demands "Blood, blood!" he does not deliver the coup de grâce. To the contrary, he grants his rival a break, he enjoys the affection of the people, allowing his enemy to recuperate. And then he's treacherously attacked from behind.

The nicknames, the masks, the defining traits (the cannibal who munches ears, the Adonis with a broken nose who stares at a small mirror): all of that makes wrestling intensely narrative. Nothing that happens there demands any truth but the truth of theater, and, moreover, the truth of a melodrama, which aspires to the highest point of representation. When a bad guy among bad guys loses the battle in which he bet his hair, etiquette requires that he get down on his knees in the ring, beg for mercy, watch the barber who will shear him approach, and weep disconsolately listening to the shouting that humiliates him. Only the excessive is normal in that setting. Every wrestler competes dramatically with the moment when Tosca leaps to her death from the prison wall.

Wrestling is all about hyperbolic scale: its psychology rejects small size. Anyone with doubts about that can visit the *tortería,* The Ring, founded by Superstar in the center of Mexico City, on the corner of Pescaditos and Luis Moya. There the *torta* named "Gladiator Junior" challenges all comers to eat it.

I used to go to that temple of gastronomy for giants when I worked at the newspaper *La Jornada,* just a few blocks away. One *torta* was sufficient to feed half the editorial staff. Ever since that time, I've been plagued by a question that can only be answered in mythological terms: does the "Gladiator Senior" exist? Some claim to have seen it, and others add with disturbing certainty: a colossus who worked in the Arena México devoured it with no difficulty and then ordered dessert.

It's impossible to think about the ring without a legendary spirit. As a boy, I read the magazines *Lucha Libre, Box,* and *Lucha* with the curiosity of someone following a thrilling comic strip. *Thousand Masks, Blue Demon, Aguayo the Dog, Hurricane Ramírez,* and *Black Shadow* dramatized a saga that demanded in no uncertain terms a continuation beyond the ring. How did those heroes live when they weren't under the blazing spotlights of the arena? Did they lead double lives like spies, or did they follow the dictates of their stage character in private life? In his novella *The Pleasure Principle (El principio del placer),* José Emilio Pacheco explores the theme of lost innocence using a boy who is a wrestling fan. He grows up in a nasty way when he discovers that outside the ring the most bitter of rivals are friends. The drama between good and evil is nothing more than a simulation.

Himself a great fan of wrestling, Pacheco was one of the first to discover that *The Saint* was none other than Rodolfo Guzmán, who had wrestled under the nickname *Rudy.* In *The Pleasure Principle* he uses the spectacle of the pin as a symbol of the rite of passage for the adolescent: losing naïveté means understanding that the world is not inhabited by good guys and bad guys, pristine figures of a lost childhood.

Learning that heroes do not exist is a jolt to fantasy. Nevertheless, what was first believed as truth can be understood later as theater. Wrestling fans fall into two groups: those who absolutely believe in their idols—the eternal child who has never seen rival wrestlers having a beer together—and those who know that it's all a lie, but who adore the way the promised holds are carried out.

The justice the wrestlers impart in three pins with no time limit is too tempting to be relegated exclusively to the ring. Beyond the arena, a needy world demands avengers. It's no accident that the ring has inspired social wrestlers like *Superbarrio, Superanimal,* or *Brother Tormenta* (this last alternated pastoral duties as a priest with those of the professional gladiator and sponsored an orphanage that produced a wrestler willing to prove that muscles are an article of faith: *The Mystic*).

In the realm of comics and movies, Héctor Ortega and Alfonso Arau imagined a wrestler armed with a smart mouth rather than a strong arm, a kind of local anti-Batman: the Barefoot Eagle who patrolled the streets on a useless bicycle.

Cinematic references to wrestling abound. José Buil created a masterpiece about the private life of a popular icon: *The Legend of the Mask.* The scene where the hero's wife is ironing her husband's masks is unforgettable! In the history of Mexican film, this movie occupies a place equivalent to *The White Sheik* in Federico Fellini's filmography. Fellini's Alberto Sordi plays the part of a pop culture hero offstage. For years, Nicolás Echevarría had plans for a version of the ancient Mayan collection of myths, the *Popol Vuh,* where the actors would be wrestlers wearing masks designed by Francisco Toledo, who had great success when he took up the theme (in the Museo del Estanquillo, which contains Carlos Monsiváis's personal collection, an eloquent corner contains ceramic figures of wrestlers and ring scenes painted by Toledo).

But it was in popular movies that wrestling found its greatest sounding board. The book *I Want to See Blood! The Illustrated History of Wrestling Films* by Rafael Aviña, Raúl Criollo, and José Xavier Návar, is the definitive guidebook for a visit to the elusive world of extremely low production budgets that brought the mythology of the ring to the most diverse zones of exterior space, with, of course, an obligatory stop in Mexico City.

The founding film in this genre has a title that is so eloquent that it summarizes everything that came after: *The Magnificent Beast.* Filmed in 1952 by Chano Urueta, it was more a melodrama about the conditions surrounding the wrestlers than the creation of superheroes. In it, everything revolves around the artists of the kamikaze dive, the headlong attack of an opponent standing outside the ring, but what's really at stake is saving the human race—provisionally of course. The saga of the Saint would be the culmination of this ideal within a modest but excessive time frame: the local hero keeps the neighbors, that is the Men from Mars, under control.

For a couple of decades, wrestling films prospered thanks to the complicity of a public willing to believe that a ball of papier-mâché was an atomic bomb. While some movies deployed a fascinating visual design— *The Shadow,* for example—most disdained all notions of verisimilitude. If fiction suspends disbelief, wrestling movies annihilate it with a drop-kick. You either totally accept the setup or you don't. This explains the obsession with technology as a theme in a genre unable to utilize it as a device. Instead of mitigating their defective creation of flying saucers, the set designers emphasized their unreality. No one could doubt them for the simple reason that they could only be believed as obvious nonsense. In *Saint, the Man in the Silver Mask v. the Invasion of the Martians,* Wolf Ruvinkis, leader of the Martians, points out that earthlings are suspicious of their space suits. So he subjects his crew to a change of shape in a chamber that modifies identities. After being covered by a foreseeable cloud of smoke, the Martians reappear dressed as odalisques and Roman gladiators! In the enjoyable nonsense the script puts forth, these are perfect disguises for beings who do not want to be noticed in Mexico City.

The conventions of wrestling movies are as flexible as those of Elizabethan theater, where characters die in iambic pentameter. In the many laboratories that appear in them, the only decisive factor is a flask with smoke pouring out of it. The most delirious adventures are set in the most common places. In almost all the wrestling films there is a scene set in a place that looks like the home of one of the actors, a living room with sofas where the fate of the universe is decided.

Another of the genre's strange obsessions is the inclusion of dance scenes, serenades, and shows of all sorts that have absolutely nothing to do with the plot. But the most curious thing has always been the masked men incapable of acting. What special merits do those faceless actors have?

The success of the genre depended on the heroes' double presence: they could be seen in Arena México and in the unreal space of cinema. Rarely has popular culture had representatives so near and yet so far. The same person who gave you an autograph at the Friday match would be facing extraterrestrial challenges in the Sunday film. In the films, the catalogue of enemies was more varied than Don Juan's amorous conquests. Canonical rivalries, of course, were maintained (Saint against Blue Demon, good guys versus bad guys) but to them were added creatures from the other world, Martians with only one eye, vampires, mad scientists with Russian accents, imperturbable butlers, and celebrities in for the nonsense, like the boxer Butter Nápoles or the comedian Capulina, "champion of white humor." Also, the movies allowed for the arrival of the erotic rival, the stupendous evil woman. Gina Romand, the Classy Blonde, who first appeared as the star of Superior beer commercials, would become an essential icon of the genre. This put the peculiar sex appeal of the wrestlers to the test. Even if they worked naked from the waist up, the heroes were chaste. Their commitment to humanity was so great that they could not individualize their affection. So they rejected the seductions of the Blonde.

Although there have been contributions by wrestling cinema to pornography, the canonical works treat the protagonists as if they were the martyrs of early Christianity, beyond any pleasure but social service. Beneath the tights, the wrestler's sex is simply decoration.

In the perfect nudity of his *David,* Michelangelo revealed that the discretion of a body does not depend on clothing: the statue arouses not the slightest erotic curiosity. Its intimacy is that of a superlative marble shape. Wrestlers work under the same rule: they appear before the blondes as moral statues. The buxom body of the woman is simply an additional temptation that allows the heroes to show their fortitude. Trained to suppress their intimacy, they also suppress their libido.

Wrestling movies are unabashedly ideal for recycling. The same scene could be used in several pictures and the remix of scenes could be a new movie. This vampire technique recalls the working methods of José G. Cruz, the creator of the Saint comic strip and promoter of the myth beyond the ring. Cruz photographed the hero is various poses and then placed him in unusual settings. His frenetic ability to use scissors and glue created a montage showing the Saint leaping from a building in one scene and at the bottom of the sea in the next (the photo of the protagonist was identical in both cases). "What matters is not what [the spectator] believes but what he sees," Roland Barthes wrote with regard to wrestling. This logic governs the bouts, the comic strips, and the Saint's movies. Truth is determined by the eyes, not by the mind.

The screen resolved once and for all this question: What do the heroes do when they leave the ring? They save humanity from its own perfidious tendencies. The private life of the wrestlers took place in films, and most of them spoke with the voice of Narciso Busquets, a virtuoso at dubbing. Since they could not show facial expressions, the masked heroes depended on tone of voice.

In the saga of Charon, this trick reached its limits: all the characters who put on the mask of the wrestler whose name was the title of the film spoke like Busquets. The mask gave an identity, but the mask was dubbed.

According to the authors of *I Want to See Blood!*, there were characters who existed in films without ever entering a ring. That was the case of the Avenging Shadow. Faithful to his name, he never showed his body. Another notable exception was the wrestler who did not use a mask—very common in matches but difficult to use in film: the bare face demands acting skill. Wolf Ruvinkis was convincing because of his features, offering a necessary contrast to the all too common heroes without a face. He became a star in *A Streetcar Named Desire*.

Wrestling movies have lived out their life cycle: ultimately its naive initial meaning acquired the charm of the archaic, and later was revalued as a cult object: its awkwardness represented the moving creative impulse of a technology from an earlier age.

The genre, which stirred the dreams and passions of Mexico during the 1960s and 1970s, passed through the purgatory of kitsch until it achieved the posterity of the DVD. On the fringe of commercial programming, it found space in pirating and the most varied levels of fetishism.

The last speech in *The Shadow* summarizes the condition of the masked hero: he does good in silence, without looking for heroism, from the shadows.

Places

Public Government Ministry

Juan Antonia Ruiz?

    Antonio.

    Be seated, Mister Antonio.

Thank you, sir.

Have you brought your statement?

Here it is.

Well now, let me see . . . Lord, what bad handwriting. What is your profession?

I'm a writer.

No disrespect intended, but you don't know how to write.

So I've been told.

If you are a writer, you'll understand me better because your handwriting is so awful.

Thank you.

What happened?

I wrote it all down there.

Yes, but you didn't know how to write it down.

I went to the United States, and someone hacked my credit card.

Did they hack it while you were there?

No, they hacked it later, I'd already come back to Mexico. I have my boarding pass to prove it.

Don't tack on documents: they're just distractions. The credit card never left your possession?

Correct. I noted that in my statement.

Stop telling me what you wrote. You didn't know how to write it down.

Certainly, sir.

Why have you come before me?

The bank asked me to make a formal statement at the Public Government Ministry.

But all this happened abroad.

Yes, it did.

Well then, that's where you should make your statement.

But I live in Mexico, and everything happened after I'd returned.

We have no international jurisdiction.

In that case, what should I do?

You've got to write better. There are people who can help you. Me, for instance.

What should I do?

In the first place, we must justify your presence here. What is the reason for your being here?

Almost five thousand dollars was stolen from me, in a store called PJ Wholesale, of which I have absolutely no knowledge!

Don't get distraught, Mr. Antonio. You'll get nothing that way.

I'm sorry. All I'm asking is that you understand me.

Exactly what I'm trying to do, Antonio. Do you mind if I call you Antonio?

Not in the slightest.

In which neighborhood do you live?

In Coyoacán.

Excellent. Then that's the police precinct you must visit even if the crime took place in the United States. Where did you go?

To New York.

Wow, that's super. Did you have a good time?

Yes, until my credit card was hacked.

But by then you'd already returned.

Yes.

So that in New York you did have a good time?

Yes.

You've got to be precise, Antonio. Everything will work out if you write clearly. Shall I show you how?

Yes.

When someone says yes to me three times in a row it means they're not understanding me. Are you understanding me?

Yes . . . I mean I do understand.

Now concentrate, and don't say yes again.

Okay.

Look, for us to have jurisdiction over the case, the crime had to take place here.

What do you want me to do? The hacking took place in the U.S.!

Did they hack you or your card? What a guy this Antonio is! You must express yourself clearly.

I know, forgive me.

Would you allow me to show you how to write your declaration of what took place?

Please.

How did you find out your card had been hacked?

The bank sent me an email.

Where did you receive the email?

On my computer.

And where is your computer?

In my home.

You live in Coyoacán?

I do live in Coyoacán.

See? The events took place in Coyoacán! That's where you found out about everything! That's what you have to write. Don't talk about the United States, we're not Interpol you know.

I understand you, sir.

And as long as we're at it, Antoñito, maybe you can improve your handwriting. It looks as if you were tense when you wrote.

I always write that way.

You've got to relax! If you like, I can take you to the cells so you can see people who really have problems. Your problem is mental. It's all a matter of understanding where things actually took place.

At home.

There you are. There is no other crime scene: everything happened in your home. There's nothing like the truth.

Living in the City

My Grandmother's Outing

The first writer in my family was my grandmother, María Luisa Toranzo, widow of Villoro. With that ancient name—more appropriate for conferring prestige to a tequila label than for the spine of a book—she published self-help books that were genuine best sellers in Catholic schools during the 1950s. *Orange Blossoms, Thorns and . . . Roses, Chats with My Daughter, Silly Atoms* are just a few of her titles.

A love child, she grew up in the countryside near San Luis Potosí, where her father had two haciendas: Cerro Prieto and Puerto Espino. She was a distant relative of Teresa Toranzo, the green-eyed woman courted by the poet Ramón López Velarde when he was a judge in Venado, a town in the state of San Luis Potosí.

The family's money came from distilling mezcal. Even though she grew up in a rustic environment, she was given a first-rate education. This, by the way, was not infrequent among hacienda owners. She spoke four languages and played six instruments, including the mandolin and the harp. Along with her works of moral pedagogy, she translated Giuseppe Steiner's *The Soldier's Guitar*. A great opera enthusiast, she attended the Bayreuth festivals and became a friend of the pianist Arthur Rubinstein, whose autograph she possessed. None of her descendants was as versatile in terms of art, and her musical instruments became decorative rarities that arouse the interest of visitors:

"What the devil is this?"

"It's Grandma's harp," answer my cousins, in the same way my mother answers, "It's Grandma's mandolin."

Separated from her mother and country business, María Luisa Toranzo grew up surrounded by encyclopedias and record players. To complete her education, the family (made up of María Luisa and my great-grandfather) decided to move to Mexico City. They lived on the Alameda, next to the place now occupied by the Laboratorio Arte Alameda.

The house was demolished, but I managed to see it in the first full-length feature film in Mexican cinematography: *The Gray Automobile*. Based on real events, the movie combines scenes reenacted by actors with elements of what would later be called cinéma vérité: the lead was played by a real policeman, Juan Manuel Cabrera, the filming took place in the houses attacked by the thieves, who fled in a gray automobile. The movie ends with a documentary sequence about the execution of the criminals. One of the assaults takes place in the Casa Toranzo. My grandmother was ashamed of the movie because the actress who played her flirted—using the techniques of silent film—with one of the handsome thieves.

The events took place in 1915, and the film was made four years later. In a certain way, the scene in which my grandmother appears was prophetic. María Luisa did not flirt with a bandit, but a revolutionary did try to seduce her in the style of Pancho Villa: he gallantly warned her he was going to seduce her.

It all took place during the Revolution, and the family had abandoned the country in search of the relative peace offered by Mexico City. A great collector of knickknacks (among which were some genuine works of art), my great-grandfather moved into town with no intention of ever returning to the country.

Strolling across the Alameda, my grandmother was in the habit of stopping at the most erotic sculpture in the city: *Malgré Tout* by Jesús Contreras. A beautiful, naked woman strains to drag herself along, as if she wanted to flee the block of marble. According to the poet Amado

Nervo, the greatest mythographer of sentimentality, the title *Despite All* had nothing to do with the efforts of the woman, whose sensuality tried to free itself from its mineral prison, but with the fact that the sculptor had lost his right arm and had to finish the piece with his awkward left hand. "Despite all," he succeeded.

Nervo's tale is not completely accurate. Jesús Contreras finished the sculpture in 1889 and lost his arm in 1902, shortly before dying at the age of thirty-six. But nothing can hold a poet back, and Nervo explained that the cancer which had invaded that right arm earlier made the artist a virtual cripple. Inspired by Nervo's tale, Manuel M. Ponce, in 1900, wrote a work for piano, *Malgré Tout,* a composition to be played exclusively with the left hand.

Contreras also created twenty of the bronze sculptures along Paseo de la Reforma as well as the statue of Cuauhtémoc on the same avenue. For my generation, that monument acquired singular importance in 1988, when the engineer Cuauhtémoc Cárdenas became the left's presidential candidate. In the demonstrations his supporters carried out, we would stop at the last Aztec emperor made immortal by Contreras and shout the name of our hope: "Cuauhtémoc!"

As we all know, that election ended in an outrageous fraud. In 1997, almost a decade later, Cárdenas became the first head of government democratically elected in the Federal District. This belated recognition of the fact that we citizens of the capital deserved to govern ourselves began in the nine years of our shouting as we stood around the statue Contreras created.

Another unusual detail is that Cuauhtémoc's pose was imitated by the exceptional soccer forward, Cuauhtémoc Blanco, who for about twenty years (1992–2012) was the supreme virtuoso of Mexican soccer. Born in the Tlatilco neighborhood, Blanco dashed about the playing field with the sassiness of someone who came from a place where soccer was played dodging cars from which players often stole rearview mirrors. He regularly copied the pose of his Aztec namesake until the prim authorities asked him not to disrespect a symbol of the nation.

But it's Contreras's *Malgré Tout* that interests me most. In prudish times, a naked woman was crawling, rather disturbingly, on the Alameda. Her body was perfect, but what was even more perfect was her combination of power and surrender. With her hands chained behind her back, her feet chained to a rock, and her gaze fixed on the void, that woman surrendered and did not surrender, destroyed by a trance, over-whelmed, she wanted something more.

My grandmother contemplated her every day, and years later she talked to me about the statue. What did that woman feel—this not phys-ically attractive women who'd been courted by schemers perhaps only interested in her money? We know that thanks to the many languages she spoke and the many instruments she played that she used euphony to sublimate her desires. She would speak with enormous liberality about the fleshy bodies of Italian painting and the need Renaissance artists had to lead erratic, irregular lives. In her everyday life she was conserva-tive but suspicious. My parents concealed their divorce from her so she wouldn't be disillusioned, but her diaries reveal she knew everything. She said nothing about it in order not to deprive my father of the illusion that he was tricking her.

Malgré Tout condensed the confusions of an era in which public art could be erotic to the breaking point and women, as in López Velarde's poem, shortened their skirts "up to the wish bone."

The Alameda, about which my grandmother spoke so much, repre-sented in my childhood the place with the most balloons in the world, the colorful place Diego Rivera painted in a celebrated mural, *Dream of a Sunday Afternoon in Alameda Park,* where he gathered together all the famous people of his time and which reminded me of the jacket pic-ture on the Beatles' *Sgt. Pepper* album. The Alameda was also the place we'd visit on January 6 in order to have our picture taken with the Three Kings, whose fake beards competed in texture with the cotton candy sold in the same place.

It was in the Alameda where I absorbed the initial protocols of spoon-ing with a girl and where I first touched a bosom with the awkwardness of Jesús Contreras's maimed hand. On the night of our high school grad-uation what we least wanted to do was go home. An inventive genius suggested we go to the Alameda. As couples accidentally created by the evening's events, we sat on one of the semicircular stone benches. Out of the corner of my eye I saw the clock on the Torre Latinoamericana count-ing out the minutes of my anxiety. Nearby was the sculptor's woman whose body was much more striking than the one I couldn't quite manage to decipher by touch. I never again got close to that girl. For a few hours the utter strangeness of being there and our mutual desire to test our innocence joined us. We didn't love each other. We were nervous being together, but we were able to experience something we'd never done before, and that was our transitory way of loving each other.

Many years later, we met again to talk about literature and about what life had done with us. The adolescent who trembled on that stone bench was an intelligent and wise woman. We saw each other several times, but the city that bestowed on us the miracle of touching each other in a mystery of unknowing prepared another story for her. She was attacked in a taxi and shot. She died a few hours later.

I never again walked by the statue of *Malgré Tout*. For me that sculpture was no longer the disorderly representation of desire but instead of death. In my imagination, it remained at the Alameda. Only when I was writing down notes for this book did I learn that in 1983 it was moved to the National Museum of Art to protect it from vandals. The strange thing—and this speaks explicitly about the tricks memory plays—is that I saw the statue in the museum without completely understanding that it "was there," that is without mentally removing it from its place in the park and where today there is a replica. The city is a strange place: you live in it one way and remember it in another.

My grandmother, who from an aesthetic point of view admired the frozen sensuality of the woman in *Malgré Tout,* began to identify herself with another aspect of the figure: the desire and the impossibility of escape. Courted by a revolutionary, she thought only about leaving the country. The family had a Basque friend with an unforgettable name, Celestino Bustindui. To prevent my future grandmother from ending up pregnant in some revolutionary encampment, Bustindui accompanied her to San Sebastián.

On the shores of the Bay of Biscay, she met a doctor born in Mataraña, the strip of land that separates Aragon from Cataluña. Handsome, charming, and a great talker, that doctor loved the good life as only a person who's suffered penury can love it. His family names revealed that he came from a town so small that there proximity blended with incest. His double last name was Villoro Villoro.

He fell in love with my grandmother or with what she represented. As I mentioned, María Luisa was not pretty. She had owl eyes (the only Oedipal trace in her son Luis is that he collected owls). Among her virtues: intelligence, irony, an ability to take charge, culture, generosity, and honor. But libido is usually discriminatory. I suppose that Dr. Miguel Villoro Villoro was also attracted by the idea of giving a woman who'd never had one a family. Exiled, bereft of relatives, María Luisa needed some affection to hold on to. Besides, she was a millionaire. Newly married, she and my grandfather moved to Barcelona where my father and his two brothers were born.

Once married, my grandfather abandoned medicine, a profession for which he didn't seem to have much passion, and dedicated himself to administering properties, which he did badly but with sympathy. Among other blunders, he sold the Alameda house "with everything it contained" to Mr. Larín, owner of the celebrated chocolate factory. My grandmother called that episode the Great Harvest—among the furnishings that were included free of charge were two dressers painted by Watteau.

As a boy, I heard the story of that lost forever greatness. Certain names and certain brands were ingrained in me as symbols of the intangible. My grandmother traveled in a Hispano-Suiza automobile, wore Balenciaga, stayed at the Hotel Carlton in Bilbao, and took part in the Wagner cycles at Bayreuth.

When her husband died (victim of a bad operation), she sent her sons off to Belgium, to Jesuit-run boarding schools, and went on with her luxurious lifestyle. Her income derived from the exploitation of peasants and from rental properties. The consequence of this was that her great political adversaries would be Lázaro Cárdenas and Manuel Ávila Camacho. The expansion of the agrarian reform during the 1930s and the rent freeze of 1942 damaged the fortunes of idle property owners, the class to which my grandmother belonged.

My father would completely reject that bourgeois life based on injustice. The same went for his elder brother, Miguel, a Jesuit and a lawyer. The most interesting aspect of this is that in old age even my grandmother would regret her extravagant life. She didn't repent because of an ideological conversion but a moral one.

When I first met her, she lived in the Departamentos Mascota, later known as El Buen Tono, on Avenida Bucareli. That mass of one hundred and seventy-five apartments was built in 1904 as a model project by Eugenio Pugibet, owner of the tobacco company El Buen Tono. He commissioned Miguel Ángel de Quevedo, who produced spacious, well-lighted rooms with high ceilings. There were basements ideal for storage, and the apartments faced agreeable interior patios.

However, between 1942 and 1992, the rent freeze caused El Buen Tono to be maintained like a building during time of war.

Nowadays, those apartments have a hipster charm, but during the mid-1960s, when I would visit my grandmother, they were a ruin. She lived there to expiate her guilt in the same way she prayed for the blind with her eyes closed as she walked through the house. This was risky, and on two occasions she fell down the stairs.

The rent freeze harmed María Luisa Toranzo when her world was a succession of ocean liners, restaurants, and opera festivals. Even so, she could have gone on with her lavish life, but a radical conversion caused her to cross the property line and she spent her old age renting an apartment in a building falling to pieces.

Sorry she hadn't taken a hand in bringing up her own children, she spoiled her grandsons rotten. She assigned each one a wall to paint. As a result, the decoration of those walls was worthy of a psychiatric hospital. My cousin Ernesto, who had a splendid drawing skill and would become an architect, painted an immense devil with a single word below it: *me.*

My grandmother focused on charity work and extended her late vows of poverty to her clothing. She wore two gowns, which, as an homage to the great comedians of the time, she called Cantinflas and Tin Tan. Someone told her that her teeth could cause infections, so she had all of them pulled. Since she did not wear dentures, her grin was identical to the old crones in the illustrations to children's books. She had a skin condition on her ankles that obliged her to use cotton pads, themselves covered with purple cardboard.

This precarious appearance contrasted with her splendid humor. She had no television, but she listened to radio soap operas. She would recount her favorites to me in detail: *Great Soul,* the saga of a rancher handy with a gun and eloquent in pronouncing the sayings of a rustic

Jesus, and *Kalimán,* an adventure series whose best feature was its credits. After reciting the names of the different actors, a voice would say: "And in the role of Kalimán . . . Kalimán himself!"

That action hero, whose mystical motto was "Serenity and Patience," even took the time to visit the radio station.

In her old age, my grandmother stopped writing self-help books, but she still kept her diary. I got one "in a raffle," as she noted in pencil. Many years later, I read it, surprised at how acute she was in judging others.

In handwriting ruined by arthritis, my grandmother noted her concern for me, the most depressed and timid of her grandchildren. My father, always hermetic, she called *The Knight of Silence.* In those pages, she attributes my introverted nature, which burdened me to a pathological degree until I reached adolescence, to my parents' imminent divorce—which they tried to hide from her.

Maybe the raffle in her diary was a fiction. Maybe she gave it to me so I'd read it years later and understand the pain I'd endured and dare not speak to others. I suppose after all she never stopped being a self-help author.

On Saturday, we'd eat at her place, and she would give each grandson ten pesos—an undeserved fortune—to spend at the Juárez Market just around the corner. That was my first incursion into the motley world of Mexico City markets. Few places offered such a mix of fragrances derived from such a variety of sources: tripe and chocolate define the density of the air. You step on blood, sawdust, seeds, and a chicken bone; then the air smells like flowers or fish. The sellers call you, with less insistence than the hookers in bars or the employees at the duty-free shop at the airport. Some don't even bother to mention what they're selling: "How much I sell and how much I enjoy myself," one would shout. "Here you have tenderness!" answered another, while a third preferred to promote his prices: "I sell cheap!"

In those days, I focused on the zone of cheap toys. I was after a translucent, psychedelic yo-yo, a wooden top, a plastic cowboy covered with burrs you had to cut off with scissors, but which you sometimes left intact because they looked like Cherokee feathers. Like Andy Warhol paintings imitated on a deliberately defective press, out of focus, over time those burrs became for me the most valuable aspect of those toys, made by an imperfect technology, sold in order to be improved by the buyer. "If you ever feel that something you've written is impeccable, add a defect," Augusto Monterroso told me in his unforgettable short story workshop. Sometimes, I feel there's a burr on a literary passage, an impurity that alters it but doesn't ruin it and renders it dear to my heart in a world where only the unreal aspires to perfection.

The principal toy bastion in that era was the Ara toy shop, owned by an Armenian family. Their infinite shelves were full of scale models ready for assembly, plastic storage boxes, wooden horses, electric trains, and highways. The opposite pole was the Mercado Juárez, where the toys followed the logic of tomatoes: they got there because of capricious causes and effects. If you did not buy, on the spot, an Indian with a spectacular headdress, you might never buy it. The supply did not derive from a measured mass production but from whatever they managed to get at the moment. The fluctuations of whatever was being sold conferred on purchases the prestige of rarity. Like fruits in season, the marbles of one Saturday were different from those of the following Saturday.

The Argentine critic Beatriz Sarlo says that part of the charm of modern shopping malls (*el shopping* as they say in Argentina) derives from establishing a contact with products you can't buy but which are right there before your eyes. Like television, the mall follows a "logic of celebrity." Just because you don't have the money to buy Armani clothes doesn't mean you can't admire and even touch them. Sarlo writes in *The City Seen (La ciudad vista)*:

As if it were the same as the beauty of some celebrity or a cooking program, what the mall offers does not require a purchase every time, even if a purchase is the shared objective of both the mall and the customer. There exists a kind of zone where frustration is neutralized. The spectacle of the abundance of merchandise, in many cases financially out of reach, is the basis for the probably minor attractiveness of the merchandise that is actually bought and which is thus ennobled.

Liverpool, a cathedral of consumption built on Avenida Insurgentes a few blocks from where I lived, revealed to me the fascination embodied in hierarchically organized products where, as Sarlo observes, while the most expensive are out of reach they are not less desirable for that reason—like movie stars.

The Mercado Juárez provided me with the opposite experience. The area set aside for toys and Superman or Batman costumes was not really separate from the vegetable market. My ten pesos could metamorphose into the cooking herb espazote, chicken parts, a tamale, quicklime, iodine, nails, goat cheese, calf's liver, roses, or even toys.

Unlike the mall, the general market gives you the impression you can buy anything. The thing you buy does not acquire prestige just because it belongs to the same universe as what is unattainable (the Rolex on display in the Palacio de Hierro). It's part of an organic totality and belongs to the same environment as the sticky floor, the confused aromas, the stands with their crude mosaics. Although fortunes are made there, and suddenly we find out that so-and-so is the king of garlic or the czar of beans, the bad condition of the place suggests that all sales are fair, that outwardly at least no one is getting rich. The option to haggle confirms that the prices are conjectural and that the merchandise can be affected by feelings.

That worn-out setting constantly receives fresh merchandise. The market functions like a stomach, and sales are like digestion. The jolly colorfulness of the stands and the drawling humor of the sellers—"Step right inside, madam. Come along, please. Just taste this mamey."— contributes to the sensation that usury has nothing to do with sales but with a way to survive a difficult life with joy. Even if the abalone has the same price as a jewel, no one imagines a fancy emporium sits behind the broken-down fish and seafood stand.

The markets remind me of the years when María Luisa Toranzo decided to be poor, her voluntary incarceration in a building where the rent was frozen, her repudiation of the world of prestige she flirted with when young.

But the decision to move to El Buen Tono was accompanied by another even more interesting: never to leave the place. She renounced the exterior world and restricted herself to walking from one room to another.

She heard the voices of the dead and knocks on her headboard. None of that alarmed her. Once she heard the buzzer and went downstairs to open the door that opened on to Avenida Bucareli. It was a priest friend of hers. He'd come to announce he'd be taking a long voyage. The next day she learned that the priest had died somewhere far away.

She accepted this condition of being a seer with the same tranquility she accepted her bad clothes or the sores on her calves. After traveling the world, she experienced plenitude behind walls scrawled over by the hesitant hands of her grandchildren.

For decades, the city for her was an unknown place that made noise. One day my parents came up with the idea of taking her for a walk. I don't recall any other project into which they invested so much effort. They rarely did anything together. During vacation, my father would take us to the beach without removing his suit or taking off his tie. We would get to Mazatlán, unpack, he would hand the car keys to my mother and go back to Mexico City on the first bus.

The idea that they would decide to set my grandmother into motion seemed incredible to me. My sister, Carmen, who at the time was probably six, also remembers that moment as unique in our lives. Grandma's outing was something unheard of, but we remembered it because of an even greater surprise: for a few hours, our parents had a shared project.

It wasn't easy to convince the recluse to abandon her chosen prison for a while. My father spoke to her with the rhetorical skill of a prize-winning debater who had become a professor of celebrated eloquence. Most certainly, Mother added the emotional details that made her into an expert in stimulating the feelings of others.

As she listened to them, my grandmother flashed the curved smile of her toothless mouth. And then she agreed to go with them. Why? My parents couldn't convince her of anything. She lived at the far edge of the street. Besides, her reclusion was an emblem of her moral conversion: María Luisa Toranzo, Villoro's widow or the Hermit of El Buen Tono.

At this historical distance, I can imagine a hypothesis. She knew my parents were not made for each other and that they'd soon separate. She wrote that in her diaries. She also knew she would die soon. She accepted that sojourn in which we pretended to be a family and which in fact represented something more definitive: she was saying goodbye to us, and my parents pretended to be what they couldn't be.

We would lose the ties that bound us, but something of that outing in which we had the illusion of proximity and belonging would remain: the things we saw. We might not be a family, but we belonged to the city.

The objective of the outing was to see the Christmas lights downtown. My grandmother must have felt like Proust in the last volume of *Remembrance of Things Past,* returning to the scenes of her youth, places that were not the same. The Alameda had lost its air of a fancy park, where rich people strolled among pinwheel vendors.

My father, who had just published his book *The Ideological Process of the Independence Revolution,* might have preferred to see the patriotic spectacle of September. My mother, for her part, hated Christmas. Once divorced, she would repeat a nihilistic mantra: "We are not a family." And then she'd use any pretext to defame the holiday in which everyone feels obliged to be part of a tribe. Her most radical moment in this struggle to annihilate the sentimental hypocrisy that makes soft hearts long for nonexistent reindeer and snow would take place in 1970. I was fourteen; my sister had gone on a trip with my father. I was left at the mercy of her maternal impulses. "Are we a family?" she asked me. "No!" I shouted to please her. "Perfect. Then we won't celebrate Christmas." We got into her Valiant Acapulco and headed north. Christmas Eve surprised us in León, in the state of Guanajuato. We were hungry, but we weren't going to celebrate anything, so we walked into a Vips. I ordered cornflakes, just to make my contempt for the day perfect. Our waitress had bright red hair. In her eyes, despair mixed with sadness. She did indeed have a family and hated being there, waiting on the only customers in the place. That was our heroic Christmas.

Also the worst.

On the other hand, I remember our outing with Grandma as a holiday. My father's white Opel with bright green trim could barely move among the other cars, and we were on the verge of colliding with a streetcar. I wished the traffic would stand still forever while my grandmother stared at a city that was too modern for her and too old for the present.

The French poet Jules Laforgue describes himself writing at the moment the light goes out. The poet finishes his verses thanks to the glow that condenses in the eyes of his cat.

I don't know what my grandmother saw on that ride. I suppose nothing interesting for her, but she agreed to go out with us, perhaps so her grandchildren would remember the scene, her toothless smile in the presence of colored lights on a Christmas that would not be for us, her way of being fine in that place, now unrecognizable, but not so for the person who is finishing this chapter with the light that condensed in her eyes.

Places

Tepito, El Chopo, and Other Informalities

The Nile is plied by feluccas, small boats that have been transporting merchandise on the river since time immemorial. That Arabic word gave birth to the Mexican term *fayuca,* which means contraband. The other significant term that defines our informal economy is *tianguis,* which derives from the Nahuatl word *tianquiztli,* market.

Tepito is the place in Mexico City where those two words are used most. Seen from the air, the neighborhood is a pretty mosaic of magenta, orange, and yellow canopies. By day the swarms of people recall Hong Kong movies. The similarity is more than physical: the Chinese ability to produce pirated goods is identical to Tepito's ability to sell them. By night, this centrally located enclave, just a couple of kilometers north of the Alameda, takes on the dark prestige of danger. For decades, it's had the nickname Barrio Bravo (Tough Town).

Tepito was the birthplace of legendary boxers: Raúl *The Mouse* Macías, Ricardo *Birdie* Moreno, and José Medel. It also witnessed the drinking of another star of the ring fond of the local cantinas: Rubén *Spikes* Olivares, pride of the Bondojito neighborhood.

At the same time, this zone, which some have survived thanks to knockouts, has also been the seat of the counterculture movement Arte Acá (Art Here), founded by, among others, Armando Ramírez, who in

1971 took Mexican literature by storm with *Chin Chin from Tepito (Chin Chin el teporocho)*. Narrated by a street person, this novel brought up to date the research of the U.S. anthropologist Oscar Lewis, whose 1964 *The Children of Sánchez* unleashed a torrent of scandal.

A cynical policy of negation has led many to think that what's bad about Mexico is not our problems but talking about them. The authorities accused Oscar Lewis of defaming Mexico with his testimonies about Tepito, and his editor at the Fondo de Cultura Económica was fired.

A symbol of the struggle to survive, Tepito is also the territory where the composer Juventino Rosas, author of the celebrated waltz "Over the Waves," functioned as the bell-ringer in the church, and where people connected with valor if not contraband have also lived. The journalist Ricardo Rocha was born there, the man who had to resign from Televisa in 1995 because he dared to report on the massacre at Aguas Blancas. And in the same building on Allende Street, four of the most eminent members of Mexico's scientific community grew up: Marcos Rosenbaum, Pablo Rudomin, Carlos Gitler, and Samuel Gitler. All sons of poor immigrants in the Jewish community, from families who trafficked in junk and other waste without apparent value, the four future researchers began their studies of the mysteries of the world on the streets of the neighborhood and in the Jardín de los Topos on the other side of Paseo de la Reforma, where later the Secretariat of Foreign Relations would be built and where they still search for the mythical treasure of Moctezuma.

The Rudomin family moved from Allende Street to Jesús Carranza. Many years later, Pablo wanted to show his sons and grandsons the place where he'd discovered the streets and the scents of the city. He visited Tepito with his offspring, not as numerous as one of the tribes of Israel, but easily recognizable. The locals stared at the scientist with his white beard and liquid blue eyes with a defensive curiosity until he found the very building and said: "I lived here." People of a certain age remembered his grandfather Isaac, and the welcome was immediate. "I felt better there than at any academic congress," smiles the man from Tepito who would grow up to study neurons in the human brain.

I visited the area first in 1971. Inspired by Alejandro Jodorowsky's happening-play, *The Game We All Play,* a group of friends decided to stage a work of collective creation about the commonplaces (for us quite novel) of the Age of Aquarius. The title of the piece was *Melting Pot* and generated a dialogue with the audience about peace and love. Those were the times when wild hair was in itself a sign of freedom, a time when the patience inculcated in us by the Franciscans of the New World could be described as "lighten up." In other words, we found an audience able to resign itself to be before us. Only that explains how we came to act in many different places. Héctor Azar, director of the Theater Department at Bellas Artes, went so far as to give us a season in the Teatro Comonfort, in the Peralvillo neighborhood, right next to Tepito. That was my first paid job. At the end of the month I would get an envelope with a salary so thin it was made up of more coins than bills.

Jaime Nualart, who later would be Mexico's ambassador to Egypt and India, was our leader. He wore a tunic decorated with purple anemones, used a fork folded around his wrist as a bracelet, and appeared in a gas mask bought in an Army-Navy store. This outlandish appearance, which could hardly be a preview of his diplomatic career, conferred on us the security of carnival (people walking around in costume are rarely attacked). Even so, we never wandered far from the Teatro Comonfort and barely dared to take a quick look at the streets where the celebrated geniuses of the left hook to the liver practiced their art.

After the earthquake of 1985, the artist Felipe Ehrenberg moved to Tepito. I often visited the house that he and his partner Lourdes transformed into an extraordinary example of Mexican folk art. So nothing would happen to my Volkswagen, my host would place a sign on the windshield that read "Friend of Felipe."

The novelist Fernando del Paso later defined Ehrenberg as a "neologician."

Even so, his predilection for the avant-garde did not keep him from establishing a fertile contact with popular tradition—to such a degree that he had bones tattooed on his left hand as an homage to the great illustrator José Guadalupe Posada. With that indelible gesture he perhaps honored, as would only be fitting for someone of German blood, Wilhelm Röntgen, inventor of X-rays.

In the lingering dinners and lunches at the Ehrenberg house, the infamous dangerousness of Tepito was nowhere to be seen. Did an invisible wave surround us while we enjoyed Lourdes's imaginative dishes in the eye of the hurricane?

It would be snobbish of me to derive a genuine knowledge of the place from only those visits. Just knowing an anthropologist's campsite doesn't mean you know the tribe he's studying.

In his play *The Green Cockatoo,* Arthur Schnitzler puts a group of French aristocrats on the stage: they take a "plunge into the people" and feel the "temptation of mud" in a tavern. For them, there's nothing more chic than rubbing shoulders for a short while with criminals.

Tepito has been demonized as an enclave of evil, but, though to a lesser degree, it has promoted variations on extreme tourism for those who wish to feel, for a few hours, the stolen life of "the other." I confess that I gave in to the high-brow illusion of being in a place forbidden to most of the city's inhabitants, a closed, hard enclave, when in reality I was simply visiting Felipe's house.

Excursions to tumultuous places can be inspired by the best desires, but they rarely produce an experience except discomfiture. I remember the night when a bunch of us thrill-seekers went to the gay bar Spartacus in Ciudad Nezahualcóyotl. That was at the end of the 1980s, when that far edge of the city still retained the appearance of a place yet to be urbanized—no public services, no zip codes, a time when sexual deviation had few places to speak its name. In the Zona Rosa, citadel of tourism and refined bohemianism, the Bar 9 was the precursor to the gay movement. It was much harder to find an equivalent place in poorer areas. At the end of the 1970s, José Joaquín Blanco published a decisive text in the *Saturday* supplement of *Unomásuno,* "Eyes It Panics You to Dream Of," about the double condemnation the "fucking fag" suffers.

The night I'm bringing back to life here seemed animated by the spirit of *The Green Cockatoo.* We'd gone to Bellas Artes to see Richard Strauss's opera *Salomé,* directed by the outrageous Werner Schroeter. The excursion to Ciudad Nezahualcóyotl arose out of a desire to prolong Oscar Wilde's libretto on a local scale. We were looking for "The Other" the way you take part in a highly dangerous sport that brings dangers you survive in a delicious way.

The main attraction at the Spartacus was Alexander the Erotic, a stripper who copulated with a papaya. Years later, I would read an article by Empar Moliner about the Bagdad, a live sex show in Barcelona, which also invited the audience to explore other levels of human experience. There, a boy would spread a gelatinous substance on his stomach and then stroll among the audience members to be licked by them. The journalist did not abstain, and she tasted the seasoned torso, covered by a light, slightly fruity film that reminded her of the subtle foams of Ferran Adrià. Opposite poles of taste became identical, pornography and molecular cuisine. Sometimes "high" is another name for "low." Moliner's experience is very similar to the one we tourists in the lower depths had in the Spartacus. That night we believed we were part of an underworld to which we did not belong. A rapid dialogue should have alerted us from the start about our condition as outsiders. A man at the next table heard my wife say something, and he asked her if she were a foreigner.

"What kind of accent do you think I have?" she asked.

The man thought up a remote place and answered, "Maybe Tijuana."

The outstanding lesson of the evening was this: after the erotic show, we danced, and when we came back to our table we discovered that our sweaters had been slashed, an eloquent sign that while that reality did exist, it was not ours.

Knowing the city implies butting in where you don't belong, sneaking in, being out of place, running the risk that someone may tear your clothing or whatever is under the clothing. At the same time, butting in for a moment does not mean that you fully understand situations alien to you. Embedded journalism usually fails for that reason. When the reporter tells how he passed himself off as someone and something else and that he lived a reality not his own, the most interesting thing is not the anecdote about that other world but the problems he had to solve to narrate it.

I'll state it frankly: I don't really know Tepito and don't think I ever could. But I wouldn't be a chilango unless I knew it exists, unless I felt the temptation to go there from time to time.

The place is a bastion of frenetic labor, except that they work in a different way there. In fact, their principal income source is not that eccentric. According to the official page of the International Labor Organization: "the informal economy generates between half and three fourths of all the nonagricultural jobs in developing nations."

Within the zone you find toys, school supplies, scissors, nail clippers, domestic electronics, clothing, combs, umbrellas, and other products worthy of a twenty-first-century adaptation of the bazaars of the *Thousand and One Nights*. None comes with a guarantee because they're all contraband. None of that would matter much if smuggling and drugs didn't pass through the same circuit. The feluccas of the third millennium carry more damaging things than those that sailed the Nile of the pharaohs.

As a result, Tepito has never stopped being in the sights of the police, especially when it's not a matter of fighting crime but of offering a spectacular representation of the fact that it is fought. The fame of Tough Town, only a few meters away from the historic center of the city, makes police interventions seem more convincing because they take place there. A long saga of crimes—sometimes real, sometimes legendary—confers on those streets the aura of an impregnable place.

The melodrama with which the antiriot vehicles knock down stands, and the way the police "strategically" seize control of the zone has a clearly symbolic function. In Tepito, the war on the underworld is more newsworthy than it is in other places.

In 2007, the police seized a property known as The Fortress, supposedly the headquarters of organized crime: later it was discovered that the criminal world's center of operations was elsewhere. In 2012, an antismuggling unit came to the zone, but it was repelled by two hundred people armed with nightsticks. In 2013, there was a new offensive after four people were murdered in the Body Extreme gym. That same year, after twelve people were kidnapped and held in some dive, the prison of Tepito was spoken of more and more, because it had strong connections with the Zeta, the gang most dedicated to contraband.

Just how serious is the situation? Aristegui News reported in 2013 that Tepito was one part of the fifty-seven demarcations of the nation where forty percent of the crimes are committed.

Real or fictitious, Tepito's challenges alter the fact that after every police cleanup, the selling of contraband merchandise returns to the streets with the same constancy as its vernacular dish: the *migas* (crumbs), the food of poverty, made of bread, pork, and bones.

The Apostle of Rock in Tepito

A few years ago, I went with José Xavier Návar to buy pirated DVDs in Tepito. I wanted to go with someone familiar with the place. When I asked Pepe how often he went there, he answered in the tone of incombustible enthusiasm he uses to speak about anything: "At least twice a week."

We met in 1977, when he was press officer for PolyGram records. Extremely generous, he gave me myriad Roxy Music albums to be played on the radio program *The Dark Side of the Moon* for which I wrote scripts. A journalist who supported numerous lost causes, producer of the progressive rock group Chac Mool, a wrestling specialist, Pepe only interrupted his search for artistic rarities in order to write about them in the press.

Those of us who discovered the counterculture in an era prior to globalization took on the task of acquiring books, records, and magazines as if it were a safari chasing elusive white tigers. The quest became an essential part of our passion, as if overcoming obstacles in order to reach the Work conferred moral merits on us that enabled us to deserve it. "Pray that the road be long" says Cavafy in his celebrated poem "Ithaca." In our hunt for talismans, the avatars of the search could be more interesting than the goal.

More than thirty years ago, the Tianguis Cultural del Chopo (Cultural Market del Chopo) arose in the Santa María la Ribera zone, as the principal free market of the counterculture. The market prolonged the alternative influence generated by the Museo del Chopo. According to some rumors, that cast iron building from the nineteenth century was built following a plan devised by the architect Alexandre Gustave Eiffel.

The street stands of recordings, posters, T-shirts, and other memorabilia mitigated the consumer anxieties of the industrial era tribe. But even after the arrival of internet, there are things you just can't get. The romantic poet seeks the intangible blue flower.

Pepe shares the lineage of those who suffer insomnia if they know that a fascinating recording has yet to enter their collection. His interest in the most recondite expressions of high volume won him the nickname Apostle of Rock.

It's to Pepe I owe one of the most terrifying moments of my life. A fanatic of terror movies, in their richest gore variations, he enjoyed creating false alarms. In 1980, the Police gave a rare concert in Mexico City. For years, the Hotel de México was a delirious project. It never housed any guests, but it promised to do so and grew to be the tallest, most striking building in the southern sector of the city. A block structure right out of science fiction, huge and challenging, the ideal building to be demolished by Godzilla.

In 1980, it had its moment of glory in a banquet room on the second floor. The Police, a dazzling New Wave group, agreed to play for a rather limited audience. I was running *The Dark Side of the Moon* radio show so I had a press pass. I also wrote for the magazine *Melody / 10 Years Later,* edited by Víctor Roura. It was there I published a more or less devastating note on Pako Gruexxxo and his Tlatelolco Rock Symphony. Known for dominating the concerts in the Tlatelolco zone with support from the Institutional Revolutionary Party (PRI), for striking fear into his musicians, and for having a voice more suitable for a harangue than for a song, Gruexxxo was, in wrestling terms, a bad guy detested by the good guys.

Pepe and I walked over to the table where press passes were being handed out, and we ran straight into the fearsome mass of almost one hundred kilos that was Pako Gruexxxo. The Tlatelolco rocker instantly asked Pepe: "Have you seen that son of a bitch Juan Villoro? I'm going to kick his ass."

Fully enjoying the moment, Pepe answered: "No," then, turning toward me, he asked, "Have you seen him, Juan?"

For a second, I considered the possibility of dying the death of a martyr of music journalism in a country where rock was utopia. But that instinct for self-preservation called with some simplicity *fear* made me say: "I don't know him."

Even now, Pepe the memorious recalls the scene in which I denied myself and does not accept the philosophic argument that says no one really knows himself from the inside. An irreplaceable friend, Pepe is a compulsive reporter of marginal aesthetic phenomena. Since his expeditions are even rarer than his prey, he himself has become a popular icon.

People wave hello to him in Tepito, as just another neighborhood guy. On Jesús Carranza Street, known as "the most dangerous street in Mexico City after seven p.m.," we visit fifty-odd stands whose principal characteristic is to offer products not available on the rest of the national market. There is an ethical disconnect between buying a legal DVD of *Birdman* and an illegal one. But there isn't if the only possibility you have to acquire that product depends on the informal economy.

When I went to Tepito with Pepe, my daughter was thirteen. She gave me forty Japanese anime titles, hoping I'd find a couple. Following her samurai code, she wrote out the names in the original language (although she was respectful in not using ideograms). Pepe led me to two stands that specialized in Japanese fantasies. I bought Inés's entire list—at under one dollar per DVD. The only words we exchanged in Spanish were related to the prices.

The secret of Tepito's pirated trade resides in the immense variety of products offered, but also, above all, in the specialized form of presenting them. Foreseeably, there are stands dedicated to pornography. More unusual are the sanctuaries sacred to the prolific production of India's Bollywood, auteur films, documentaries, science fiction, cartoons, and the many types of gore. The long-suffering national cinema industry is divided into so many sections that you'd think it was a success: there are "Golden Age" stands, stands from the Echeverría opening period, experimental movies, bar girl movies, romantic comedies, B-level films, and even films never released.

Erudite in wrestling films, Pepe has augmented his invaluable collection there. As I said, I was surprised to find all the titles Inés wanted. Even if that can be attributed to the fact that Japan has colonized the world's collective imagination, the fact that not a single film was missing is notable.

Even more noteworthy is the fact that I found what I was looking for. I'll transcribe my list, which no doubt leaves me in a snobbish light, but it's useful to show what's available at that market. Each stand is the size of a middle-class guest bathroom. There are little floods that form puddles everywhere. The air smells of sausages cooking on a nearby grill. Some knockoffs have top-notch packaging and carefully imitate the originals. Most have been wrapped in honest photocopies of labels.

In this precarious setting, you'll find Borges's Aleph with regard to film. I snagged Alexander Kluge's *Capital,* Jean-Luc Godard's *Histoire(s) du Cinéma,* the director's cut of *Blade Runner,* the history of the Helvetica typeface, Lacan's Sorbonne courses, an interview with Foucault, the documentary Louis Kahn's son made about his father, Gore Vidal's senatorial campaign in the United States, and other rarities of that kind. Is there any other store in the world where all that is on display? Tepito shows that cultural products rejected by the major sectors of commerce are in demand there. If videos about Castoriadis and Heidegger are sold there it's because someone will buy them. Should it happen that for some inexplicable reason something is not available, they'll get if for you in a week.

Mexico City offers numerous surprises when it comes to the circulation of cultural goods. Out of nowhere, a vendor walks into your subway car and offers Aristotle's *Ethics:* three people buy it in under two minutes. It's true that doesn't happen every day and that the next vendor has a loudspeaker strapped to his back broadcasting Shakira's spasmodic lamentations, but there can be no doubt that one of the most peculiar traits of our urban life is the bootleg promotion of the most sophisticated culture. All this is to say that if one of the critics from *Cahiers du Cinéma* is missing a film by Raúl Ruiz, he'd find it in Tepito.

In their abusive division of the planet, transnational consortiums have created designated regions for products, slicing up the continents like pizza. Mexico belongs to region number 4. What is to be done with all the DVDs that do not belong to region number 4? In Tepito, that problem is solved with another illegally imported product: the *humilliator,* as Pepe Návar calls it, an extremely cheap device made in China that can read any DVD on the planet.

The fayuca and the market create a tension for a theme that has accompanied civilizations since the Phoenicians: what you find there is unique, but it got there by questionable means.

The makers are like the people who create programs for commercial television: they think they know what people want. The bootleggers on the other hand let people ask for things.

The Zetas kill people to keep their hold on the contraband circuits. It's impossible to defend the activities of people who have stripped various nations of their sovereignty. Numerous DVDs carry the last letter of the alphabet as a sign they were approved by that criminal group.

Ever since Felipe Calderón launched his unfortunate "war on narcotraffic" in 2006, Mexico has been devastated by a bloodbath in which various criminal groups fight to recover control over certain marketplaces and which the government strikes the top end of organized crime without solving the problem—which involves the state itself. A problem that cannot be resolved through military means. Tepito is part of the disputed zones. The confrontation between legality and illegality belongs to the very fiber of cities. In Tough Town, this fiber is a harsh, living tapestry only understood by the people who live there. On their busy streets, informal commerce weaves its picture every day and then unweaves it before anyone sees the hidden side of the story.

City Characters

Paquita la del Barrio

In a nation where sexual life is a hermetic subject, passion requires complicated strategies to be "legitimate." Although some intrepid types promote their most intimate depilations in print and the last car on the subway, during nocturnal hours is the scene of casual gay encounters, a good number of Mexicans still depend on romantic songs to transmit or temper their emotions.

Up until the 1950s of the last century, serenades stimulated timid young girls to step down from balconies in houses over in Colonia Roma or Villa de Cortés because those balconies were so favorable to such scenes. But the same serenades never got the girls of the 1970s to come down from their condominiums.

Nevertheless, the bolero still contributes to the form by which we administer the misery of heartbreak with the vast repertory that runs from unrequited love to the spite caused by being dumped.

The double task Ovid took on as a love poet—helping out during courtship and consoling after rejection—becomes flesh among us in voices accompanied by guitars.

During the last years of the twentieth century, the city witnessed the triumph of a high priestess of the capital's heart: Paquita la del Barrio (Paquita from the Hood), who rarely ever appeared in venues distant from her popular ballroom in Colonia Guerrero. Beginning with its opening, the place acquired a fascinating decorative aspect. It looks like a union hall transformed into a cabaret after a rapid decision made at a meeting.

Do Max Weber's social theories contain a feeling able to classify the social archetypes that make up Paquita's public? The sadly traditional Mexican man, whose manliness is called into question if he changes his children's diapers, rarely turns up there. The same thing happens with women who bear their dignity in their eyes and stare at the floor as if it were an inexhaustible spectacle. Also consolidated married couples— that is, those who neither separate nor speak to each other—would rather avoid that sanctuary of romantic exaltation and feminine freedom.

One of the many secondary effects of a shared life is slander. A good part of the population is committed to imagining the sins of others rather than daring to commit their own. "Have you noticed how she eats crackers?" asks someone who affirms his own virtue by proving someone else's fall, and adds: "She must have mental problems." Those who fall into that category are involuntary disciples of Jean-Paul Sartre, because they believe "hell is others." They cultivate malicious gossip to protect themselves from its opposite, impudence, as exemplified by the diva of Colonia Guerrero.

Mexico is so addicted to tradition that it accepts change only in order to cultivate nostalgia. After being in power for seventy-one years, the Institutional Revolutionary Party (PRI) left the presidency. But our social collapses are rarely definitive. Every farewell provokes the maria-chis to sing "And come back, come back, come back . . ." The antihero of democracy, which had organized all kinds of electoral frauds, began to be missed, and in 2012 it regained power.

Fully aware that in Mexico renovation is an opportunity to long for the past, Paquita combines temporalities in order to redefine amorous protocols. Atavistic and avant-garde, she defies convention. Born in 1947 as Francisca Viveros Barradas, she was ahead of Juan Gabriel in combin-ing the bolero with the ranchera. Starting with her debut, her stage pres-ence attacked standard show codes. In a territory where female romantic singers are usually sylphs with flaming hair, and décolletés cut not by a tailor but by a plastic surgeon, Paquita from the Hood carries her extra pounds with serene aplomb and faces the audience with the gravity of a professor. Wrapped in immense dresses that look like tunics, usually embroidered and spangled, she looks like a grande dame from the Academy of the Language on the night of her inaugural speech. Her furrowed brow anticipates the vertigo of her dissertation. Then she immediately speaks messages of ardent eloquence.

Paquita terminates once and for all the conventions of chaste Mexico, where women only sing if they are sluts or if they're washing clothes by hand (an intimate and solitary form of psychoanalysis), while men have at their disposal an immense musical repertory to catalogue the problems caused by women (not only the ones who sing but also those who leave or who are there but refuse to obey, or those who kiss other lips without knowing they will suffer the curse of remembering us). The most popular poet in Mexico in the late twentieth century, Jaime Sabines, summed up this attitude in two verses: "Blessed art thou among women / you who don't get in the way."

In the most well-known of her hymns, Paquita answered: "I was unfaithful to you three times: the first out of rage, the second as a whim, the third for pleasure." With the gasoline of rancor, she lit the fire of passion.

At three or four in the afternoon, Paquita's place fills up with unaccompanied women, fugitive housewives who just finished shopping and leave their bags of vegetables at the coat check. They rarely drink anything but soda and leave the hall with enough time to make dinner.

A bit later, a contingent of office girls arrives armed with a discreet desire for chaos. For some unfathomable reason, during the transition from the twentieth to the twenty-first century in office-culture Mexico, it was considered sexy for women to have a curl on their foreheads, like a feather on a tropical bird. That was the defining trait in those years of the secretaries who came to Paquita's place accompanied by bureaucrats in brown suits. The solitary curl, tubular in shape, came to define the appearance of Rosario Robles, provisional head of the city government. That hairdo went out of fashion, but the office girls found other ways to complicate their hairstyles. What is decisive is that the audiences who arrive after six or seven, when offices close, are dominated by bureaucratic elegance. The men wear tie bars, bracelets, medals of the Virgin, and watches plated with phony gold, and the women, nail polish, excessive makeup, and hairdos fresh out of the oven.

A little later, the hall becomes the seat of a consolidated, quasi-family institution: the second front, the long-term mistress, who handles herself with the ostentatiousness of someone who has forgotten that her situation is clandestine and knows her partner better than the wife who washes his shirts.

The singer's calls to freedom make some women accept the savage idyll they longed for ever since they contemplated a distant TV soap opera and abandoning their useless husbands, but most of the time they produce a more limited rebellion. The manager who invites the receptionist to Paquita's place is not intending for her to free herself like some Madame Bovary with orange fingernails but, in the confused breaking of old bonds, to accept the transitory conditions of a "forbidden love."

At around ten p.m., people appear with wandering eyes, surprised to see themselves reflected in the mirrors. These are the solitary types who've made a blind date on the internet. According to Manuel Vicent, cybernetic conquests follow a trajectory opposite to those in the third dimension. In the virtual world, people fall in love from the inside to the outside.

The sophisticated hypocrisy of Mexican life causes many lovers to prefer expressing their deepest feelings on the web. Facing the choice of a place that is strangely true, cyberlovers opt for scenarios so peculiar that they seem virtual. In Paquita's salon, couples who already love each other with digital shamelessness study their features to the rhythm of her songs of rebellious love.

The next-to-last to arrive are those nocturnal chameleons who look like narcos, magistrates on a break, or mere extras with no defined role, who contribute to the local color with their leopard-patterned, imitation-silk shirts. The very last are the tourists from alien territory, university people, and independent film producers eager for authenticity and vernacular values (in order to know what is genuine, which is only yours in part, you've got to practice anthropology).

From the stage where she works with the imperturbable power of a contemporary myth, Paquita examines her public. Her facial expression is that of a member of parliament during a government crisis. Suddenly she locates in the audience a man with a beatific smile or ferocious mustache, that is, someone who for one reason or another accepts being there. The culminating moment arrives, the kabuki gesture when the rebel goddess interrupts her own song to lash out at the spy (what man there is not a spy?) with the question that has made her famous: "Are you listening to me, you useless thing?"

The best part of the evening is that the men never answer.

Ceremonies

The Virgin of Transit

We citizens of the capital have turned our cars into chapels for saving our souls. That's the only possible explanation for the fact that we accept embarking on this road of expiation involved in city driving.

Traffic has disordered behavior, producing an annoying being: the driver (man or woman) only too willing to prove that the traffic is not a problem, at least for them.

I'll try to explain this encounter of the third kind. Every time I'm late for a gathering I say out loud: "I only hope they've invited the Jiménezes."

The Jiménezes are a happy couple who think it matters not the slightest that they arrive only in time for dessert. I'm almost always more punctual than they are. Which is why I consider them essential friends.

But there are situations that transcend shame in which even the Jiménezes arrive before I do. The only way out is to wear an expression that says you've run over some poor soul (you before you became the madman who hates anything that doesn't move) and say something about the inconveniences of not living in Calcutta. It's then the Road Genius appears:

"How did you get here?" he asks, quite proud of himself.

No one who arrives two hours late knows how he got there. What you should have done was to turn on Añil to exit at Tepezcohuite, as an act of faith you drove on the unknown Social Prosperity Street, crossed Héroes, and reached the inevitable Rancho San Felipe Boulevard. It was there that someone recommended a route to nothingness.

A Mexican who drives around for half an hour looking for a street named Zapata knows he is irremediably lost. The name of the Warlord of the South is repeated less out of patriotism than to create the illusion that it's actually possible to get someplace. Faced with the abyss of national heroes, I never ask where the street I'm trying to get to is but where the nearest Zapata Street is.

I say none of this out of presumption, I know, but the Road Genius is not satisfied with the fact that you've suffered:

"Don't you know about Alijadores Street?" he asks, as if that unknown thoroughfare led directly to the Zócalo. In the face of your ignorance, he lowers his eyes, surprised that you're really wearing shoes.

It is possible that this detestable being manages to drive around without problems (which, of course, makes him all the more detestable), but the fact is that traffic has annihilated our way of life (which in itself was nothing much). I have friends who call me only because they're in a traffic jam. To kill time, they tell an incredibly long story which interests them very little (and me not at all). Others take advantage of the fact that the car barely budges to buy stuffed animals, small bronze, vaguely Tibetan bells, Korean tea sets, and superheroes that may perhaps be liked by people they've yet to meet, but who exist somewhere (that's how my friend Chacho started his Sunday bazaar).

Our traffic has been unbearable for much too long. On March 31, 1972, Jorge Ibargüengoitia wrote: "Mexican drivers combine the clumsiness of Italian drivers, the sadism of French drivers, and the ill humor typical of the Shah of Persia's relatives." In 1976, he again reviewed the disasters of the capital: "The future twenty years from now is a vision very few dare to speak of." We've already gone past that future, and it's much worse than what Ibargüengoitia foresaw.

Traffic attains apocalyptic splendor on the avenues that lead out of the city. It's perhaps the hope of abandoning the horror of thousands of drivers subjecting themselves to the purgatory of going to paradise in slow motion.

I'm going to tell now what happened to me with the Navas, a hospi-

table couple who suffer from a local variant of Moses syndrome. They
think Insurgentes Sur is the Red Sea and that it will instantly part so their
Tsuru can reach the Promised Land.

The Navas live around the corner from me, but they host stupendous dinners in Chipilo, where they have a farm. Instead of walking
two blocks to see them, I have to take the highway to Puebla, pass along
Ignacio Zaragoza, where it's advisable to repeat, as if it were a mantra,
the celebrated declaration of that national hero: "Our nation's arms are
covered with glory."

The exit for Puebla, like the rest of the country, is usually under construction. Besides, it has accumulated such an extreme level of ugliness
that it could only be improved for the worse as a set for some sacrifice. In
his novel *Miss Mexico (Señorita México),* Enrique Serna's female protagonist is sorry for committing suicide, but she lives on Ignacio Zaragoza;
when she looks out the window and sees the horrifying scene, she concludes that it's not possible to go on living just to be there.

The improvements make the situation worse. Suddenly (just a manner of speaking: in slowness there are no surprises), the lanes narrow; on
the left, forbidden and conjectural, is the fast lane, protected by a fence,
marker lights, and an ironing board.

In the paralyzed traffic, a lady is squeezing oranges and a guy stretches
out in a chair to offer sunblock. On the shoulder, a man administers a
shortcut of his own invention (he's dug a path so cars can get to the side
road in exchange for some small change).

The Virgin of Transit was conceived to help in our passage to the
great beyond. Insofar as we reach that final landscape, we chilangos
honor her with the penitence of driving. Unlike Islam, Christianity is
fond of slow martyrdoms. There is no instant immolation on the road to
eternal life. You have to drive the length of Añil, Tepezcohuite, Social
Prosperity, Heroes of 1932, and Rancho San Felipe Boulevard in order to
reach Mexican heaven, which is to say, the corner of the city where the
closed-off Emiliano Zapata Street appears.

Living in the City

The Conscript

The military had no prestige whatsoever in my family. The fact that it constituted an impoverished army unable to win any war was less serious than its repressive role in the 1968 student movement. During those days of hope and anxiety, my father was a member of the Teachers Coalition, and several friends of his landed in jail after October 2.

Despite my father's repudiation of all things military, I decided, at the age of sixteen, to do my military service two years early. During the 1970s of the past century, the "civic" routine of the middle class consisted in buying a military identification card or going every Sunday to pay a fee to enter the vacant lot where a battalion ran around in order not to exercise. My father warned me that would be impossible in our case. He hated the army, but he hated cheating even more. Sooner or later, I would have to march wearing the cardboard-colored uniform of conscripts.

The activities involved in Mexican military service were practically nonexistent. You had to get a crew cut, carry a rifle that was last fired in the De la Huerta rebellion of 1920, and endure the sun for two or three hours. The greatest martial challenge was to know the difference between quick time and double time.

Beginning when I was four, my best friend was Pablo Friedmann. For two decades we made up an unbreakable binomial. If someone saw me by myself, they'd ask: "Where's Pablo?" He was a year older, but he was in my grade because of a cruel rule of the German School: he'd repeated the second year of kindergarten.

When we entered high school, we decided to advance our biological clock, which in our case included the army. We thought that when we were eighteen, we'd need time to lead a tumultuous life—chasing girls, standing out in youth soccer, creating a rock group, taking a class on Marx's *Das Kapital* and starting a revolution. If we got past military service, I at the age of sixteen and Pablo at the age of seventeen, we could do a better job of carrying out the crowded agenda of our coming-of-age.

In one of his early stories, Italo Calvino divides the city fauna into the "alreadys" and the "stills," those who are *already* awake and those who *still* are not. I longed to be eighteen so I could immerse myself in the mysteries of night life and watch the sun rise on the street after an epic orgy. In the future, I would passionately belong to the awake group.

At the age of sixteen, I'd have been content being one of those guys who go out early into the city. With an esoteric sense of compensation, I thought that marching early would contribute to the frenzy I'd experience at eighteen. I was an "already" who was buying his right to be a "still."

My decision to do my military service early was also influenced by my recent reading of Mario Vargas Llosa's novel *The Time of the Hero*. In the shaping of that admired author, Faulkner had been as decisive as his years as a cadet at the Leoncio Prado Military School.

Even though getting sunstroke on a vacant lot had little to do with the epic, I thought that military service would take me to unforeseen zones of reality. With egoistic masochism, I supposed that the insults of the army would be useful for transforming humiliation into narrative.

The first Sunday, an abusive lieutenant decided that our hair did not comply with the rigors of the crew cut. He took a pair of scissors and trimmed us severely. That day barbershops were closed. So, on Monday, Pablo and I went to class with haircuts perfect for the insane asylum.

At the third or fourth Sunday, an olive green jeep pulled up to the dustbowl where Battalion 21 was marching. The lieutenant who'd shorn us came to attention with disciplined servility opposite a man about fifty or so years of age whose insignia showed him to be of a higher rank. We halted and formed into ranks to be inspected.

The officer from the jeep picked out the tallest. Pablo and I were in that group. He told us he was creating escort groups for the Flag Day parade, when conscripts swear allegiance to the nation. Our reward would be that we'd continue our service in Military Camp Number 1. We'd have to march twice a week, but we'd finish basic training in half a year and leave with the rank of buck sergeant.

Pablo had lent a book by Marx to a girl, offering her his "communist heart," and I'd written my first ever book review on the Chilean Marxist Marta Harnecker's *Basic Concepts of Historical Materialism (Los conceptos elementales del materialismo histórico)*. Going to Military Camp Number 1, where the leaders of 1968 and other dissidents had been tortured, would mean being in the belly of the beast. The idea seemed wonderful to us.

For six months we got out to Naucalpan, in the State of Mexico, the northern point of the city, by taking a complicated succession of buses. Near the Military Camp stood the Israelite Sport Center, where my team, Necaxa, trained. It was a favorite place for the Jewish community. Other sites of interest in the area were the Four Roads Bull Ring and the Mexican Olympic Sports Center.

At that far end of the capital, sporting interests blended with military life. Not very far from there, the Ministry of Defense and the Military Hospital coexisted with the Americas Hippodrome. This contiguity suggested that, in Mexico, sports and war were prepared for in the same way: you have to train for competition with no hope of ever winning.

Military Camp Number 1 had a ten-foot stone wall around it. The entrance was in the Federal District, but the buildings themselves were in the State of Mexico. A door allowed the restricted group of Presidential Guards to enter. At their entrance, the guards wore a white armband with two green letters: PM (Military Police).

In his book *The Policeman (El policía),* Rafael Rodríguez Castañeda, editor of the magazine *Proceso,* investigated the unpunished behavior of Miguel Nazar Haro, creator of the White Brigade. He writes:

Opened for the first time to police and civilians under arrest in 1968, Military Camp Number 1 became the coordination hub between the army and police divisions in the struggle against "subversives." The White Brigade was born there and had its command center there. The White Brigade was a kind of death squad made up of military men and select elements from different state and federal police forces. The White Brigade worked as a paramilitary organization with no control other than that imposed by its leaders.

Even without a knowledge as precise as that of Rodríguez Castañeda, I knew that those arrested in 1968 ended up at Military Camp Number 1. I was expecting some kind of revelation during my time in that mansion of terror, but everything took place with monotonous normality.

We in the escort did not learn to march with the rhythm verging on levitation of the cadets in the Heroic Military College, but we did learn to march in time.

We were served lunch in a half-empty dining room (chicken soup, red rice, chicken cutlet, a roll, and Jell-O), and during our idle moments we talked with the privates who'd been out on the most remote highways cutting down the weeds in the asphalt with rusty tin can tops, never seeing any other part of the nation. Those poor men, who spoke awkwardly, had helped the civilian population during floods and had participated in fruitless operations in which they very rarely seized a weapon or a shipment of marijuana. They weren't really soldiers but uniformed workers, unskilled labor used to carry bricks, cut branches, seal a well, and, most of all, to cut the weeds that never stop growing on highways (the verb they used to define that work was *chapear,* to clear). The highest aspiration of most of these soldiers was to rise and be in the service of some colonel. That meant going from worker to butler. The members of the military elite had an olive green car at their disposal: the chauffeur, for example, might accompany his boss's wife to the supermarket and carry her bags for her.

The military camp I knew resembled a public school more than a fortress. The only notable thing was its immensity: an underutilized space.

Pablo and I were middle-class adolescents in search of a powerful experience, tourists in alien territory. Obviously, we didn't think of ourselves in those terms: we were future warriors learning to shed our social class.

The fact is that my rebellious pup fantasies fell to disillusion, and I could not view the soldiers as repressive enemies. They were closer to the people than I. My time at Military Camp Number 1 only emphasized the privileges of my class. Height is a form of racial discrimination. All of us in the escort group were middle-class. We would be given the rank of sergeant simply because of a biological trait.

I accepted marching the way anyone carries out a bureaucratic chore until knowledge of another reality came to me in an unexpected way. One afternoon, the bus I would take on my long trip home was late in arriving at the stop near the military camp. So I tried a different route. I ended up in Nonoalco, near the Buena Vista train station, a neighborhood I only knew from Fernando del Paso's novel *José Trigo*.

Most of the houses were old and evinced a beaten-down splendor. Mansions whose ground floors were turned into repair shops, tailor shops, chicken shops, and whose upper floors had been subdivided into small apartments. The palazzi of the late nineteenth century were now broken-down tenements. I saw propane tanks tied onto balconies, oil cans turned into vases, cages filled with canaries, dogs that barked from terraces. The air smelled of burned tortillas and stoves fed by sawdust.

I was wearing my uniform, so no one paid me any attention. Just another conscript.

I walked over to a lady to ask about buses going south, and she, speaking with a man's voice, turned to a third person: "This here soldier needs help."

Two or three boys stopped playing hopscotch. They came over to talk to me. One asked how much my boots cost. I lowered the price I'd paid in the El Tranvía store. Another took off a baseball cap with a Tigers shield on it and rubbed his forehead, as if his ideas would pop out of it.

I noticed they were playing hopscotch with huge coins. I stared at them long enough for the one with the baseball cap to say: "The trains flatten them out."

I carried a lucky coin flattened by streetcar over in the Del Valle neighborhood. It was a twenty-centavo piece, the ones with the pyramid of the Sun, a Phrygian cap on one side and the eagle on the other.

"Heads or tails?" asked the one interested in my boots.

I understood he wanted to bet my flattened coin against his.

I chose heads. I lost, and he got my coin.

"Want to try again, this time for your boots?"

Before I could answer, the lady with the man's voice insulted me with compassion: "Poor little soldier boy, they've got you by the short curly ones!" Then she turned to the others: "Don't be assholes. You're robbing the kid blind."

I imagined myself walking barefoot to the southern part of the city. A bus stopped right near us. It was filled to overflowing, but there was still space on the step.

"It leaves you in Salto del Agua, and from there you go to Nativitas," said the lady.

The offensive compassion she'd had for me spread to the kid with the cap. He pointed to me and said with offensive affection: "You're a hopeless bastard. If you fall off the step you'll end up worse than your coin. Have you had dinner?"

That Sunday was his sister's fifteenth birthday.

"You have to pay to get into the party," he smiled, "but you already gave me your coin."

As far as I can remember, his name was Fernando. His father worked as a brakeman for the National Railroads of Mexico. We walked to a one-story house with an interior patio, decorated with flowerpots covered with glittering pieces of mirror. All of them contained ferns. From the walls hung wooden cages filled with colored birds.

We entered a half-darkened room. The light switch was in the form of a small swivel. Fernando rotated it, and the yellowish blaze illuminated a room filled with boxes, presided over by an altar to the Virgin. On a shelf covered with turquoise blue oilcloth, there were glasses, unlit candles, and toy trains.

The gathering, which had yet to reach the level of party, was being celebrated in the next room. Fernando introduced me to his father, a man predisposed to conversation. Seeing my uniform, he talked about soldiers who traveled free, third-class, on trains. He was surrounded by three or four inseparable friends. Over the course of the afternoon, they asked him to tell stories they knew almost by heart but which they wanted to hear again.

"My aunts," Fernando pointed to some fourteen women sitting in a semicircle, very stiff, their knees together, made up to the point of excess.

It was curious that someone could have so many aunts. They all began or ended every sentence with the expression "oh you":

"Oh you, you brought a soldier," one said to Fernando.

"What's your name?"

"Juan."

One aunt started singing in a low voice, *Oh I'm a girl who works the rails, and I have guy named Juan.*

"All of us work the rails, oh you," said another.

They offered me a little cup of guava pulque. I asked if the pulque shop called the Four Hundred Rabbits, which I knew from the novel *José Trigo,* still existed.

"There are only two rabbits left, oh you!" said yet another aunt.

At the request of one of his friends, Fernando's father talked about the railroad car called La Guadalupana, the first to arrive in the twentieth century at the Buenavista station. The railroad men at that time lived in cars, like an Indian encampment. He'd met the first conductors.

I'd traveled to Veracruz in a Pullman car several times and had heard the conductors before departure: "All aboard!" By then, the cars were as outdated as the army rifles. I remember the bottle-green curtains made of thick cloth that separated the berths, the nets where we stored our gear, the lamps shaped like tables to read by. Many years later I'd see Edward Hopper's painting *Compartment C, Car 293,* where a woman reads sitting on a folding seat that during the night became a bed. That car was painted in 1938, and it was identical to the ones still traveling between Mexico City and Veracruz thirty years later.

Fernando's father was part of the railroad workers' movement that paralyzed the nation at the end of the 1950s. In the most remote train stations in Mexico, it was still possible to see freight trains with "Long Live Vallejo!" painted on them—in support of Demetrio Vallejo, the leader arrested in 1959 who became one of the most celebrated political prisoners in the Lecumberri prison, a man I'd meet in 1974, when I joined the Mexican Workers Party, of which he was the secretary.

Our host knew him well. A man of spotless character. Vallejo hadn't inundated him with political slogans but off-color jokes.

Fernando's father told one about a burro who had such a huge erection that it bounced off his chest.

"There you go with the burro again, oh you," said an aunt.

"There you go with the drinks again, burro," he said, holding out to me a shot glass filled with something I took to be aged tequila. It was whiskey.

"I don't like rotgut," he said, referring to tequila.

It still wasn't fashionable to drink tequila and much less mezcal.

The air swelled with the asphyxiating fragrance of unknown flowers (except for roses, carnations, sunflowers, and daisies, they were all unknown to me). They might have been spikenards.

I walked over to the table, covered by a royal blue plastic cloth stamped with peaches and apples. I took a handful of peanuts without noticing that I'd also picked up some garlic and a dry chile. I downed the whiskey, and my mouth burned even more.

With tears in my eyes, I walked back to the circle of friends. The host never stopped talking. He'd taken part in the railroad workers movement repressed by President Adolfo López Mateos. That was the epic part of his life, but his narrative soon switched to another. In Mexico, you can't talk about trains without eventually talking about the Revolution.

Fernando del Paso evokes railroad culture in *José Trigo*:

He'll tell you that the Revolution happened by train. He listens to his blood that runs through his veins like liquid gunpowder, that becomes a rifle and sings to him as it did that time a Holy Thursday in 1915 or so (run run locomotive don't leave a single car behind we're on the way to Celaya): that Revolution, that blessed Revolution of blue hoods and thirty-thirty rifles, of canteens filled with water and sotol tequila and days and days with nothing to eat but biznaga weeds and nopal or pinole and dirty water and men who slept out on the abandoned tracks like ammunition belts and bottles of gin that spun and jumped like merry go round horses in the groups of men clanking buckles, that Revolution, the one that went away went away a white morning on the rails it went north went and never came back: that Revolution was made by train.

Del Paso uses stream of consciousness, omitting commas, mixing neologisms with archaisms. In 1966, *José Trigo* looked like a super-modern novel (some said it was the first novel "made by computer") that at the same time recovered a lost era.

In that house of relative poverty, I discovered that the precarious life refers back to earlier times. Fernando's family wasn't living badly, but they depended on old things. The furniture, the tableware, the very walls were touched by the patina of time. Poverty is a vicarious form of memory; it alludes to wear and tear, deterioration, loss: memories that don't belong to you.

The father sang with his friends

> The train that ran
> On the wide gauge track
> Made a crash and broke its back
> Hit a plane flying low
> Flying low low low

The next verses were accompanied by fits of laughter:

> The engineer stood
> With his guts in his hands
> Staring at the pilot
> Who lost his head
> But called for his hat
> To protect him from the sun

One of the aunts said: "Oh you, toot toot and on your way!"

That was the moment when Lucía, the birthday girl, accompanied by various girlfriends, made her appearance. It was then I learned that the actual Quinceañera had already taken place and that we were taking part in a kind of afterparty. The father, absolute center of the house, had been working on the train during the ceremony and it was only now he could enjoy this daughter's introduction to society.

Starting then, I no longer felt I was in Fernando's house but in Lucía's.

A man with a Zapata-style mustache stood up to make the presentation in the style of a lottery announcer:

"Soldier boy, now you'll be introduced: The Soldier!" he pointed at me and then at Lucía: "The cute little lady: The Lady!"

"He's drunk, oh you," said one of the aunts.

Lucía asked me if I was a friend of Fernando. I talked about the lost coin, and she wanted to know more. Until then, my presence had been perfectly normal for everyone. My uniform erased social differences. They allowed a conscript into the party in the same way they might have included a balloon seller or an organ grinder. My presence added variety to the scene without completely changing it.

Lucía was still curious. I said my father was the doorman in the building where we lived; I had six brothers, and I was the youngest. I wanted to study architecture.

I wasn't ashamed to tell lies, but I was ashamed those things weren't the truth. I hated being the son of neurotic university people who'd separated without that fact being in any way interesting. I longed for the tumultuous life of the slum, which I had before me now.

Lucía's black eyes glittered, as if she made things better through visual effort. She listened to my basic information and said, "Would you be afraid to go to war?"

I told her that the only thing I knew how to do was march. If there was a fight, I could move toward defeat in an orderly fashion.

Those two sentences I spoke between stammers. Grammar had deserted my brain. Lucía's cinnamon complexion, the birthmark on her neck, her small but well-defined nose, her upper lip turned slightly upward were stimulants for a racing heart, not for language.

I fell in love with her so intensely that I never again spoke to her or asked her to dance.

I went back to Fernando and his friends. He hated the Mexican Red Devils because they were tacky. "Damn bunch of Indians," he said.

"How much for the boots, blondie?" insisted the one who from the beginning was obsessed with them.

Lucía's friends chattered in secret and glanced at me from time to time. They represented Lucía's Greek chorus, her public opinion.

Her brother, who seemed like such a great guy when he invited me, I began to think was an idiot who put on airs of superiority, who held the fans of the Red Devils in contempt, calling them "Indians." As his alcohol consumption increased along with the hours I was spending there he became my latent adversary, the obstacle between me and Lucía and the accomplice of the other idiot who longed for my boots.

A soup made of greens was served along with tacos de tinga—tacos with shredded chicken in sauce. Out of a record player set up on top of a console made of polished wood about the size of a coffin came hideous tropical music.

I had to get out of there. I'd peeked into that house the way you peek into a well. I saw what I wasn't supposed to see. I liked Lucía too much to feel comfortable. I had to leave.

I tried to go to the bathroom before I said goodbye. I thought it would be near the patio. I headed in that direction, but Lucía stopped me. "May I have this dance, Sergeant?"

She held out her hand so I'd follow her to the dance floor. A few seconds later, I'd stepped on her foot with my boots. She called me "idiot" in a fascinating way. She didn't want to go on dancing.

I went to the bathroom, which was at the end of a corridor. The sink was a pitcher and the water heater was fueled by sawdust. The used toilet paper was not flushed away but thrown into a can that gave off a nauseating stench. The poverty I'd sought out so romantically was there just as it's always been: shit.

As I left the bathroom, I ran into Lucía. "Come along," she said, "I want you to meet Mom."

She led me to a nearby room. She opened the door, half wood, half frosted glass. In the dim light, it was hard for me to make out a person among all the pillows, a person covered by three or four sarapes.

"Mom, I'd like to introduce you to Juan, a sergeant who's going to lose the war," said Lucía.

A groan came from the bed. Little by little, I distinguished the haggard features of a woman with curly hair. A sour smell dominated the atmosphere.

"She's been like this for two years. She had an operation, and it didn't turn out well."

She paused, went over to a piece of furniture, picked up a hairbrush, and said to her: "Sickness is afraid of pretty people." Here Lucía smiled sadly. "I comb her hair every morning," she added.

Then she began to sing, in an extremely soothing voice. From her throat came the shadow of a voice.

Her mother smiled, and her eyes filled with tears.

"She's such a romantic." Lucía daubed her eyes with a handkerchief.

Her mother couldn't speak and had perhaps lost understanding. Lucía could tell her delirious tales, but she didn't hear the words, only the tender, affectionate tone.

"Juan wants to die for his country, he came to say goodbye, he wanted to meet me before they blow his brains out. Cute, isn't he? People do strange things before going to war."

She spoke to me through her mother. I awkwardly kissed her on the cheek. Resolute, she turned toward me: "That's not how you win a war." She kissed me on the lips. I felt her quick tongue. Then she stepped back and began brushing her mother's hair again.

"Go back to the party or they're going to think you're raping me," she said. "Fernando likes you, but he could cut your balls off. I imagine you'll need them in the war."

Lucía revealed to me how marvelous it could be to be insulted affectionately.

I went back to the party. Before she left the room, she again said to her mom: "Sickness is afraid of pretty people."

Lucía's father's friends were all wrapped up in a strange game. One of them had a bullet lodged in his leg. It was a wound of honor, the result of the repression of the railroad workers' movement. "I don't want to have it removed: it's my American part." He explained: "The only thing I'd ever accept from those damn gringos is a Remington bullet."

Another friend passed a circular device over his leg. Every time he got close to the bullet, it made a noise that made everyone fall down laughing.

The candles surrounding the Virgin had been lit. The air shuddered with the flames. It smelled of soot.

When they got tired of locating the bullet in the railroad worker's leg, Lucía's father told the story of a freight car loaded with contraband store dummies.

"Where'd you get to?" Fernando asked with a touch of aggressiveness. Then he handed me a bottle of liquor. Maybe he wanted to see how much I could hold, maybe that was his way of either getting even or making up. I couldn't say no. I drank, knowing that whatever I swallowed would keep me from getting home.

I went out to the patio to get some air. It was dark now. The birdcages were draped with cloths and towels. When I went back to the living room, the numerous aunts had already left. I found an armchair. I dropped into it and fell asleep.

I woke up at dawn. A single candle was burning next to the Virgin. I tried to stand up and discovered I was barefoot. Someone had stolen my boots! That kept me in the armchair. With the calm of a drunk I concluded I could go nowhere, so at least I could go on sleeping.

Hours later I felt a hand on my cheek. I opened my eyes. It was Lucía. She said something hard for me to understand: "You'll need these in the war." She had my boots in her hands. "Blondie wanted to take them, but I stopped him. Come along." She held out her hand to me. We walked up a spiral staircase to the terrace.

The sun was rising in Nonoalco. I heard a locomotor whistle. I saw the triangular Banobras building, myriad low houses, and the bridge where Carlos Fuentes's novel *Where the Air Is Clear* (1958) ends.

And Gladys García pauses on Nonoalco Bridge, she too quick in the dust, and she lights the night's last cigarette and drops the match on the zinc roofs and breathes in the dawn of the city, the steam from the trains, the sleepiness of the flesh, the whiffs of gasoline and alcohol and the voice of Ixca Cienfuegos, which runs with the silent tumult of all memories amid the city's dust, I'd like to touch her fingers, Gladys García's fingers, and say to her, say to her only: This is what fell to us. What can you do. In the place where the air is clear.

In 1996, Fernando del Paso concludes the first chapter of *José Trigo* in the same place:

Also in the distance the railroad workers look like toy soldiers. This happens when you see them from up on top of the Nonoalco Bridge or through the windows of a train. In the distance you see row upon row of old cars full of dust and a few men in blue uniforms who rest on benches or walk arm-in-arm. You don't see their faces. You don't see, as I did, an old, disabled railroad man using a chocolate grinder to scratch the stumps of legs he perhaps lost in a railroad accident. You don't see the man urinating into a soda bottle. You don't see the

women hanging out yellow sheets and colorful skirts between the
tracks abandoned long ago, as if they were carpeting the rails of a
train that may never arrive.

My fate was inscribed on those words. I was a "toy soldier" waiting for "a train that may never arrive," condemned to the "tumultuous
silence of all memories."

The sky took on a violet tone split by television antennas. Way back
in the far distance, you could make out the silhouettes of the volcanoes.

"How long does it take you to get to Nativitas?" Lucía asked.

"Depends," I said, without knowing that my vagueness gave me
away. I'd told her I lived in that neighborhood because I was ashamed of
my own.

I don't know if she was suspicious of me from the start. In any case, it
does me some good to think I didn't trick her, or at least not completely.
She gave me a long kiss, and we silently watched the city for a while, as
if each one of us were calculating the paths, the possible futures, the lives
that would fall to us. I was a virgin, and she most certainly was as well.
I remembered tales—fantasies perhaps—told by friends about making
love on terraces. I didn't dare do anything more than hold her hand, until
she said: "There are buses now. It's better Fernando doesn't see you."

Her brother's rage was proof of her interest in me. I left the house
with that conviction and reinforced it while I tied my boots on the next
corner, as if I were tying up the certainty of loving Lucía.

I decided to run away with her, to be, forever, someone unreal, a
phony soldier who would shape his identity on the road. I found some
money at home in the drawer of the kitchen table, enough it seemed
to me to get to the border. I took it, mentally writing the letter which
would explain to my mother that I was running away for love.

We marched on Thursdays and Sundays at Military Camp Number 1.
Four days after the party I was again in Nonoalco. She had no telephone,
so I couldn't warn her I was coming. I knocked at the door, and Lucía
gaped at me in an enormous state of shock: "I thought you would never
come back," she said, showing no joy at our reunion. "I can't come out.
I'm studying."

I'd run away from home. I had stolen money. I could begin a new life.

I'd strip off the uniform to be another man. I said nothing about all that. Calmly, almost as if she were bored, she shut the door.

I was an intruder in her life. What happened only made sense for a few hours one Sunday. She certainly sensed I was lying. Once she said to me, "You smell like new." Perhaps that was a way of underlining my naïveté, my being a rich boy, the lie no one believed any longer. Or perhaps everything was simpler, and the rare bird she liked one Sunday became a bother when he turned up again, that I was threatening to transform the caprice of a few hours into an uncomfortable custom.

No one found out I'd run away or that I'd stolen money. I put the money back in the drawer when I got home, with no relief whatsoever.

I never went back to Nonoalco, but I never forgot my afternoon in that neighborhood, the freight car loaded with contraband dummies, the aunts who repeated "oh you," the railroad man with the bullet in his leg, the mother, prostrate among the pillows, the guy who tried to take my boots, the guava pulque, dawn on the terrace, the final kiss exchanged by two bodies that never managed to join in that city, and, most especially, the desire to be someone else.

I never heard anything about Lucía until fate granted me a ghostly contact, which may well have been nothing more than a fantasy, but one that rounds off that memory so worked over by desire, something more resembling legend than firsthand account.

In September of 2012, my wife was going to be operated on in the Santa Fe ABC Hospital. We moved into that absurd sector of the city, an enclave of corporate luxury built at top speed over the past two decades facing a ravine where the earlier inhabitants of the zone live in shacks made of corrugated iron and cardboard.

On September 15 or 16, the hospital staff was diminished because of the national holiday. My wife was recovering from a hemorrhage and needed analgesics. I left the room, looking for help. There was no one on that floor. I wandered along corridors that made me feel I was in a haunted place. I passed through a hall with large windows. Far away, the lights in the ravine looked like a nativity scene under a Christmas tree. By day, the landscape would be opprobrious again.

I went one floor down and walked along a hallway that promised a luxurious efficiency, but where there was no one. Finally, I found a room whose door was ajar, from which came voices. A nurse was saying something.

I was about to push open the door, desperate to find someone, when I heard an unforgettable consolation saying: "Sickness fears pretty people." It wasn't Lucía's voice, at least not the voice I remembered. Could forty years have changed her tone and her accent? Was it another person who was speaking? Was the phrase just an old saying I'd never heard but once? Was it simply a coincidence?

In case it was Lucía, what could I say to her? The only thing she knew and appreciated about me was a disguise that made me into any conscript in the city. A sergeant who'd lost his way in the war, who'd stolen a kiss, who thought he loved her and want to run away with her without her knowing about it.

If it really was Lucía, what could I say to her?

I heard the sound of rubber soles on the linoleum floor approaching the door.

There are things worthwhile because they are impossible. Before the nurse got to the door, I retraced my steps with the urgency of a faker.

Was that a different woman? Was it the same woman? Insofar as this book is concerned it was both things: the opportunity I lost but that I remember.

City Characters

The King of Coyoacán

There was a time when Coyoacán was a monarchy. But the only person aware of that fact was the monarch himself.

I moved into the neighborhood in 1969. We took over a house which had belonged to the owner of a cabaret, the Quid. The décor made you think of seduction in the French style. Inside, the wallpaper imitated a style at Versailles and a wall mirror recalled Madame de Staël's salon. On the façade, there were bull's-eye windows, a cornice with curved flower tubs, and a tin mansard window conceived for snows that would never come. My mother softened that boudoir ambience using an inflexible method: accumulating knickknacks.

Among her captures, there is a green ceramic soup tureen in the shape of a giant cabbage. When my uncle Pancho saw it, he eloquently asked: "Does that tureen have a history?"

My mother's collection deserves a digression. That tureen traveled in her hands by plane from Portugal to the house where we began our lives again.

We were neighbors with a bakery, which brought aromatic advantages and rodent problems. When we went to complain to the neighbor (a Spaniard who floured the dough as if he were angry with it), he calmed us down showing us a pistol for killing rats. When he learned that I was twelve and that there was no "man of the house," he promised to take us under his wing, as if he were the local sheriff.

It was under those circumstances that we came into contact with His Majesty. Perhaps he came to our home because of its phony aristocratic air or because it was next-door to his bakery. The fact is he rang the bell and said in a matter of fact tone: "I am Antonio Gaitán, the King of Coyoacán."

For years we would hear that rhymed introduction, but what we heard most were his songs. Gaitán had been in a seminary and had a beautiful baritone voice. At any hour, he would break into his hymn: "Rum, beer, water from Tehuacán: who is the King of Coyoacán?"

The reference to alcohol was no accident. It was an obligation in his kingdom. Every third day, the monarch would greet the dawn drunk in his doorway. Even though neighbors lent him a room on the other side of Avenida México-Coyoacán, he sometimes couldn't manage to get there.

His physical features were peculiar. He had enormous feet and walked taking rigid strides, like Popeye the Sailor. The fantastical words that came from his huge jawed mouth together with his burning gaze made you think he'd spent some time in a psychiatric hospital.

He would read for hours outside the bakery. A single sentence could hold him up for a long time. Once he asked me: "What does *from l. to r.* mean?" "From left to right," I answered. "Like in politics?" he said enthusiastically.

Every September 1, His Majesty delivered a chaotic government status report. He spoke to his imaginary Congress of the Union when he was drunk. His delirium, usually tranquil, would go off the tracks in those cases. He confused the government secretariats with secretaries who painted their nails in government offices. Accordingly, he would go on to insult "miss secretary of the Navy, who is an authentic slut." The cabinet deserved not the slightest respect. After announcing the dithyrambic figures of his achievements, as unverifiable as those of the incumbent president, he would revile those dubious female collaborators.

Another of his peculiarities was his superfine sense of smell. Through the front door he could know what my mom had cooked. "The lady doctor made tamales," he would say with thunderous delight. On party days, we were accustomed to prepare a serving for the King. It goes without saying that his appetite was imperial.

On one occasion, I functioned as his escort. As I've already said, I'm a kind of fanatic when it comes to obligations, the kind of guy who isn't happy with merely fulfilling his military obligations but who has to fulfill them early. On September 15, 1972, I paraded through Coyoacán with the squad that carried the flag. Behind us came the band that usually played in the kiosk in the plaza.

It all looked like a neorealist Italian movie until Antonio Gaitán perfected unreality and made it Mexican by stationing himself at the head of the parade. He greeted one and all with vigorous salutes, accustomed as he was to making that gesture from the tribune. People cheered him enthusiastically under a cloud of streamers and confetti. Not a single cop tried to chase him off.

"The King, the King, rah rah rah!" chorused the crowd.

Then came another cheer: "Mé-xi-co, Mé-xi-co!"

That insanity defined us. Led by a monarch, he formed an ephemeral army that would never go to war. Beneath our itchy uniforms, we recruits felt in our skin that defending this hallucinated nation was worthwhile.

The functions of His Majesty Gaitán were as absurd as those that allowed me to get a military ID card. He would sing to show he held the keys of the kingdom, and we would march to pretend that the country had new troops at its disposal.

Sometimes, the document that identified me as a buck sergeant in the Mexican Army turns up in one of my drawers. Useless by now: a long time ago, I went from the first reserves to the second reserves and from there to the demobilization of the soldier who won no battles. Nevertheless, the document has a usefulness in memory. The photo in which I appear with the downy cheeks of a boy who's yet to shave reminds me of the afternoon under the sun in Coyoacán when we were something more than a neighborhood and something less than an empire, the day of glory when we celebrated—with an impassioned sense of belonging— the monarchy proclaimed by a madman.

Ceremonies

The Bureaucracy of Mexico City—
Giving and Receiving

There exist tedious countries where routine has the bad taste of looking like routine. Mexico is an interesting nation where you have to guess at what tradition is.

I don't think I'm the only one who feels out of step with our baroque society. Suddenly, some grudge-charged eyes announce that you've committed an indecipherable offense. It often happens that it's fun to bother someone with justification and with full consciousness of what you're doing; the bad thing is to commit a gaffe without knowing it and without enjoying it.

Living in Chilangopolis implies being an expert in bureaucratic formalities. The capital is the unique seat of seals, numbered pages, the infinite tasks of government. Many people come here from the provinces just to go through formalities. I've seen people suffer nervous breakdowns when the bureaucrat in question tells them to go back to Culiacán or Tamazunchale for a missing document.

As we know that such matters are very complicated, we arrive at the office two hours before they open. We haven't had breakfast, so we succumb to the provocations of street gastronomy, which veteran citizens of the capital prefer to avoid. We buy a torta de tama that smells divine.

That sandwich of corn meal wrapped in corn meal works as a tranquilizer, but only as long as you're chewing it. After, it becomes a long-term annoyance, harder to digest than the bureaucratic business itself.

It's possible there are worse bureaucracies than ours, but the city is incomprehensible without those immense offices, badly constructed halls with their sickly light, where the doors are usually rat gray or pistachio green, and where thrive meddlers who, in exchange for some cash, make the transaction extremely long instead of eternal. These men (only rarely do women practice this profession) are the famous *coyotes*. At the entrance, they greet the policemen on duty with a triple handshake, ask if Rosa's feeling better, give away candies, and reconnoiter the building with the calm of someone looking for leaks. These are the bureaucrats of the bureaucrats, the underground economy that relieves the lag time of the public economy.

Modernity has sanctioned the registering of citizens in various areas of their lives. This increases the number of documents necessary for a person to be properly equipped for his fate.

A driver's license or a passport is not enough to validate you in the city, or they're only sufficient for validating the fact that if you are here it's because you have enough money to leave. To receive a payment, you have to identify yourself with documents thought to possess the highest degree of reliability, documents that derive from the labyrinth of acronyms: you have to show you have CURP (Clave Única de Registro de Población or Unique Population Registry Code), REC (Registro Económico Común or Common Economic Registry), and the interbank code CLARE. Sometimes, finding those papers in your drawers deserves a GPS and sending them requires other wonderful initials, UPS or DHL.

Foreigners are surprised when they're asked for proof of address when they want to make a payment in this country. "What does it matter where you live or if you're in the process of moving or if you don't have a fixed address?" the Argentine journalist Martín Caparrós asked me, in despair at the sheer quantity of papers asked of him in order to be paid in Mexico. Does payment for your labor depend on where you sleep? What happens if the water or electric bill are not in your name? And to top it all off, the proof has to be for the past three months. A man who has a fight with his wife and temporarily lives at his mother's place: Does he lack legal status to be paid? What is the relationship between having a fixed residence and receiving a payment?

We find ourselves facing one of the most deceptive subtleties of our bureaucracy, itself founded on two axial values of Mexican society: suspicion and superstition. The person who requests a document lacks something; therefore you have to be suspicious of him; if that person hasn't slept in the same place during the past three months, he's suspicious. And of what importance is it to possess a piece of paper that says Mártires Irlandeses 34 (bis), Héroes de Churubusco? That generates the superstition, not only that we may be able to find the person in question there, but that we'll be able to find the street.

Fixed-abode laws stand in opposition to our freedom of movement, consecrated by the constitution and in opposition to a citizen's right to a nomadic life. Nevertheless, this rule brooks no exceptions. It is a supreme irony that a city founded by pilgrims from Nayarit should invest so much judicial importance in the sedentary life.

What happens to people who've been living not only three months but thirty years in the same place but who lack bills for services in their name? From a bureaucratic point of view, such people are pariahs.

We find ourselves confronted by a security principle founded on a theology of documents. You have to have a lot of faith to believe that in a paradise of counterfeiting like Mexico every single document is authentic. In the same way that many honest people do not pay a light bill that bears their name, other folks pay bills at addresses that are not theirs.

Fixed abodes prove nothing definitive, but in Mexico they are required because in Mexico annoyances are a form of efficacy. Besides, those documents seem decisive because of the difficulty we have in finding the places. The paper containing your abode suggests that, should the case arise, the police could go to that place. Ever since the Aztlán tribe reached Anáhuac Valley searching for the image of an eagle devouring a serpent, we've depended on the myth in order to move around. Such is the function of constancy. Like our national shield, it offers a symbolic address, the hope that such a place actually exists.

Sometimes you're asked for an even rarer document: your university degree. I understand that a doctor should show his before cutting open a body just as an engineer should show his before building a bridge. In other cases, it's simply absurd. I studied sociology at the Universidad

Autónoma Metropolitana-Iztapalapa (Metropolitan Autonomous University at Iztapalapa). What technical knowledge does that major guarantee? If I were going to give classes on the subject, it would be logical to ask me to show the appropriate degree. But my profession is literature, a profession in which Juan José Arreola achieved remarkable erudition having finished only the fourth year of primary school.

The offices demand a photocopy of the degree to make a payment totally unrelated to academic life. The objective is to make the payment difficult.

I'll tell an anecdote related to the Ministry of Public Education. I wrote a children's story for one of their textbooks and then set out on the road of expiation to be paid for it. Among other things, I was asked to show my bachelor's degree. What connection is there between sociology and a story for children? None.

But our dealings with bureaucracy are a solemn moment, and there is no way to dodge them. We don't hand over documents: we yield them, knowing that the last will be our death certificate. I shall die a Mexican, but when I'm up against the bureaucracy I get the feeling I'll die for being a Mexican.

The SEP (Ministry of Public Education) demanded twelve different documents. More difficult than gathering them up was handing them over. It isn't always easy to enter an office. You have to give the complete name of the person you've come to see, that of his secretary, and the telephone extension number that must be dialed at the reception desk. That last part is indispensable because the guards have no idea who works in the building. Besides, you have to carry some form of identification to leave at the entrance (a different form of identification from the one you'll have to show to carry out the process on the upper floor) and sign the security log, which, as I'll point out in another chapter, no one looks at and where you can sign in as Jack the Ripper, but which, at the same time, suggests that scrutiny is possible.

Taking those precautions at the SEP was useless. After several phone calls, the guard was instructed not to allow me to enter. I ran to a public telephone and called the person who'd commissioned the story. He gave me this fabulous solution: "Don't say you've come to drop off documents but to receive them."

Which is what I did, and the Red Sea parted. It was something entirely new in my office experience. "What is the difference between giving and receiving?" I thought in the elevator as I rode up to the tenth floor. Once there, the person who'd given me the advice explained: "The person who brings something has come to make a request; the one who receives something has already made the request."

I thought I understood that the business of the present was seen as an annoyance and that the business of the past was seen as an accomplishment. The real reason was something else: "It's a matter of security. If you've passed through here before they think you're fine."

Obviously, it's impossible to pick up a document without having initiated the process beforehand. The strategy for overcoming the rigid security of the office depended on a lie.

The *Homo bureauocraticus* is the key issue: although that process took me two hours, when I was out on the street again I felt terrific and concluded that government offices were spaces for soothing social souls: it's so relaxing to get out of there that people don't go back to their normal lives feeling they'd like to burn down the capital building, but instead long to celebrate in Garibaldi Plaza until they exhaust the repertory of the resident mariachis. In few places does malaise have such a happy denouement.

Unfortunately, that curative vision of bureaucracy was short-lived. How wrong I was to think that a bureaucratic process was a perverse form of therapy! The acquaintance who'd commissioned the story was kind enough to take personal charge of my file, write up the contract, and send it to my home. Everything seems in order. I used black ink because blue ink is illegal in many cases, including those of the national university (UNAM), whose colors are blue and gold. I placed my rubric in the margin of the first pages and signed on the last.

I felt the relief I hope to feel when my children graduate college.

The next day my acquaintance called: "We've got a problem."

I thought perhaps the messenger had been mugged and that the contract was lost. The situation was odder: "You put your rubric in the left margin."

"So what?"

"The contract has to be bound."

"I still don't get it."

"They bind on the left side."

George Steiner observes that a cornered man becomes eloquent. I improvised arguments I had no idea I was capable of producing: "The contract is totally valid; it's like laminating a license *after* it's been granted; it loses none of its juridical validity because it isn't being altered or destroyed. It doesn't matter if they perforate the contract to put it in a binder."

"Let me talk to legal."

That sentence never ends in a solution. Legal is the legal name for impossibility.

The contract was declared invalid. In a gesture of pride, I refused to sign another. I chose to throw out the window the dealings carried out until that point, assuming that in the bureaucracy, giving and receiving mean the same thing: nothing.

Places

Fairs, Theme Parks, Children City

After two thousand years of believing that work is a curse for earning our daily bread with the sweat of our brow, Children City arose. There the condemnation of adults is the fun of childhood.

In this theme park, located in a commercial center itself in the wealthiest neighborhood in the city, Santa Fe, and with a branch in Cuicuilco, to the south of the city, visitors below the age of twelve play at being employees of great corporations.

A group of impresarios with a nose for modernity discovered that you can make money by allowing children to pretend they are adults. The project is the antithesis of other forms of child's play: it does not involve accentuating what makes children children per se, but in allowing them to take off their childish shell and anticipate their destiny as adults.

Without proposing it, the park returns to an idea of play anterior to the Age of Reason, when being a minor meant nothing more than a long wait to be an adult. Just as medieval children played at killing one another, anticipating battles to come, the visitors to Children City (also called KidZania) disconnect from their present moment of stuffed animals and cartoons to dedicate themselves to something they will hate in a few years: honoring the neon emblems that illuminate urban nights. If medieval heraldry depended on the House of Orléans or King Arthur, the heraldry of our time derives from corporate logos.

In most theme parks, fairy tales are connected in a secondary way to consumption and market technology: a toy train carries you from a mechanical game to the souvenir stand. In Children City, you don't have to walk around to reach marketing because the fact that you're playing is part of commerce. There they don't sell objects but functions: the children pay in order to consume their own labor.

The Invention of the Child

Starting in the Age of Reason, the child could be seen as a complete subject. No longer were children potential beings—a small-sized adult—but individuals with their own destiny and with their own merits which they could lose over the years.

The discovery of childhood virtues allowed literature to speak about people addicted to childhood who want to postpone adulthood forever: Peter Pan in Never Never Land; Oskar Matzerath in the beating of his tin drum; the eternally shaven face of Tarzan.

"It's Rousseau's fault!" shouts the small Gavroche in *Les Misérables*. Even though Rousseau wasn't the only party guilty of the pedagogic twist that understood the child as father to the adult, the author of *The Social Contract* made a noteworthy theoretical contribution to the subject (as with so many intellectuals, within the limited world of facts he behaved otherwise: he delivered his five children to an orphanage).

In *Emile, or On Education*, Rousseau sees his protagonist as one who should develop his own abilities before trying out adult abilities, which are still alien to him. This idea does not seem especially original in a world spattered with options for children—a day care center named Snow White and colorful clothing stores for babies—but there was a time when it did mean a break.

When the child stops being viewed as the puppy-state of human kind and becomes a creature with special rights, the question arises: How do we amuse him? This creates a problem with no solution: the children tribe does not make its own decisions, so entertaining it depends on the criteria of the elders.

Local Fairs and Theme Parks

Fairs and theme parks offer vertigo and din imagined by adults. Their principal characteristic is supplying zones of unreality, separated from the logic of the city: an alternative dominion where it's possible to enter a castle or be part of the crew of a miniature ambulance.

In the new section of Chapultepec Forest rises the roller coaster drivers contemplate with envy when they are stuck in a traffic jam on the Peripheral Ring. To one side the Museum of the Child stretches out like a suggestive fable in blue mosaics, the conception of the architect Ricardo Legorreta. This building does not house the collections its name announces. It's actually an immense and attractive play center. To the south of the city, at the foot of the Ajusto volcano, is the Six Flags theme park, which was born with a more attractive name: Adventure Kingdom.

Both the theme parks and the local fairs that set up for a few days in city plazas and parks link childhood amusement with machinery. In the Museum of the Child, a sophisticated laboratory enables you to put a cloud into a bottle. At the local fairs, a hoarse motor makes tin ducks spin so they can be knocked down by pellets. The child plays at hunting. Depending on his marksmanship and the quality of the fair, he might win a Captain Hopper made of plaster or a koala bear the size of a washing machine. The economy of rewards is a part of the unreality of the place. The absurd commerce of trophies confirms the fact that normality is left outside the fair.

In the fairs of the globalized world circulate artisanal, vernacular objects and dazzling Chinese artifacts. Every time my daughter (at the age of six or eight) triumphed in the art of catching kryptonite-colored plastic trout, she was faced with the dilemma of choosing between an artisanal rag doll or a flying saucer with lights that annoy you in six different ways. The shocking thing is they cost the same. The underground economy has equalized the price of a home-grown doll and a minor league UFO. A little while ago, I went into a store and bought deodorant and an alarm clock. I was surprised to see that the deodorant was more expensive. "It's that the alarm clock is made in China," a relative explained, a person who understands reality, that is, whatever comes from Shanghai, better than I.

Chinese products offer—at a low cost—functions they only perform during the purchase. Seconds later, the intergalactic ship stops emitting rays, and the alarm clock sticks at Taiwan time. These simulacra of objects are the order of the day at fairs, where we play to get rewards.

Temporary and local, fairs occupy a slice of the city, like an expansion of the school or neighborhood carnival, where everyone knows one another, where volunteers sell sandwiches for the price of a slice of ham, and where a girl exchanges kisses for chocolates. To this NGO of fun, the fair adds technology: gadgets that go from mirrors that distort to fantastic mechanical vehicles.

These carnivals may be gratuitous: the fair depends on a system of exchange that has a bit of trickery built in. If you ride the merry-go-round once, you pay one price, but if you ride ten times it's only six times that price. The beleaguered father has to decide beforehand if his children have strong enough stomachs and a tendency toward repetition for the larger sum to be a real savings.

The fairs set up in plazas, vacant lots, empty spaces where the city pulls back and defers its logic of constant advance, exceptional spaces left to the pigeons, to the statue of some forgotten hero, weeds that grow wild, the dusty or paved esplanade.

In their subtle invasion of the city, street fairs alter habits. There are pickpockets, balloon sellers, rosy-cheeked women bearing baskets that smell delicious. And of course, the culinary excess of pancakes decorated with multicolored sparks and asterisks.

Fairs are the last industrial attraction operated by people. In theme parks, the employees are simply guides who lead people to rides that work on their own. By contrast, at local fairs each stand depends on a man who is always missing at least two teeth. I imagine there is no harder task than setting up and taking down a carousel with rotating swans. The fact is that the person running the ride is usually someone overwhelmed by life, with a face crisscrossed with scars, whose fingernails are black from dealing with a fallible motor.

In Europe, the people in charge of rides speak with a whirlwind of consonants that seem to come from the far side of reason. They've got the furtive eyes of men who've seen too many wars and too many highways. In their calloused hands, the ticket looks like a flower petal. According to legend, they must be Gypsies.

Even though they're in Mexico, some employees—almost always the local variants of worn-out men—curse in Romani. Perhaps because their hands are so big they prefer extremely small cups or glasses that emphasize their fabulous condition as giants. They drink strong things in small doses: a coffee that gives off smoke that smells like a barn fire or the rotgut liquor drunk by polar explorers.

Parents fear these men of few words and prison-yard beards who lift their children into a wheel that spins, but the children trust them with the respect we allot to good ogres. The best part of local fairs are those examples of the hard life amid all those childhood illusions. An impassive fat man chews gum a few inches away from the target shooters, convinced that no child will put a bullet in his head. A strong man with no thumbs meticulously examines the chain protecting a little girl on a swing. Another, released from a coal mine, smiles blissfully at how well the tin panels of his bumper cars creak. It's thus that the children of the postindustrial age come into contact with the groundskeepers of tender harshness, who in fairy tales prove that only one monster can save another monster.

Something different takes place in theme parks, which shun links to the city. These are closed spaces beyond the reach of the curious, the nosy bodies, informal participants. Those who work there have not carried the attractions on their backs and have no biological relation to the insane. Unlike the traveling circus or the migratory fair, the park does not chase after its clients: like a cathedral of leisure, it awaits them. The first thing that defines their greatness is the lines of people who have made the pilgrimage to enter.

These places with their elaborate architecture conform to Michel Foucault's definition of a *heterotopia*. We enter a space "which has the power to juxtapose, in a single, real place, multiple spaces, multiple sites in and of themselves incompatible with one another."

If local fairs depend on robust but damaged bodies, theme parks have an invisible electronic brain that controls the little trains at a distance. In that space, removed from the cares of the city, the employees brandish a corporate joy. Dressed as fairies, mice, or golf tournament judges, they do nothing other than move the visitors along and push the occasional button. They work as if they were enjoying themselves: "Have a good time," they say with mechanical friendliness.

At street fairs, no one encourages you to have a good time. The workers seem to have seen innumerable troubles; they don't promote their rides or try to be friendly. They stand there by way of contrast, proof that only others can be lucky. The world may burn down, but children will play. If something breaks down, the man in charge will stick his hand into the screeching metal risking either losing it or picking up another scar. No one thanks him; nor will he ask for any thanks. These giants may save you, but they don't smile. The flying seats are rickety, and everything seems on the point of falling apart. But someone is on the lookout so joy can take place.

Terrible and benevolent, the ogres of the fair are strange representatives of the law in a nation where everything is uncertain.

The Panda Tohui and Keiko the Killer Whale

In 1964, The Fair was inaugurated in the Second Section of Chapultepec Forest. It was there the vertigo of my generation found its place—on the Roller Coaster, the Hammer, and the Mad Mouse.

Two decades later, Adventure Kingdom offered mechanical fantasies at the base of the Ajusco volcano. The most singular moment of that park was related to a killer whale, Keiko, captured in Iceland and trained in Canada. In 1985, Keiko came to Mexico City, and his popularity competed with that of Tohui, the first panda born in captivity outside of China (on the unforgettable day: July 21, 1981), the emblem of the Federal District's demographic explosion.

If Yuri had sung for Tohui (which means "child" in Tarahumara), Lucerito (now Lucero) sang to welcome Keiko (whose name means "lucky girl" in Japanese). One exotic black and white pet prepared the capital's imagination for getting excited about another.

In 1993 (the year Tohui died), Keiko starred in the movie *Free Willy*. Three years later, reality imitated art: *Life* magazine published an article that described the killer whale's living conditions in the Ajusco theme park, conditions similar to those of a high-risk criminal. As a result of the protests that came about because of the *Life* article, Keiko followed, halfway, the route of his movie character. He was taken from Adventure Kingdom to the Oregon aquarium, where he had the conditional freedom of a larger tank.

Later on, he was set free in Iceland, in compliance with the ecological ideal that says animals would rather live in their natural habitat. But Keiko had grown up in Mexico, where solitude is a labyrinth, as the poet Octavio Paz once wrote. Faced with the challenge of freedom, the killer whale swam more than a thousand miles in search of company. He reached Norway and found out that there were no Mexicans there, none of the people who'd sung to him and shouted encouragement. He traveled the fjords without finding what he was looking for, went into a depression worthy of one of Ibsen's characters, and died of pneumonia in December of 2003.

What did he miss? I remember those intense days of farewell, when we chilangos went to Adventure Kingdom to sing him "Las Golondrinas" or "Swallows," our farewell song. We sang to a killer whale trained to say goodbye waving a fin. At that level of sentimentality, he was a Mexican mascot.

Life without ties isn't easy for someone who's known Mexican tenderness. For Keiko, freedom was a place where no one sang him "Cielito Lindo" ("Cute Sweetie"), with its refrain "sing and don't cry." He died of pneumonia, like our national poet Ramón López Velarde. This sickness associated with emotional ecstasy seems strange for a whale, but not so much for a whale plagued by Mexican nostalgia. Keiko was twenty-seven years old, a respectable age for one of his species, but the people's verdict was different: Keiko died because he missed us.

KidZania

It was in 1999 that the main character of this chapter of neoliberalism, this sanctuary of neoliberalism, arose: Children City, also known by the maniacal name KidZania. Those who protested about Keiko's living conditions would be wise to take note of the treatment children receive in this amusement zone. If painters view their work as play, the visitor to Children City views play as work.

Since the days when Engels denounced child labor practices in the factories of Manchester, capitalism had not found as efficient a means to take advantage of children in the name of progress. Children City belongs to late capitalism, the bastion of monopolies. There, no brand competes with any other: all present have exclusive control of their area. The hamburgers are from McDonald's and the programs from Televisa. This helps recruit investors interested in creating an "image seedbed" so children grow up devoted to their products. Nevertheless, it is possible that the excesses of the park will produce a paradoxical effect, that there a generation of diabetic globalizationphobics will be incubated.

As I mentioned above, there is a branch of KidZania in Cuicuilco, very near the most ancient pyramids in the nation, built about four thousand years ago, when urban settlement almost didn't exist. This southern section of the city has become an emblem of insane development. It's there that Olympic Village was built, a group of very well-designed structures designed to house the athletes participating in the 1968 Olympics. But right next door stand some of the most horrible buildings in the city, the Elektra building and the Mexican Telephone building, the first the property of Ricardo Salinas Pliego, who also owns Televisión Azteca, and the second the property of the billionaire Carlos Slim. In that area, there once was a paper factory that gave off an agreeably rotten smell. It was closed for ecological reasons, but it did not become a park, which would certainly have improved the environment. Instead, it became a business center of which the new KidZania is a part.

In 2005, I went to the original headquarters of this amusement business in Santa Fe. I visited the site with my daughter and two of her best friends who were attracted by the name Children City and hoped to find an alternative urban life, with streets they would be fortunate enough to wander without fear. But this is not a space with houses and open zones but an enclosed bulwark of amusement. Within six thousand square meters, the park stretches out like a two-story, plastic village.

The entrance is a very effective rite of passage: visitors walk to an American Airlines counter as if they were going to take a plane somewhere, and they receive a receipt in exchange for their admission fee. In turn, the receipt has to be exchanged in an HSBC bank for the local currency: kidzos. From that moment on, the children may use kidzos to play games or earn them working within the games. In this economic model, there is only one free activity: jail. It costs nothing to snore on one of its cots.

The city offers seventy-five professions in which children can approximate—with greater or lesser veracity—adult life. Being a fire-man is an ideal job for a five-year-old since it only involves climbing onto a little fire truck and ringing a bell; on the other hand, to be a reporter for the newspaper *Reforma* (where I work) you must be at least eleven in order to carry out an interview and type it out on a computer that prints it on the front page.

Since there are no explanations for the work options, there may be twenty-minute waits for an inappropriate game. But that's the least of it: the lure of the place does not depend on a ludic logic but on the many options you haven't yet reached. The most diligent child can practice, at the most, a dozen professions: what matters most is what he could have done, not what he's actually doing. "What can the hospital be like?" wonder the children leaving the veterinary clinic. Destiny maintains its magic aura to the degree it is not reached.

In this social system, all tasks are a matter of business, even those that approach the archaic world of art. When my daughter and her friends discovered there was a theater, they enthusiastically ran in to take part in that profession devoid of logo. But the dynamic was limited to the restrictions of commercial television: a show was being prepared in which all the girls would be models and all the boys would be clowns. As long as the muses do not carry a franchise (with logo) in their bosoms, art will have no interest in KidZania.

In 2000, every family spent about eighty dollars during their five hours there. But very few seemed to come from the prosperous Santa Fe district. "We prefer Disney World," said a lady friend of mine who lives in that zone.

Mexico is a land of castes: your appearance reveals which way you'll vote, your level of education, and the kind of church you visit or stop visiting. The people crowding the halls and fast food spots in Children City seemed to be middle management government employees imbued with upper mobility, people who make a pilgrimage to Santa Fe as if it were a consumerist Lourdes.

KidZania is a *paideia,* a formal education, where children of the vacil-lating middle class can be educated to be corporate beings. None of them want to grow up in order to put the pepperoni on a Domino's pizza, but the fetishizing of the merchandise foments illusions of rising higher: if you played at being a cashier at age six, at the age of thirty you might be a manager.

No modernity prospers without precedents. In Children City there are modest and common amusements: little cars like the ones in fairs, a wall of artificial stone you can climb, a corner stocked with mats where the flexibility of little bodies can be demonstrated. These amusements are the least used and the only ones that stimulate repetition: "Do you think we came here so you could jump up and down on a mat?" a mother reproached a boy who was really having fun. In a contradictory form, some "amusements" are really tasks that are too simple: the candy factory is a boring place where they give you an insipid palette and two envelopes of flavor so you can mix it up and make it into candy.

Sometimes the children inject a personal element into the work: those who play at painting the façade of a house, to the benefit of the Comex paint company, choose a delightful bubblegum color, which they combine with pistachio tones, and end up satisfactorily covered with paint.

Although the maintenance of the city is impeccable, most of the levers and panels with buttons are merely decorative. Parents do nothing but watch over their children. Although one space is set aside for adults, I never got closer than ten meters. That area represented something like a club for soulless parents who stopped supervising their children.

Children City is a theater where the set designer triumphs. The director and the dramatist are secondary. The important thing about the gas station is its recognizable shape: "Look, my boy, a gas station," says the eloquent father when he sees it. We're in a work environment devoid of products, labor conflicts, stimulus packages, or losses, with no other function but appearances.

This turns parents into snoops. Since each attraction takes place in a setting equipped with windows, the adults look in from the "street" with the anxiety of those who only participate through their DNA. From that perspective, the theme park could be named the Children Zoo. The main actors do not behave as they would if they were free, but also not as they would at a circus where they were trained to perform. We witness them in an intermediate world, a closed space with simple, unbreakable rules: the human zoo.

There are exceptional cases in which a child does come into contact with a profession. The veterinary clinic distinguishes itself from what is merely representation. The animals are real, and the clinic is run by authentic veterinarians who teach children how to use a stethoscope on a chicken. By contrast, the hospital for humans, sponsored by Johnson & Johnson, has plastic bodies in its beds and offers the dubious pleasure of slicing a leg so that it looks like a bicycle repair.

The invitation to play at working in a country with 55.3 million poor people and high levels of unemployment represents a compensatory utopia. It's no accident that it's a success. In 2001, a second Children City was inaugurated in industrious Monterrey, and in 2005 the franchise debuted in Tokyo, where it perhaps represents a nostalgic return to primitive capitalism. Following the line of capitalist expansion, the company has entered Portugal, India, Thailand, Chile, Malaysia, the United Arab Emirates, South Korea, Indonesia, Kuwait, Egypt, and Turkey. Created by the Mexican Xavier López Ancona, KidZania found a gold mine by transforming mercantile labor into a children's game.

For a few minutes, my daughter visited Walmart, the earth's principal supermarket. There she played at filling a shopping cart with the ten products allowed her, then she wheeled it to another girl who was working as cashier. Together they reviewed her purchases with an optic pencil, then she returned everything at the entrance. The exercise might be amusing for a four-year-old housewife, but since my daughter was already six, she was expecting something more.

Shortly before the loudspeakers urged us to leave, a boy came up to my daughter, who was holding the candy she'd "manufactured" in one of the games, and ran off with it. I chased him down and stared him in the eye. For a few seconds, we exchanged furious looks. Perhaps he was less interested in the candy than he was in attacking the orderly setting by means of risky behavior. As for me: all I wanted was to be a real father again. We stared at each other with primitive hatred. He gave back the candy without saying a word or even saying he was sorry. I snatched it up with patrimonial intensity. Explanations were unnecessary. We went back to fighting in the spontaneous setting of the tribe.

During the visit, the children and I wore bracelets with a chip that linked us. No other father could leave with the three children I'd brought. This protection is essential in a country where one of the main industries is kidnapping. Even so, there was something uncomfortable in that cybernetic linkage, not only because two of the children were not "mine," but because it affiliated us with the dominant criterion of the place: the series and the chain. When an employee cut off my bracelet, I felt like a freed slave.

As we left, Chinese wisdom reconciled us with the forms of the world. All three children wanted the same toy: a translucent tube whose function was to emit lights. After practicing numerous professions, they wanted something guaranteed to be useless. "Made in China," I read with satisfaction. Even before we left the parking lot, the three toys were broken. The Chinese know how to satisfy: while others design overwhelming utopias, they sell promises that only last for a minute.

If Children City dissolves the fairy tale on which the other theme parks are founded and substitutes for it the hyperrealism of work, Chinese trinkets allow us to return to the primal gratuitousness of play.

On the long road home, my daughter and her friends had more fun with the broken toys than they did in KidZania.

Places

A Square Meter of the Nation

How do we measure the importance of a news item? The invention of the fork passed unnoticed, and the invention of the napkin is only remembered because some people attribute it to Leonardo da Vinci. Can we connect the grand line of history with the minute episodes that also affect us?

From the point of view of information, national reality is a place where people fire weapons. Crime constitutes a narrative only interrupted by some scandal. Can we link the news with our daily perception of the world we live in?

In the way people write the name of the person they love on a grain of rice, I'd like to summarize here the front page of a newspaper. The topic of the day is the price of corn, a talisman of our culture. As the cyclopean ears of corn painted by the Muralists remind us, Mesoamerica owes its origin to corn. Nowadays, the preferred grain of pre-Hispanic cosmogony is an import. To that has been added the problem of imported genetically modified corn, which requires a supervision that is not carried out. Will our descendants confirm the fact that we ate tortillas made from a dough as dangerous as anthrax or polonium? Let's move on to the protagonists of the story: producers, importers, distributers, authorities on the subject. They all agree that, if corn prices rise, everything else must rise. In a strange way, none of them thinks that if the price of tortillas falls, everything else should cost less. The emblematic grain only seems to influence in one direction. Since those who comment on the situation want to be optimistic, they assert that a ceiling price is possible. So why is the tortilla valued in a capricious auction? What is the origin of the problem?

It's here that a character with a perfect name for a villain appears: ethanol. The United States sells us less corn than we need because it sets aside a good portion of its corn to make ethanol gasoline. This amplifies the problem and adds variables, like the structural dependency of our economy, the initiatives that other nations have undertaken with regard to alternative sources of energy, global warming, the importance of the Kyoto Accord, the absence of snow in the European winter. In sum: for the news about corn to be dealt with seriously, it would take a monograph about the length of a Tolstoy novel.

We are condemned to cover partial news, fragments of fragments. The more imperfect societies become, the more obvious are the unavoidable themes: murder, embezzlement, fraud.

Is there any space left in the news for the adventure of the ordinary? I'll limit my analysis to a square meter of the nation. I stopped at the corner of Miguel Ángel de Quevedo and Avenida Universidad. On the median, there were no people, nothing going on. A bit of the original grass remained, green splotches covered with dust. The rest was litter. I saw a worn-out girl's shoe, the kind of shoe that even when new says poverty, a shoe made in haste and at low wages by some desperate Chinese person. Why was it there? I thought about the children who spend the greater part of their infancy on the curb while their parents try to sell chewing gum. Was the girl who wore that shoe dead? Did a lucky break get her better shoes? Did it no longer fit? Next to it, I saw the box for a Barbie doll. Maybe there was a connection between the box and the shoe, both used by the same girl. Certain folds in the cardboard led me to conclude that the box hadn't been the container but the toy.

A soda can, a takeout food container, an empty cigarette pack confirmed that in this corner of the city cleanup services were as absent as the civility of drivers. I kicked aside the packing and noticed it formed a first layer of refuse; underneath I found trash worn away by time and footsteps, pieces of pieces, random bits of news, a mosaic of deterioration. On one cardboard tab and in a confused mass of wrappers I recognized a few trademarks, almost all foreign. I was in a garbage dump for things sent from Hong Kong. Globalized misery. Then I found a local newspaper torn into strips. It talked about a crime that happened two years ago and had yet to be solved, as if the investigation had remained in the same place as the junk in the dust.

Would it be possible to improve that place, plant the corn we need, create a small farm plot in that idle hole? Few things depress you as much as staring attentively at a square meter of the country. Our most habitual use of the soil. The most dramatic thing is that the sensation of disorder and waste the place transmits can be applied to many other places.

We descendants of the men of maize are garbage men who make a garbage dump without even producing what we throw away. The front page of the newspaper I'd like to summarize is this: a square meter of the nation, a metaphor for the news that doesn't circulate because it seems insignificant and yet, news that defines what we are.

I thought about Ulysses, the man whose great deed was nothing more or less than getting home, and I went on my way.

Ceremonies

How Does the City Decorate Itself?
From the Foundational Image
to Garbage as Ornament

Our megalopolis owes its existence to an image that appeared in the transparent air, at an altitude of 2,200 meters. It all began far from the Anáhuac Valley, in the moist caves of the pre-Hispanic era, near the Pacific coast, where Nayarit stands now. According to the myth, the founders chased after an emblem to raise their city: an eagle devouring a serpent.

The most interesting thing is that the story was constructed retrospectively to give greater symbolic relevance to the founding of Tenoch-titlán. Very important elements condensed into the image that became our national shield: the eagle devouring a serpent, a unique national emblem, which is an act of depredation.

The anthropologist Alfredo López Austin has found traces of the story in contemporary tales told by the Huichol Indians of Nayarit. The confrontation of the animals represents the struggle of the Sun (whose avatar is the eagle) to dominate the water (whose avatar is the serpent). Their struggle allows fertility.

According to the legend, the Aztecs found the scene on an islet in Lake Texococo, in Anáhuac Valley. On a nopal, the eagle breakfasted on the snake. To nuance this foundational violence, the most celebrated song that alludes to our shield, and which bears a gastronomic title, "I Must Eat That Prickly Pear," includes these lines:

> The eagle being an animal
> Has its portrait on money.
> To climb up the nopal,
> It asked permission first.

The lyrics capture hermetic Mexican courtesy. The bird of prey asks permission to climb up on the cactus in order to liquidate the viper. It kills without sacrificing amiability. Thus begins a long tradition in which grievances do not preclude manners: you can murder with formality.

Always following the legend, the people who sought out the triumph of the sun came from Chicomoztoc, "the place of the seven caves." In pre-Hispanic cosmogonies, neither beginnings nor ends take place outdoors. The origin is usually represented by a grotto, and death by the underworld. What happens between, the brief life, is the period of the sun. It's only logical that a tribe that came from a dark space would seek a luminous image.

Faithful to that photosensitive tradition, the Nahua people, whom the outsiders called *Aztec,* built their capital where they found the foundational image, hundreds of kilometers from their original cave, on the brilliant highlands.

More historical weight has been given to that emblem than to the action it represents. We aren't interested in what happens (the depredation): we're interested in the fact that it did happen. Although their relations aren't the best, the eagle and the serpent share a rough moment, it is our moment, when the nation is a union of opposites. What came after, the voracious digestion, is not mentioned.

The city derives from that convulsive picture. The eagle and the serpent offered a fierce prophecy: the Sun would eat the water. Understanding the scene implied feeling sorry about it. The ecocide to come was announced in that minimal bestiary.

The shield is a fixture on all official stationery, on money, and on the monument that stands to one side of the Plaza de la Constitución, next to the Supreme Court of Justice. What other decorative elements derive from the pre-Hispanic world?

The symbolic center of the National Museum of Anthropology is the Aztec calendar. Its glyphs measure *ties of the years.* What can we read in that mineral disc? "Hours of light the birds already peck, / forebodings that escape the hand," writes Octavio Paz in *Sunstone,* the chain of eleven-syllable lines of blank verse with which he seeks to bring Aztec time up to date.

Avid for omens, the modern gaze is in league with the circular designs of mythic time. In our culture, the grandiose is something that returns. Numerous monuments and buildings in the city refer back to pre-Hispanic culture. In this way, our daily chaos and progressive de-urbanization acquire a simulacrum of order. Everything is a disaster: the bus doesn't come, the street is full of potholes, the mugger is before our eyes, but a pattern on a façade indicates that the place is "historical." The disaster zone doesn't improve with that sign, but it does acquire tragic grandeur by being linked with an earlier era, distantly splendorous. Knowing that the present is a degradation of something that in its day was magnificent offers a melancholy consolation, nostalgia for what we didn't have.

Which images define today's city? Frequently, the various megalopolises poke their way into landscapes difficult to associate with the notion of "place." In certain zones, the "identification marks" are neon logos. You know you're moving forward, because you've already seen the parabolic M of McDonald's. About this, John Berger says:

Trademarks and logos are the toponymics of No Place. Other signs that indicate Freedom or Democracy are also used, terms stolen from earlier periods in order to create confusion. In earlier times, the defenders of the nation used a technique against invaders which consisted in changing highway signs; so, the sign that pointed the way to Zaragoza ended up pointing in the opposite direction: Burgos. Today it is not the defenders but the foreign invaders who change the signs in order to confuse the locals, confusing them about who governs whom, the nature of happiness, the dimensions of grief, or where one finds eternity.

The reconversion of the citizen into a client makes him confront the city as a network of stores and recognizable logos. The symbolic fabric depends on consumption.

Amid this dislocation, historic details of Mexico City (the eagle and the serpent, pre-Hispanic symbols, the geometries of the triangular Mayan arch and the patterns at Teotihuacán) refer to an age that has disappeared.

Suddenly, a pyramidal office building with mirror windows interrupts the urban landscape. It little matters that the glass triangle seems like a futurist delirium about Asia Minor: all archaeological reminiscences, even a Mesopotamian ziggurat, must be seen as "ours."

The same thing happens with designs in Mexican Pink, a hue we never favor in anything we buy, but which an established rhetoric of taste obliges us to interpret as an identification mark.

Low reliefs inspired by pre-Hispanic culture don't manage to configure a modern architectural style; they suggest, in the mode of a placebo, that urban expansion, no matter how chaotic it is, "belongs to us." It's almost always a matter of decorative fragments that mix with other historical references. In this way, ornamental nationalism unites forces that are historically enemies: Aztec foundations, the three crosses of Golgotha, statues of revolutionary leaders who fought among themselves. If the mix turns out motley it's because our tradition is too rich to seem simple.

The popular imagination understands the passage of time in another way. It doesn't look for a legacy but for refuse. André Le Nôtre, the architect of Louis XIV's gardens, was in the habit of saying: "Chaos is welcome, whenever and as long as it conforms to the budget." Streetwise people don't subordinate their desires to a sense of order. With voracious creativity, they take deterioration as a vast decorative possibility and with enormously pleasurable scenography transform the environment. They don't use signs of details of "elegance"; they concentrate on the junk; they recycle what no longer works or never worked, the useless stuff we like.

In *Ornament and Crime,* Adolf Loos observes: "As culture develops, ornament disappears from daily objects." In primitive civilizations, artisanship blends with art. The capricious angel of progress causes aesthetics to specialize: a can used to preserve soup completely separates itself from painting worthy of having a place in a museum, until Andy Warhol appears on the scene, and the object again blends with art.

Mexico City is intensely Warholesque. Here, everyday objects exist to become ornaments. What is significant in the chain of wear is that the final result becomes an adornment. In order for that to happen, you have to have an eclectic sense of decoration and assume that every utensil becomes greater when it is stripped of its use.

Decorative Trash

Walk into any public establishment in the capital and you'll find a bizarre altar of postmodernity: a television screen festooned with Christmas tree lights with the head of a doll on the antenna (the aesthetic touch is that the television set doesn't work but the lights do). It would be an oversimplification to say that the city is a pop-up gallery for installation artists. The trash repurposed into decoration is not there to destabilize the gaze and break up the autonomy of art. It belongs to a classical modality: it hopes to endure, liberated from its original function.

The citizens of the capital make the street their own by altering it and inscribing a trace of themselves on it. Only rarely do these gestures coincide with an aesthetic codified by modern art. Their guiding principle consists in showing up. Someone proclaims: "I was here" and leaves a mark, like the red hand in Mayan cities or the footprints in Nahua codices. A testimony that says this space could be crossed.

The first thing I see as I leave my house is a precarious installation: from an electric power line hangs a pair of shoes. On the next block, a rectangle of grass is covered with plastic bottles filled with water to protect it from the scatological intentions of dogs; a short distance later, a tree trunk is covered with chewing gum. Going out onto the street means making contact with a strange decorative passion.

"Vienna is being demolished into a great city," Karl Kraus wrote. Despite Kraus's complaint, Vienna, until now, has been a bourgeois city, well ordered and conservative, at least compared to other places as mutable as the sands of the desert.

Built on top of ruins in order to produce more ruins, Mexico City is never finished being demolished into a great city. Wherever you go, the racket of drills or picks; most of the time you can't tell if the building is going up or coming down. In the air float bits of plaster, light pieces of what once were houses, columns, statues, neighborhoods.

It isn't even necessary to move to change scenes. The city migrates toward itself, moves along, acquires a different skin, a mask waiting for another mask.

In this theater of transfigurations, taste opposes the transitory in order to impose its will on the tide of trash. The stray piece, detached from its original use, acquires its second life as ornament. No craft is practiced as much in Chilangopolis as recycling.

You suddenly come upon an ironing board to which tools have been attached, making it look like a bull suffering the torture of the banderillas. The piece resembles a cross between Gabriel Orozco, who placed ironing boards on terraces in Holland, and Abraham Cruzvillegas, who has created several series with elements used for "self-construction." If it were shown at Documenta or the Venice Biennale, the "wounded ironing board" would be conceptual art and be understood as a suggestive destabilization of everyday objects. In Mexico City, it's routine, because the whole place looks like an installation. Orozco and Cruzvillegas are not alien to this way of seeing the city. Their works enable us to understand objects in a different way, so we can find in them a creative intention which is perhaps only the result of chance and the caprices of our eyes. Nature imitates art to the same degree that art allows us to know that such a thing is happening.

The jumbled mix of decorative trash is a constant in this hyperactive and precarious city, where everything is destroyed but nothing is abandoned. What falls apart is used as adornment. The simple gesture of gathering up junk reveals the pleasure of intervening in the order of things. Apropos of the passion for arranging stones in a capricious way, John Berger observes: "Wherever you go, one stone touches another. And here in this cruel soil, you approach the most delicate thing: a way to place one stone on top of another that irrefutably announces a human act as different from natural chance." To mark a place with a stone is a way of convoking a presence. A cobblestone is the first syllable in the grammar of the world.

Spontaneous installations depend less on an artistic will than on an urge to express identity. Even though someone decides that such and such looks good (or "pretty"), their essential motivation consists in transforming garbage into a sign of identification, of belonging.

Which sense of taste does it put into play? The chilango fond of tossing shoes up onto electric wires is not thinking of the intrinsic beauty of his materials. On the one hand, he resembles the Baroque artist who abhors a vacuum and distorts reality to its final possibilities; on the other, he resembles the postmodernist, who incorporates quotations from the past (what occurred in a different way becomes yet another fragment, an assemblage of times that speak to one another).

This decorative culture does not depend on any aesthetic tradition, and it cannot subject itself to current criticism. It simply puts into play the possibilities that imperfection has of lasting. The useless, the thing that has exhausted its possibilities, becomes a sign, a presence that accompanies us, a tribal talisman. By means of chance, the installation artist achieves one of the central intentions of art: the unique object.

In the bulwarks of consumption, the latest-model cars and luxury clothing create a mirage of singularity. They put themselves forward as "exclusive," but only rarely are they truly exclusive. In that regard, the Argentine novelist Juan José Saer observes: "The obsession with detail of engineers and designers seeks in vain to create the illusion of the exclusive model, barely managing to conceive minor variations of the prototype." To the contrary, wear and tear makes vehicles and ordinary clothing acquire a curious personality. "An old truck from the plains earns, from the vicissitudes of its own evolution, that status as unique object which is the principal finality of art," Saer adds. The dents, the decals, the signs, the plush-covered steering wheel, the fox tail on the antenna, and above all, the wounds of time on the chassis charge the old truck with meaning. On the other hand, the shiny model displayed in a showroom lacks any identification marks beyond those planned by the designer: a catalogue product, incapable of individuality, affiliated with the series, that's an edition for collectors.

Gallery of galleries, Mexico City rises above pre-Hispanic foundations and everyday practices in order to express an archaeology of junk: what broke yesterday drops out of chronology, remains at the margin of use, and carries out, perhaps eternally, the function of being seen. Saer continues: "A TV set just out of the factory summarizes the servile conformism of our era, but a TV set smashed to pieces next to a garbage can reveals the ridiculous emptiness of the world." The accidental installation artist transforms garbage into a long-lasting retable that comments on the fugitive nature of the environment. That installation artist does not seek to overturn tradition but to secure it. An antiquarian of the instant, he knows that the only long-lasting urban custom is trash. His inventiveness places itself at the service of salvage and conservation.

Seen from above, Mexico City is an urban stain; seen face-to-face, a showcase of wreckage. A formless city, it finds meaning in the deformation of the broken piece of apparatus, the shattered glass, the stone painted yellow, the row of empty bottles lined up on a terrace railing.

The city streets are a parking lot that sometimes moves. There can be nothing more logical than that automobile graveyards should look like residential units. In an accidental installation captured by the photographer Francisco Mata Rosas, cars are piled on top of one another like buildings of the future.

Shoes hung on electric lines offer another parable of transit. Since the streets are dead ends, the final steps must be made aloft. The dead shoes reach that desired beyond, the paradise where the pedestrian strolls the sky.

The appropriation of detritus cancels official tradition, which assumes prestige with recognizable signs of the past, but shares with that tradition the idea that junk adorns. National discourse places the remains of time in stone (it incorporates ruins into new construction or imitates those ruins with other materials); for its part, popular reappropriation discovers the perennial value of junk (in emblematic fashion, one of the tender nicknames for the Federal District is Federal Detritus). The flavor of chewing gum doesn't last an hour, but the tree coated with gum shows that the useful life of an object cannot compare to its posterity as garbage.

The city disintegrates in order to decorate itself. "Our era associates beauty with disappearance," says the writer Guillermo Fadanelli. He's not referring to the evanescent, cinematic condition Paul Virilio noticed in the macropolis viewed from mediums of transportation, but to extinction as a form of art. In our urban phantasmagoria places disappear but adornment remains.

Ambiguous Adornments: Tlaloc, the Virgin of Guadalupe, the Angel of Independence

The use of Aztec nomenclature reveals that the city can be conquered but not understood. The Nahua names lend prestige to today's chaos by suggesting that at some point there existed a previous model, that those names share space with nineteenth- and twentieth-century names, which mostly allude to spilled blood.

The most recognizable heroes are distributed over space following a "hit parade" criterion. A national hero matters if he is in more than one spot.

This toponymic urban mess generates the mysterious seduction of the unfindable. Not to be left in the dust, our statuary is nomadic: the Diana the Huntress, the effigy of Cuauhtémoc, the Green Indians, and the equestrian monument to Carlos IV have changed location several times.

What symbols endure in this moving scenario? Three effigies aspire to the incessant novelty of myth: the Virgin of Guadalupe, the statue of Tlaloc, and the Angel of Independence. In all three cases, we have phantasmal talismans.

The facts surrounding the manifestation of the Virgin are so feeble that they've even been questioned by the Church hierarchy. In 1996, Father Guillermo Schulenburg, who had been abbot of the Guadalupe Basilica for thirty years, cast doubt on the existence of Juan Diego, witness of the revelation of the Mexican saint. Even so, the occasional rationality of the Church has not mitigated a cult whose only evidence is its own faith. Guadalupe exists because nine million of the faithful visit her on December 12 and because a good number of cantinas and pharmacies—and even a brand of safflower oil—take refuge in her name.

The Dark Virgin is an alien deity we interpret as being our own; she has an Arabic name, Guadalupe ("river of love," according to Gutierre Tibón), and she poses on a half-moon. Her original mission seems to have been as pacifier of Near Eastern peoples, but she found a better position in Mexico. We don't see her as what she originally sought to be, a mirror to convert Muslims, but as our patron saint, the indigenous woman who appeared before Juan Diego.

Another myth that works overtime belongs to the pre-Hispanic world: the myth of Tlaloc, god of rain. His statue outside the National Museum of Anthropology is the most resounding presence of the pre-Hispanic legacy in the city. That mass, with no other adornment than some stone rings, seems to represent a science fiction superhero. Covered with scum opposite a reflecting pool, it bears on top the remains of graffiti. Someone tried to write the word *Tlaloc*.

I remember the day the statue came to Mexico City. It was April 16, 1964. I was eight years old and went out to the street with my father to witness the arrival of the monolith. Instead of following a direct route to the museum, Tlaloc took a victory lap like an Olympic champion. We saw it pass by on a truck suitably tricked out for an extravagant god. Naturally, on that day it rained a lot. My father told me the same thing happened in the towns Tlaloc passed through on the way to the capital.

Thanks to its colossal size, the statue was perfect for expanding the influence of the museum out to the street. After its arrival, our rainstorms had a cause. In 2004, Armando Ponce, a reporter for the magazine *Proceso,* showed we'd been believing in the wrong god. The monolith does not represent Tlaloc. Even today, no one knows its divine specialization. The original idea was to place an Olmec head at the museum's esplanade, but when President Adolfo López Mateos saw the scale model for the museum he thought the piece was too small to be appreciated at a distance by passersby and drivers ("It looks like a golf ball," he observed). The architects came up with a god to his dimensions.

Did the prestige of the colossus change when its story as bogus deity was revealed? Of course not. After decades putting up with acid rain, it's become the Tlaloc we like.

And what should we say about the Angel of Independence? We find ourselves before a monument that confirms our ability to be byzantine or at least quite confused. According to the legend, while the Ottomans approached Byzantium, the wise men of the city were wasting time arguing about the sex of the angels. In consonance with that custom, the popular imagination of the capital mystified the sex of the golden figure who stands on top of a column breaking the chains of dependence. Born a goddess, it transfigured into an angel.

In 1910, the government of Porfirio Díaz wanted to celebrate the Centenary of Independence with a triumphal symbol, a column inspired by Trajan's column in Rome and the Victory in Berlin. They placed a Winged Victory on the column, Nike in Greek mythology (the same Nike that protects the popular sneakers and whose logo is a stylized version of one of the goddess's wings). About this theme, the Hellenist Ericka Castellanos Moreno writes:

> This allegorical figure was highly venerated in ancient Greece and used as an alternative name for Athena (goddess, among other things, of war and strategy). When they began a battle, they carried it on the prow of their ships to show the enemy that a victorious army was traveling there and that victory "accompanied them." The fact that it is represented with wings is a clear allusion to the idea that victory is sometimes in one place and other times in another.

The Victory that reached Mexico had a destiny as indecisive as that of the nation. In 1957, an earthquake caused it to fall to the ground. All doubt about the angelical sex was erased: even damaged by the fall, the effigy showed the traits of a goddess. But, as in the case of Tlaloc, the masculine angel had already taken its place in the mind of the chilangos.

When that earthquake happened, I was six months old. Ever since, the family's been telling the joke about how the earth was unhappy with my arrival. Another child of that time, five years old at the time, recalled the impact in another way. I refer to Joe Strummer, the son of an English diplomat stationed in Mexico. After the incident, the Strummer family abandoned the impious place where angels fell to earth, but the son would grow up to found a rock group worthy of that impact: The Clash.

In sum: the Angel is not an angel, or if he is, he's a trans angel, and Mexico is not independent. Appropriately, it's there we celebrate a national soccer team that almost never wins. Acclimated to our nation, Nike renders no tribute to victory but instead to divine uncertainty.

With regard to their quality as sacred ornaments, the Virgin of Guadalupe, the Angel of Independence, and the water god depend on no motives for existing except the devotion of the people. Like the eagle and the serpent, they are condensation points of meaning that allow no questions: legends translated into emblems.

It's not surprising then that in a place where trash metamorphoses into ornament, symbols too undergo transfigurations. Here the gods in danger of being disqualified also have an opportunity to get into the playoffs. Tlaloc, a monolith of Nahua origin excavated in Estado de México, became an emergency god thanks to a presidential initiative and acquired value thanks to the people's devotion. The Virgin, destined for the Orient, became our dark-skinned goddess. And, on its fragile pedestal, the winged Victory metamorphosed into the *Angelus Novus* of Walter Benjamin, and stands as the witness of the devastating windstorm we call "progress."

In Mexico City, the original version of an object represents the project for something that will deteriorate—interestingly.

Crossings

Extraterrestrials in the Capital

T he city has been prone to the otherworldly contacts proposed by Catholicism and the pre-Hispanic cosmogonies. But also to a third type.

It is possible that the nearness of the United States has prepared us to be invaded by ultratechnology and that we should take that as good news. In our algebra of domination, to be conquered by a sidereal power might be seen as a strange liberation from colonialism. Besides, we're convinced the Martians are going to like us.

As Laura Castellanos shows in her well-documented research piece *Aliens: History and Passions of Sightings in Mexico (OVNIS: Historia y pasiones de los avistamientos en México),* few nations have been as vigilant with regard to extraterrestrials as ours. The absolute record for news about the possibility of intelligent life in outer space took place in 1965, the year when presumed contacts took place every other day. The UFO expert Carlos Guzmán comments that the fervor reached its climax on October 1, when it was announced that there was a parade of flying saucers moving from Villa de Guadalupe to the Angel of Independence. Laura Castellanos writes about it:

The information, broadcast by the press and repeated by the television host Paco Malgesto, had been received telepathically by a house

painter named Clemente González Infante, who vanished from the
scene after delivering his message. Aharon Aray Amath publicized
the matter and acted as spokesperson for the painter. Aray Amath,
a young man, identified himself as President of the Association for
Astrophysical Investigation [. . .] On the day announced as the day
of the parade, hundreds of citizens of the capital, especially students,
some with binoculars and cameras, gathered in the Chapel on the
Little Hill at the Basilica of Guadalupe and at the Angel Independence. Time went by, and nothing happened. The Venusians stood
us up. In their place, the crowd of young people animated Paseo de
la Reforma. The journalist Guillermo Ochoa reported that the students took naps on the street, played the game called Doña Blanca—
where a child pretending to be after Doña Blanca must penetrate a
circle of children; naturally there was the usual sexual harasser present, the students climbed on the monuments, trampled the gardens.
Fifty policemen intervened to reestablish order.

Looking back at that event, we don't know which is more improbable: the arrival of the Martians or that fifty cops reestablish order on
Paseo de la Reforma. The fact is that we Mexicans feel more comfortable
with extraterrestrials than we do with men in uniform.

In accord with New Age archaeology, extraterrestrials were already
here, among the original tribes. At Palenque, the effigy that decorates the
tombstone of the Mayan King Pakal III has been nicknamed the Astronaut. The monarch seems suspended in zero gravity, manipulating ears
of corn that resemble possible control instruments.

My generation received an intense cosmic education through wrestling movies and the magazine *Doubt,* whose unforgettable motto was
"What is incredible is true." The gospel of otherness, *Doubt* showed just
how close we were both to the Sumerians and to the aliens; the past and
the future frozen in a plot where only the odd was true.

This inversion of the real—apparitions as the criterion for
verification—had a decisive influence on city planning in the mid-1950s
of the last century. The architect Mario Pani, the greatest urban de-
veloper of the period, conceived Satellite City, a subdivision for citizens
of the capital with an extraterrestrial vocation. The advertisements that

invited people to buy property in that zone showed two Martians ready to move to this suburban paradise, shouting "City within sight!" The architect Luis Barragán and the sculptor Mathias Goeritz designed the Satellite Towers as a mirage to be seen from a distance. Five rhomboidal parts succeeded in making the concrete simulate the fragility of paper. The number of towers was chosen using a cabalistic principle. In order to harmonize rhetorics, they were first painted red (because they had to be announced in newspapers, which only printed in black or red ink) and then in the obligatory "Mexican" colors chosen by the artist Chucho Reyes. Thus a nationalist but paradoxically archaic translation was achieved of the future. This subtle trick made us feel that we were entering if not the stratosphere at least a Japanese television set.

Over time, the inhabitants of Satellite City were given a name connected less with space travel than with ethnicity: they became *Satelucos*. As happened on so many occasions, outer space otherness was assimilated into the pre-Hispanic world, a cultural space where no one can hear you scream.

While Satellite City was being built to the north of the Federal District, the airport control tower was spotting UFOs everywhere. It isn't odd the UFO fans see flying saucers inside and outside their minds, but it is strange that the authorities should recognize their presence. Sergio González Rodríguez, in an article dedicated to reviewing the abundant bibliography about Mexico and UFOs, reports that Enrique Kolbeck, air controller at the Benito Juárez International Airport, affirms that eighty percent of his colleagues believe in flying saucers.

There are testimonies recorded from the control tower about struggles against extraterrestrials. On May 3, 1975, the pilot Carlos Antonio de los Santos was flying his Piper PA-24 over Lake Teqesquitengo, near the capital, when he lost control of his plane because of the presence of three spaceships. He managed to reach the airport at the capital without flight control and manually operated the landing gear. His dialogue with the tower was recorded second by second. The rational explanation of what happened was that the pilot suffered an attack of hypoglycemia at high altitude. But all the witnesses prefer the UFO hypothesis.

Laura Castellanos has also recounted testimonies from Enrique Kolbeck. With thirty years of experience in the control tower at the Benito

Juárez International Airport and periods spent in eleven other airports, Kolbeck is a member of the governing board of the National Syndicate of Air Traffic Controllers. Few people have his authority to speak on the subject. Among other astonishing events, he recounted what took place on July 28, 1994, over the World Trade Center. At nine p.m. an MD-88 plane owned by Aeroméxico and coming from Acapulco entered the air corridor for landing at New York, but as it passed over the World Trade Center it brushed against another ship that could not be identified. The contact was real because it damaged the landing gear, and both the pilot and the passengers gave accounts of the impact. Apparently, the ship they collided with was suspended over the building. Radar did not pick it up, but the filter for eliminating fixed echoes did.

Tales of that kind abound. The most media-friendly UFO expert, Jaime Maussan, reported about the "Azcapotzalco UFO," spotted on February 14, 2000, by six policemen, who saw it fly over the U.S.-style football field at Vocational School Number 8.

In the desert, mirages appear frequently and very often those who see them confuse them with paranormal signs. Something similar happens in nightspots. The odd thing is the sheer quantity of sightings that have taken place in the busiest places in Mexico City. One of the few female UFO specialists, Ana Luisa Cid, discovered her vocation on Easter Saturday in 1997, when she saw a silvery sphere in Río Churubusco.

In April of 2004, the Mexican Army published a curious bulletin cosigned by General Clemente Vega García, secretary of defense: the aircraft Merlin C-25 of the 501st Air Squadron had an encounter with eleven unidentified flying objects. The members of the crew, Major Magdaleno Castañon and Lieutenants Germán Marín and Mario Vazquez, reported that while they did not make visual contact with the UFOs, they did detect them with their Forward Looking Infrared camera, which picks up heat emissions. To avoid suspicion, the dispatch made it clear that the air force could not determine what kind of civilization was involved. Immediately after, the video was sent from the Ministry of Defense to the UFO expert Jaime Maussan. Thus General Clemente Vega García responded to a collective desire.

Two years earlier, in December of 2002, the nation's principal TV news service conducted a poll that showed the predisposition of the people to be mutants. A couple of questions revealed the soluble identity of Mexicans. The first was: "Are you happy?" In overwhelming numbers, those polled confessed they were living in misery. The second invited an epiphany: "Would you like to be cloned?" With not the slightest shadow of a doubt, the unhappy people accepted their desire to be cloned. I'm willing to bet that the mystery of that second answer derives from the fact that the majority of people don't assume cloning to be copying but as being abducted and being given another destiny.

Perhaps for that reason we think that contact of the third kind can only be beneficial. "We're halfway up the chain of evolution; for beings from other worlds we're the same as bacteria for us," a taxi driver, who'd witnessed UFOs, told me. He stated: "I've seen two kinds of ships: oval and spherical. The spherical one, especially, seemed very evolved. I'd like to have them take me away, with everything including the taxi. I've already left my wife . . . !" Just one more proof that abduction represents a personal transcendence.

Only rarely does the Defense Ministry publish good news. Although there was no lack of jokes, that communiqué about contact with unidentified ships was enthusiastically received, as if finally the army had done something more useful than putting into practice Plan DN3 when natural disasters take place, that they were patrolling our skies in search of a better relationship with extraterrestrials.

The Mexican-American UFO expert Rubén Uriarte, author of *Border Crossings of the Third Kind,* has compared the different attitudes held in Mexico and the United States with regard to beings from other worlds. What seems to us a blessing is seen on the other side of the border as a threat. Laura Castellanos writes about UFO experts from two worlds:

Uriarte assures us that Mexico is a kind of paradise for space aliens. In the first place, because it has a culture open to the spiritual and paranormal. And if by chance we know about it: the myth of the return of Quetzalcóatl, who traveled the stars, cost Moctezuma the Conquest. In the second place, because Mexico is not an invader, which means the phenomenon is not seen as a military risk. In the third place, because they can fly over a city like the Mexican capital and not be noticed. And in fourth place, because the geographic and natural wealth here allows them to investigate terrestrial life with complete freedom.

Castellanos lists these four reasons why we should be loved, but I'm impressed especially by the third: we inhabit the strange, dominating city where the UFOs can circulate without being seen (although everything suggests that from time to time someone does discover them).

For Marina Tsvietáieva, ghosts are "the soul's greatest condescendence toward the eyes": the spirits we want to see.

The challenging capital of Mexico improves as a specter. An image devoured by images, seat of false gods, a zone of addresses that can never be found, it stretches forth like a welcome platform for Martians.

Shocks

A Car on the Pyramid

The exalted Nostradamus predicted that by August 1999 the world would no longer exist. When the date rolled around, we Mexicans, so fond of tragedy as spectacle, put on our best glasses and went looking for catastrophes. What terminal signs did we find in the summer of our discontent? On August 20, an automobile at top speed passed through the streets of the Center and attempted to keep going through an open space next to the Templo Mayor. The driver accelerated until he noticed that his car was flying toward an Aztec pyramid. By some miracle, which we may perhaps attribute to Tezcatlipoca, god of fatality, the vehicle landed without damage on top of a temple and remained there as a strange offering to the ancestors. The driver who attempted this millennial version of human sacrifice was drunk and worked as a policeman.

People who adore bizarre accidents could confirm the fact that this was not the first Chevrolet to take that route. As strange as it seems, another Chevrolet landed in the same place in 1978.

But back to 1999. A few days after the first accident, there was another. An army officer drove across Plaza de la Constitución, heading toward the stairs that go down to the subway, as if the primal subsoil, territory of pre-Hispanic cosmogonies, contained a nocturnal automobile repair shop.

In the August of Nostradamus, law enforcement smashed into tradition. At first glance, these were everyday events, especially in a country where tequila can shape the ideas of men in uniform.

Subjected to detailed analysis, these collisions offer resounding examples of our annihilating and perhaps fertile form of mixing cultures. The impunity of the last years of the twentieth century fell on the stones where the founders of the city conducted their bloody rites. Completely right in doing so, the anthropology authorities condemned this blow against our patrimony. The paradoxical aspect of the matter is that the wrecking ball was as typical a symbol as the historical legacy it marred.

To acknowledge its hybrid, the result of the mixing of bloods, colonial New Spain chose Pegasus as one of its emblems: a creole animal, a mix of horse and bird, that effects communication between earth and sky.

"Enrico Martínez believes that the constellation that governs New Spain, and specifically Mexico City, is that of Pegasus," writes the art historian Guillermo Tovar de Teresa. The mythological animal sprang from a fountain, and the city rose up over a lake. "These facts are useful for understanding the presence of the winged horse at the main fountain of the Palace of the Viceroys," adds the author of *Pegasus, or the Baroque New Spanish World in the Seventeenth Century (El pegaso o el mundo barroco novohispano en el siglo xvii).*

The winged beast became the symbol of identity. So seventeenth-century readers could identify him as an author from New Spain, Carlos Sigüenza y Góngora suggested that the covers of his books bear the effigy of Pegasus along with his motto: *Sic itur ad astra* (Thus we go to the stars).

In August of 1999, the creole emblem of New Spain acquired a strange contemporaneity. The drunk policeman who drove straight for the Templo Mayor wasn't trying to reach the stars or recycle mythologies, but his car flew like a broken version of Pegasus.

The recklessness of this dubious representative of the law forces us to remember that the Templo Mayor came into twentieth century light because of an act as arrogant and irresponsible as driving by the National Palace at ninety miles per hour.

In his autobiography—that strange vindication of chaos titled *My Times*—President José López Portillo declares that he confirmed the reach of his power when he ordered the demolition of a squared block of colonial buildings next to the Cathedral in order to liberate the foundations of the Templo Mayor. Thanks to a president willing to confuse his office with the whims of his testosterone, the heart of Mexico City contains a huge cavity. The hole left behind by the mansions of the Viceroyalty allowed the emergence of an Aztec stone yard, exposed to our acid rain, a site the archaeologist Juan Yadeum, responsible for the Maya Toniná zone, compares to a missing tooth. The logical solution would have been for an underground restoration that would leave the surface intact, as was the case with the Louvre or what happened later a few meters away in the Spanish Cultural Center, in whose basement you can see the remains of the *calmécac,* the school for Aztec aristocrats.

But the option to reveal the destructive violence of the Conquest, to reveal it in stone, also has its intelligent defenders. The archaeologist Eduardo Matos Moctezuma, director of the recovery program at the Templo Mayor, became so popular over the course of the 1970s that *Time* magazine called him Moctezuma III. When the celebrated dual temple was located to one side of the Cathedral, the idea of rebuilding it surged. Matos, who as a young man worked at Teotihuacán, has talked in ironic terms about the excessive restoration of the pyramids, which ultimately reveals a Toltec influence—not because of any Toltec inheritance but because the restorations lead back to the Toltec Cement Company.

The architect Pedro Ramírez Vázquez, whose name has already appeared in this book as the creator of great icons in our tradition (Aztec Stadium, the Guadalupe Basilica, the National Anthropology Museum), wanted to widen his sphere of influence by remodeling the temple. President López Portillo, who identified with the enlightened god Quetzalcóatl and had actually written a book on the subject, seemed to favor the idea. But Matos convinced him to be faithful to history and show the devastation caused by the Conquest.

I accompanied the archaeologist to one of his favorite sites beneath the city subsoil, a tunnel that connects the Templo Mayor to the Cathedral. It isn't easy to follow someone who has stayed in shape for decades by climbing ladders and bending over to get through tunnels. His enthusiasm aroused by talking as he walks, Matos told the story of how the Aztec city was destroyed and led me to a place more or less beneath the high altar of the Cathedral, and where a stake that was used in the construction of the building pierces a pre-Hispanic remnant. The "meeting of two worlds," the rhetorical formula used to commemorate Christopher Columbus's arrival at the Americas, was not peaceful: "Here, sir, is the Conquest," Matos pointed to the stake in the stone.

After dynamiting enough real estate to compare himself to a Spanish viceroy or an Aztec emperor, José López Portillo could have yelled, like the protagonist of Jorge Hernández Campos's poem *The President (El presidente)*:

> I am his most excellent excellency Mister President
> of the General Republic and Dr. So and So.
> And when the Earth trembles
> and the masses bellow packed in the Zócalo
> and I shout Viva México!
> so I can shout Viva Me!
> and I place my hand on my testicles
> I feel a drunken torrent
> of life.

The driver who landed on the temple of sacrifices also shouted Viva Me! and felt a drunken torrent of life.

The Zócalo or Constitution Plaza is the place where different times incriminate themselves. The subsoil remembers that there was a lake there and causes the Baroque Cathedral to lean like a ship listing to one side. Along the railings of the Templo Mayor, techno-Indians dance to the rhythm of chirimías, kettle drums, and the music emitted by a ghetto blaster. Some wear T-shirts that pay homage to the powers of heavy rock. On the benches outside the Cathedral, unemployed plumbers and carpenters advertise with their tools in the hope someone will give them a job. Aztec, Spanish, and creole Mexico all mix in the Zócalo. Inaugurated in 1796 with bullfights, the place owes its name to the pedestal which stood unoccupied for four years to be completed by the equestrian statue of King Carlos IV of Spain. The people got used to referring to the place as *el zócalo* (plinth)—by extension, the central plazas of other cities in the nation are also called zócalos.

Oddly enough, the statue itself is not linked to that name. It's known as *The Little Horse*. The creation of the architect and sculptor Manuel Tolsá, who also designed the Cathedral, it's had the fate of a knight in chess. It was first located in the center of today's Constitutional Plaza, and after Independence was removed. It was recovered in 1822 and placed in the patio of the university. My generation saw it at Bucareli and Paseo de la Reforma, "information corner," where several newspapers had offices. After 1979, it reached its current sight in Tolsá Plaza, opposite the Palace of Mining.

The Little Horse has had as agitated a life as Pegasus, but it lacks the creole ambivalence our identity symbolizes. On the other hand, the automobile on top of the pyramid does indeed offer a contemporary metaphor for that emblem: it didn't fly to the stars, but it did fix itself in their temple.

The most typical thing in today's Mexico is thrash metal creolism, a syncretism that guarantees the annihilation of all its component parts.

Thanks to a collision, we understand that in a congested city the last parking space is on top of a pyramid.

Places

The Meeting Place

I have reasons for believing Mexico has begun its development. There was a primitive time when you got to a bus station and had to search for someone among the peanut vendors and the myriad passengers. During the 1970s, I would look for my father using his sideburns, hoping to recognize them in the indiscriminate mass. It has become fashionable that public spaces have their own original device: a green square, where four arrows meet in a white circle. The first time I saw one I thought it had to be an ad for aspirin. Not at all. We stand before one of the few logos that does not respond to the commands of advertising. If someone asks what it is, a sign tells you: "Meeting place."

There are businesspeople so proud of this service that they include it in their publicity pamphlets as one of the attractions of the hotel. Once I stayed at a Fiesta Inn where you couldn't open the windows but which had sophisticated services: jacuzzi, gymnasium, and meeting place. Since I'd never used one, I was surprised to find it advertised in the room information booklet. I decided to be modern and went looking for it.

The meeting place was in a far corner of the garden. Various arrows helped me get there. Of course, since I'm not very good with directions, I got lost trying to find the spot. When I finally did, I found a family having a picnic on the white circle. "Occupied" they said, as if it were a bathroom.

I went to speak to the manager and asked him why they'd placed the spot where people are supposed to meet so far away. He explained that the hotel is part of a chain, with hundreds of buildings all over the country. Because of a corporate decision, each one had to have a meeting place. In this case there were no empty places available, so they had to relegate the spot to a distant site. That's how I learned that the white circle is no whim, not even an extra luxury, but an essential requirement.

"In one hotel we had to put the point on the upper terrace," the manager said. I thought he might be joking, but his seriousness made me conclude it was a statistic.

All this caused me to become a meeting place spy. The first item I can report is that they're everywhere, even colonial buildings like the National College at Donceles 104, very close to the Cathedral. As you pass through the portico, the first thing you see is the point. Before visitors feel the influence of the ghosts of Diego Rivera, José Vasconcelos, Alfonso Reyes, and other founding members, they have at their disposal a meeting place. Luckily the arrows haven't been painted on the floor. They use a carpet that doesn't damage the patrimony.

By definition, there should only be one point, a kind of dogma of location, but perhaps the idea of being oriented has become so popular that in some buildings the points have proliferated and confused everyone. I'm not very sure that a proper calculation has been made of the number of people who get lost for each square meter. In a commercial center I had to make my way through three points until I found the person I was looking for.

In any case: What degree of success has this invention had? Even though my investigation is still in its preliminary phase, I'll risk putting forth some results. The important thing is not so much the human ingenuity invested in choosing the places where people may meet but the way we assimilate them into our habits.

The same thing that happens with other contraptions of modernity happens with this one. Suddenly, during a meeting, someone recalls the terrible afternoon when he lost his grandmother in the Pantaco shops and one of the people present pointed out that in the United States that would have been taken care of immediately because there are places called "meeting points." All of which makes us long for a developed society where people know where to look for one another.

But since we're Mexicans, now that we have meeting points at our disposal we've decided to use them in a strange way. Before revisiting the subject, we have to take into account another recent invention: email. Distrust is an essential feature of our national being: after sending an important email, we telephone to see if it arrived. And hypersensitiveness is another essential feature: if we're invited to a party *only* by email, we're offended ("so they wouldn't have to talk to me" we think in rage). We're an atavistic nation. Perhaps that explains why the meeting point is always empty or attracts people that want to have a snack there.

Demography expresses itself in a strange way among us: Mexicans are generally already gathered together (we have more than enough relatives). Therefore, the meeting point isn't used to find a brother who's strayed but to invite him for dessert. In the vertigo of modern life, the four arrows that meet in a white circle say that's where peace is located.

Over the entire course of my investigation, I only witnessed one real meeting, and it was a mistake: a gentleman came over to ask if I was Norberto. On all other occasions, the white circles were either deserted or occupied by people eating appetizers and smiling with the pleasure of those who appropriate a space without having to pay rent.

In essence, the meeting point reflects who we are: it announces a cosmopolitan life where people who are scattered have a way to get together in our style, to share Cheetos and play rock-paper-scissors.

After thinking this over and writing it out, I went on studying the subject and found out something I didn't know and that the vast majority of users also do not know. The meaning of the point does not respond to a need for people to meet under normal conditions, but in emergencies. That's why they're put in strange places, so they can be safe from fires or earthquakes. We aren't using a mechanism that facilitates gregarious life but a device for civilian protection. But since no one knows that, the point is used according to our gregarious habits and customs.

In the United States, forgotten things end up at the optimistically named place: lost-and-found. By contrast, in Mexico it's called Lost Objects. The administration is not responsible for finding them but in losing them in its closets.

Ever since the primordial tribe left the Seven Caves, we citizens of the capital have been lost together. The arrows of the world converge where we already are: the ideal place to eat pumpkin seeds.

If someone really does get lost, we do not go to the meeting point. Since the lost person is also looking for us, we walk until chance brings us together. Then there ensues a dialogue that defines our national ontology:

"Where the devil were you?"

"Looking for you, of course!"

Living in the City

Rain Soup

The city has grown to such an extent that it's difficult to remember the zones in which it was once upon a time strangely organized.

In 1975, I visited the location of the Metropolitan Autonomous University at Iztapalapa (UAM), for the first time and found a level stretch where the three places of reference were not especially promising: a convent, a women's prison, and a dump. On that shore of nothingness, a university was rising under the motto "House Open to Time." From 1976 to 1980 it was my alma mater, a place where I worked an extra year in the department of cultural activities.

Not far away from UAM, on the Ridge of the Star, the Aztecs would light the new fire when the calendar ran out and, miraculously, the world did not end and the sun came out again. In emblematic fashion, the auditorium of our campus bore the name Theater of the New Fire.

I first visited that wasteland—which today is overpopulated—because my father worked there as a founder of the Division of Social Sciences and Humanities. With the enthusiasm of a crusader, he showed me empty classrooms as if I were seeing things that weren't there. For him, those prefabricated walls were the prelude to a utopia of knowledge. His guided tour had less to do with the buildings than with Plato's republic and Aristotle's lyceum. As you've probably guessed, he convinced me to study there.

Over the course of half a decade, I witnessed the changes in the zone. It became urbanized with the usual disorder that goes with laying pipes and only rarely could we use the same route to reach a house open to time but not to minibuses.

On one occasion, a garbage truck stopped next to me on Gavilán Street and asked me if I was waiting for the one-peso taxi that would take me to UAM. I said I was, and they offered to give me a ride on the running board. I wasn't fragrant when I got to class, but I did get there more quickly than usual.

The challenge of actually getting to the campus forced some friends who came from the provinces to move into Iztapalapa. My thesis director, Federico Nebbia, an Argentine who'd studied at tree-lined Harvard with the functionalist sociologist Talcott Parsons, coined an aphorism to survive that precarious environment: "The only way to deal satisfactorily with a disagreeable place is to live in it." That explained the time he spent in a university dormitory in Iztapalapa.

Whenever I go back to that part of the city, I'm surprised by the expansion of multifarious urban life, so different from the half-lost village it was thirty years ago. Some of the most interesting projects in the capital are rising there, like FARO, the Fábrica de Artes y Oficios Oriente (Workshop for Eastern Arts and Professions) that supplied housing for arts and professions in one of the least favored zones of the city. Despite an oasis like that, the region simply shows the differences in services the citizens receive. One of the most serious problems is water distribution, which in 2005 turned the zone into a dry wasteland. In that year, in some schools it became normal for children to carry canteens, and the fight over pipes increased the tensions which have been present ever since the original eight neighborhoods were founded. Also, the quality of the water leaves a lot to be desired. Reporters did not need microscopes to find animal life in the muddy water, and the locals said they received "tamarind water" because of its color.

At that time, I visited a former fellow-student who'd been given an ornate watch for having served twenty-five years as a professor at the UAM—nothing seems more logical than the "house open to time" rewarding someone that way for his loyalty.

We recalled the era when it was not only impossible to find a café in the area but even to find coffee beans to make something ourselves. Italian cafés were a luxury at the time, and Starbucks had yet to initiate its viral invasion. In moments of desperation we drank Legal Coffee, which came with sugar in it and refuted its name with each spoonful.

While I was talking to my old classmate, one of those thunderstorms that flood the capital began falling. Once again we confirmed the paradoxes of a city built on a lake that used up its water, that floods during rainy season, and has trouble supplying potable water to many of its neighborhoods.

We hadn't seen each other for a long while, so we gave in to the theater of memory. Encapsulated by the storm, we fell back on our small mythology, an era when only the future existed. We evoked the flat lands around Gavilán Street, which led to the university, the dogs that wandered about there (one of them, mangy and starving, once reached the chancellor's office and died there, as if it had participated in a strange sacrifice, a propitiatory rite for academic triumph), the dumpster fire that covered the region with whitish smoke full of toxins that almost sent us to the hospital, the years in a region with a long folk tradition to which, nevertheless, we came with the air of pioneers, or perhaps more accurately fugitives.

When my friend paused, I went to a window and saw buckets, bottles, and pails of all kinds up on the surrounding terraces. People were collecting water.

The bad weather made our meeting last longer than intended. I went back out on the street with a feeling of unreality.

I walked toward my car. Suddenly a glint distracted me. In a vacant lot a fire was burning. Four little girls, about eight years old, were heating up a pewter pot.

"Toss in some onion," said one girl, "and cilantro and beans, and chops, and lungs, and pheasant."

Each ingredient was accompanied by imaginary spoonfuls.

I was shocked that they mixed lungs, poor food, favored by cats, with pheasant, which they most probably knew nothing about. To thicken their fantastic soup they tossed in a few stones and stirred them with a stick. The pot produced a tasty noise.

"There goes the *mole* and the rice and the chicken and the pizza."

The chile and the salt came last. That soup had everything in it.

As the girls played, people carried their pails of rainwater into their houses.

Did the recipe for the soup come from hunger or from a fired-up childish imagination? The only thing I knew for sure was that I was in Iztapalapa, where water is worth a lot. I wasn't surprised when the girls came over to sell me a cupful. Since I had no change, it cost me ten pesos.

"It isn't tamarind," that negation summarized the rest of the flavors in the world, "and it contains pebbles," added one of them presumptuously.

I drank as if I were tasting a witches' brew, the rejuvenating beverage of the ogres, the elixir of transfigurations, the punch of desires in a fairy tale. I'd graduated at Iztapalapa, but I'd yet to taste the soup of the region.

It didn't taste of tamarind. It tasted of city, of time, of new fire.

City Characters

The Tire Repair Man

Every three blocks, Mexico City is interrupted by a half-vacant lot where a man covered with black grease contemplates a chained-up dog. A sign with mythological resonance explains what this is all about: "Vulcanizing Done Here." The small oven where a blue flame quivers, the pile of tires, the rusted tools, the big bowl with dry tortillas and the rims that serve as chairs show that business is bad, but that despite that fact there are more and more places like this one.

Our transit is a pretext for the existence of vulcanizing shops. You might say we are idolaters when it comes to tires, not when it comes to the tire in use, but to its symbol, the misshapen hoop, just tossed aside or crumpled, the circle with patches, thick, emblem of movement, of wounds, and of their precarious cure.

More than a job, tire repair is a custom. To stop it would mean interrupting the city.

In other Spanish-speaking nations, they use other words for repairing tires. As we shall see, there is a powerful reason why this work is associated with the god Vulcan among us.

What is the source of the pleasure we get from tires? Mexico is one of the few countries where it's considered fun to burn them. On New Year's Eve, patrols roam the streets in search of fanatics who celebrate the god of fire in a double sense—by burning "vulcanized" tires.

It isn't always easy to justify our pastimes. Holding hands in an intimate circle so you can receive electric shocks, buying clay excrement—where the craftsperson had included seeds that reveal the digestion of chiles—or eating a sugar skull with your name on its forehead: doing these things causes our idea of entertainment to seem concerning. The bonfire of tires is another form of amusing ourselves by suffering. Even so, it establishes a contact with an occult tradition.

The vulcanizers do not conform to utilitarian purposes. Which is why there are so many. Their business is in the toilet and they grow in number, never thinking there are enough. In exchange for a few cents, the new Vulcan accepts the soot that covers him like a second skin and assigns a leaden consistency to his fingernails. For long hours he simply stands there, with no other amusement than spitting into a can of multigrade oil, his back to a calendar featuring blondes with pneumatic bosoms, reclining on brand-new cars.

His T-shirt is of a unique gray, on the margin of the color chart, only conceivable as a texture, the extreme limit of what wear and soot can do to a piece of fabric.

If there were motors in those places, you might think about an addiction to gasoline and its fragrant hallucinations. But the tire repair guy is not a mechanic but a patient being who tends to a tire with tame asceticism. It is possible that from time to time soap does pass over his body and that at night he fornicates with full knowledge of light. The fact is that by day and at his place of business he is an idol of waiting, of waste, of filth, of useless repairs. This last fact demands attention. In the tire repair shops they only repair tires, but there are pieces of steel and parts that come from other scrapyards and are there for reasons unclear to anyone and which may function as hermetic symbols.

If he is in fact so completely screwed, why doesn't the blackened owner close up shop? Something, a distant and mysterious cause, indicates that even though there are other variations of poverty, the vulcanizing station must remain open more in the manner of a cave than a business.

The entrance is usually irregular, as if it had been chopped out next to the bench. Some possess a convincing metal curtain, but most protect themselves with a piece of sheet metal and a rope which suggest that all work yards are utopian.

The guard dog looks like the door: he defends nothing but he does produce the impression that this is a place. Although he's got a chain around his neck, we understand this is not a wild dog who wants to go somewhere. We reach the essential point of our analysis: on that lot everything is symbolic. The calendar blondes are as unreal as the work that nevertheless keeps the man covered with black grease.

The tire repair shop is an economic absurdity. No matter how many nails there are in the city, no one prospers among these useless chunks of steel. There are no sultans of tire repair.

The disarticulated components of this place demand we give them meaning; they are signs that ask to be narrated.

The tire repair shop has yet to enter the territory of myth. It stands at an earlier stage, but it is moving toward myth. Is it possible we've missed its message?

The first key resides in the name, which alludes to the god of fire and to the geographic condition of Mexico City, the volcanic basin where Baron Alexander von Humboldt convinced himself that the Neptunists, of the water party, were wrong and that the reason for the origin of minerals aided the Vulcanists, wise in the use of light.

Earthquakes are the dramatic signal that we are living in one of the most active volcanic regions in the world. When the earth shakes because of a Richter scale 6 tremor, we do not think that it has anything to do with fire because we are too busy saving Grandma or a French poodle. In repose, relieved from the shaking, we can return to the books that take volcanoes into account. Martín Luis Guzmán declared that the principal artistic influence he'd felt was the landscape of the Valley of Mexico. The luminosity of the sky, the foliage of the trees, and the thunderstorms framed and defined the spirit of his characters. In *The Shadow of the Strongman* (*La sombra del caudillo*, 1929), climate and nature foreshadow the tragic fate of the protagonists:

It was in Ajusco, crowned with tempestuous storm clouds and wrapped in violet shadows in harsh shadows which from there tinged with night, with an unreal tone, the region where Rosario and Aguirre found themselves. And during the periods, which were longer and longer, in which the sun was blocked, the stormy divinity of the mountain totally dominated the landscape: the sky lost its luster, the bottom of the valley darkened along with the land around it, and the clouds, just a short while before as white as snow, quickly darned into somber opacity.

The volcano announced the catastrophe. Even though Martín Luis Guzmán's novel was talking about the political tragedy the Revolution became, it also foretold the dissolution of the sky. With the passage of time, the only lasting thing would be the mountain amid the mists, similar to a yoke of fire.

Mexico City has grown in order to negate water and air. Earth and fire have dominated the other elements with volcanic rigor.

In dispersed and intuitive form, writers have warned about the importance of burnings. Although other literary themes are turned to with more frequency (death, solitude, masks), fire has been a unifying passion. The space of the cold flame and the burnt water, Mexican literature has paid Vulcan his tribute in ashes, from the ashes of Sor Juana's "religious bonfires" to José Agustín's *Near the Fire (Cerca del fuego),* passing through the poems of Rubén Bonifaz Nuño's *Fire of the Poor (Fuego de pobres).*

> Mexican time is measured in Octavio Paz's *Sunstone:*
> a presence like a sudden canticle,
> like the wind singing in the bonfire

You could say that there is no way to write in this valley without having right at hand José Gorostiza's verse, which summarizes the theme with a sharp lightning rod: "intelligence, solitude in flames."

It would be a telluric exaggeration to suppose that the volcanoes, or their loss under the industrial fogs, are the only explanation for an art filled with bonfires. History and anthropology offer other clues about our predilection for flame. Alfredo López Austin has shown that the legend of the *tlacuache*—the opossum fire thief—is a shared myth among Native American peoples, who today say *fire* in more than sixty languages. The tlacuache is the Prometheus of New World fauna: he steals fire to store it in his marsupial pouch. Which is why he has a singed tail. In fables, songs, and proverbs, the tlacuache acquires a symbolic status similar to that of the poet: he is the thief of fire.

Some forty years ago, a strange animal was killed in a market in the capital. The press, fond of two-headed babies and extraterrestrial abductions, reported that it was the largest rat in the world. Then it was discovered that the animal was an opossum, the only New World marsupial, an animal closer to humans on the evolutionary scale than it is to rats. What seemed an act of horrible justice became an almost fratricidal crime. The ancestral provider of fire had been murdered.

We inhabit a volcanic plain where the automobile tire, which arose from flames, has the value of a talisman that takes us back to the *ulama,* the sacred game of Mesoamerica. The first rubber balls were invented in this land and were vulcanized with the ashes of the dead. In the archaeological site of Toniná, a frieze shows a ball that contains the head of an adversary. A representation of duality, the ball game alludes to the regeneration of night into day and of death into life. The tire repair shop, the refuge of a circular object made from fire, offers an urban link with that disappeared ritual.

Covered with a blackened second skin, the custodians of fire await their explanation. Most certainly, the mythographers of the future will decipher the true profession of this black legion. For now, we can put forward a hypothesis: the tire repair shops are chapels. It's difficult to define their ceremonies because they constitute a sect alien to proselytism, one that preaches through example. Perhaps we are observing a community that only reveals the keys to its meaning to those who deserve them; perhaps, on our streets, flamethrowers are their frenetic and fundamentalist vanguard.

The vulcanizing shops refer to the extreme times of the city: the spark in the original cave and the volcanic apocalypse that awaits us. Human life is the space between both explosions.

The carbonic men grow in number, followed by their pets, which forces us to remember that the voyages to Mictlán or Xibalbá (the Aztec and Maya infraworlds, respectively), were led by a dog.

Lords of the beginning and the end, the vulcanizers accept the second skin of pain and sacrifice in order to guard a talisman of movement which perhaps has less to do with the labors of traffic than with the cycles of time.

In the future, after the final fire, they will be sacred.

Ceremonies

The Passion of Iztapalapa

A s is only fitting with any completely Mexican gathering, the Passion of Iztapalapa lacks any statistical reality, as if the figures belonged to the mysteries of the Gospel. According to the year and the sources consulted, the festival is seen by a multitude somewhere between three and six million and the staging involves somewhere between four thousand and seven thousand participants. The truth is that those present are all those who should be there: the principal players and the gate-crashers, the skeptical minority and the myriad curious. Even those not present take part, thanks to the memories of those who do attend. Theater of memory, Holy Week recovers the route of Jesus to Golgotha, but it also evokes many family members and neighbors who participated in earlier versions of the great event. A mnemotechnical rope unites those present with uncles and grandparents, the faithful who in the past traversed the streets of the eight neighborhoods of Iztapalapa to witness the three emblematic falls of the Son of God. No one is missing. With demographic certitude, the audience belongs to an undefined but sufficient human sea.

It's also the case that the Redeemer's cross varies from year to year but without losing its solid presence. The portable gallows has weighed eighty, ninety, or ninety-nine kilos, according to the season. The cross is an opponent of regulation forcefulness. To deal with it, the Christ of the day trains like a boxing champion.

Presided over by La Estrella Mountain, Iztapalapa is the immense proletarian zone that extends eastward from the city, all the way to the Puebla exit. During Holy Week, it becomes a provisional Jerusalem where pharmacies close and ambulances arrive. On some occasions, Jesus suffers the combined tortures of sun, falls, water deprivation, beatings, the weight of the wood, the air rarefied by dust and fried food, and faints only to regain consciousness at the hands of the Red Cross.

There's no disputing the seriousness of a celebration that puts into play the physical stamina of the participants and depends on a rigorous selection process. For those involved, the Passion lasts the entire year. Some wonder if playing the part of Judas might be bad luck, while others want to rise in the evangelical ranks and move from being mere soldiers to chief dispensers of beatings; others, more of them, submit to a tribunal of conscience so they won't feel miserable shoving the lance of Longinus into the most wounded and most celebrated rib cage in the Western world.

All the actors must be Catholics of spotless reputation, and Jesus and Mary must be unmarried. In many cases, the role-playing takes up the best years in a life. A typical curriculum for the Christ of Iztapalapa: five years as a Nazarene, three as an apostle, one as a leper, one as a Hebrew, and three more as a candidate for the main role.

Although the events take place in the time between Palm Sunday and Holy Saturday, the roles are discussed, dreamed over, and rehearsed for twelve months. We are witnessing more than a play: we are seeing a way of acquiring a destiny.

There's no lack of scenes containing fine acting (especially among the women and most especially in moments of weeping), but the festival depends on the communal display. Daily life is the stage where all actors are put to the test. Once selected because of their conduct, their histrionic abilities become a secondary matter.

The props and costumes recall the night when Don Quixote stands vigil over his cardboard weapons. The actors solemnly make use of ephemeral objects. The angels wear wings with feathers gathered in poultry shops, the swords and helmets are made by honest metalworkers, Judas tosses chocolate coins, the crown has acacia thorns, and the helmets of the soldiers are adorned with bristles taken from brooms.

In his memoir, *Peeling the Onion,* Günter Grass talks about a postwar bride who got married wearing a dress made from parachute material. Recycling confers a heartwarming value on things because it reveals the urgent overcoming of a lack. No bride can appear as virginal as one who marches to the altar wrapped in a parachute, in the same way that no angel is as close to us as one who has chicken feathers on his wings.

This domestic dimension draws the epic closer to the people. The Christian poet Carlos Pellicer created extraordinary nativities and celebrated the intimate condition of that religious custom, a toy store heaven that's landed in a house where everything revolves around the child in the manger. The Iztapalapa Passion takes place with the same endearing proximity in everyday streets, bearing objects that until recently had other purposes, the people of Jerusalem go on parade.

Iztapalapa does not bet its money on the production of an event that seems real, but on creating a reality that is movingly near us. The most well-known drama in the Western world is incorporated into autobiography and becomes immediate experience. The cast for the action is a leafy genealogical tree. There are families that have supplied various Nazarenes, a pair of Pilates, numerous Jews, and even two Christs.

The seriousness and the emotion of the participants make the festival resemble graduation days, halfway between the civic and the sacred. In a double game, the neighbors affirm their belonging to the Christian faith and to the town of Iztapalapa.

It's possible that the most repeated of Jesus' expressions in the realm of popular wisdom is "No one is a prophet in their own land." Repudiated by his own people, the Messiah triumphed in posterity. Iztapalapa reverses that destiny by recognizing the sacred nature of that which is close at hand.

On Palm Sunday, Christ walks the streets. It is the moment of greatest joy, the one the participants usually prefer. A vast public waves celebratory palm fronds. Then comes the repudiation and later the betrayal. We move on to the hard part of the representation, which many wish would not happen but which confirms in dramatic fashion how simple it is to commit an evil act. Finally comes the suffering, essential in order that the injustice reach the level of horror and remain in the imagination.

Among those present are curiosity seekers who declare they don't know why Jesus died, but there are also miracle hunters who recall especially terrifying episodes, as in the year when the earth shook during the crucifixion.

At the end, the participants make their way to Cerro de la Estrella, where the Aztecs lit the new fire. There they set up the three crosses, and the condemned man is a prophet in his own land. There are even people who chase and beat him, those already converted to his faith. The populous miracle of Iztapalapa consists in revealing once and for all the Messiah is a neighbor.

The ceremony began in 1843 when a terrible cholera epidemic had been in progress for ten years. Decimated by poverty and sickness, the eight neighborhoods of Iztapalapa sought consolation in staging the last days of Christ.

Perhaps the most unusual dimension of this variation on the Passion is its mixture of the civil and the religious. Both lay and Jacobin governments have supported the ceremony. The president most hated by Catholic intolerance, Benito Juárez, offered his decisive support so the festival could get its start. It's true that that took place before the Reform laws, which confiscated Church property, were promulgated, but in later years Juárez did not oppose the ceremony. For his part, Emiliano Zapata lent his horses for one staging of the event. The fact that Holy Week is so deeply rooted in the people has created links that transcend the Christian faith.

The festival is moving because its intention is so plain. No one goes to Iztapalapa looking for *Jesus Christ Superstar*, for the Messiah overwhelmed by the temptations of a woman, for a rebel demigod who rejects his father and frees the slaves, a future Che Guevara. The staging is conventional and the purpose is simple: to reiterate what the ancestors did. This humility magnifies the ceremony. In one of his last tales, "The Bishop," Chekhov describes the death of a minister of the church who falls ill on Palm Sunday and dies without being able to transmit the sadness of a life coming to its end. What a difference there is between the public drama of Holy Week and the silent dissolution of a destiny! Chekhov's bishop, who has narrated the fall of Christ a thousand times, cannot narrate his own. His aged mother outlives him. After a while, few people believe she ever had a son in the church hierarchy. Chekhov's parable is precise: Holy Week transmits the incommunicable death of every human; art achieves the opposite: it narrates the unrepeatable death of one man.

In Iztapalapa's version of the Passion, everything is collective. No extra stands out, no gesture refutes what was done on other occasions. It may happen that the tree from which Judas hangs himself is different. This reiteration distances the drama from any rupture and reinforces its communal nature. The festival turns out, as López Velarde wished, "faithful to its daily mirror."

Obviously, not everything in the Passion impassions. There are sections when the procession passes through certain streets and nothing happens, and sometimes perspective is lost. It's impossible that millions of spectators see in detail the moving episode in which Christ washes and kisses the feet of his disciples. The important thing is not enjoying the representation but in being part of it.

In his *The Suspension of Seriousness (Fenomenología del relajo)*, Jorge Portilla wrote that Mexican festivals derive from a pretext that disappears as soon as people show up. The nonsense depends on a displacement: the original motive for the gathering fades in favor of those present, and the guests become their own spectacle. This, which is usually true for most of our social gatherings, is not true for the Passion of Iztapalapa. There the initial motivation does not dissipate, and the witnesses are also actors, because they represent the confused people of Jerusalem. Even the photographers contribute to the drama. Each change of scene passes through a transition in which the actors have to make their way through a cloud of reporters, which adds verisimilitude to the tragedy in an era when only that which is photographed exists or, as we've been seeing over the past few years, only that which is streaming exists.

Between the actors and the audience there circulates an intermediate group: the penitents who take advantage of the journey to balance their account with their biography. For them, the movement through the eight neighborhoods signifies expiation. Mixed in with the protagonists, patrolmen and nurses, volunteers of whatever kind, and prophets of no kind whatsoever. The musicians carry instruments and wear sneakers unknown in the original Holy Land.

In Iztapalapa, the king of the Jews is always two things: the chosen one and the neighbor, the Messiah and the fellow man who rehearsed his role wearing a Team America T-shirt and sunglasses.

An unbreakable mix of faith and a desire to be together, the exaltation of the people of Christ, the Passion culminates in the crosses all would wish to avoid but which allow memory to persist.

Once again, Peter denies Jesus and founds his Church. Once again, Judas betrays and repents. Through the effort of all, Christ realizes his fate: on Cerro de la Estrella, an ordinary man dies and his people redeem him. All go there in order not to forget, to not be forgotten.

At night, an unnecessary helicopter hovers over the scene, reminding us of the always distant noise of Providence.

Shocks

The Anxiety of Influenza—Diary of an Epidemic

On April 23, 2009, I published an obituary note about the English novelist J. G. Ballard. Among other things, I mentioned that his "narrative cataclysms arise from the problems generated by a community, that regulated form of apocalypse." The text appeared in the newspaper *Reforma*. In Mexico, if someone wanted to experience one of Ballard's scenarios, all he'd have to do would be to look up from the newspaper. The nation was offering Ballard a dramatic homage: Mexico had become one of his plots, a "regulated form of apocalypse."

That same Thursday the 23rd, at eleven p.m., President Felipe Calderón declared a health emergency because an unknown virus had appeared. Its effects were similar to those of pneumonia, with possibly serious consequences.

On the 24th, I flew to Tijuana for a two-day visit. At the airport, we had to fill out questionnaires about our health condition. No one picked them up, so we carried them onto the plane. It was a memorandum for ourselves, a measure typical of the Mexican government, which makes citizens responsible for the things it cannot impede. We were all traveling at our own risk.

I was seated next to a passenger who took the questionnaire lightly and sneezed for three and a half hours. I arrived with an earache and sore throat, a sensation of dizziness and indignation brought about by the lack of civility in people who travel while ill, that is, nothing that can't be fought off with three shots of tequila under normal conditions. But our conditions had ceased being normal, as I found out on Sunday, April 26, on my way back to Mexico City. Our Lord of Health was taken out of the Cathedral that day. Ever since 1691, that pale effigy of Christ had not abandoned his niche. In those days, it was used as a talisman against a smallpox epidemic and now it was being used again to combat swine flu, which, according to the news of April 27, had caused one hundred and three deaths.

Our Lord of Health traveled the streets under a cloud of incense. Then he was carried to the high altar of the Cathedral, where he would remain until the emergency was lifted.

The effigy of Christ looked like the effigy of an emergency worker fighting an epidemic which since mid-April had sent infected passengers to Australia, Spain, the United States, and Canada. The greatest alarms were sounded far away, in the offices of the World Health Organization. In Mexico, all we had were suspicions.

At the end of March, in La Gloria, a community in the state of Veracruz, where hog farms abound, four hundred people had fallen ill with pneumonia, a huge number in an area with only three thousand inhabitants. On April 2, Veratec, a U.S. biovigilance company, had announced that it was an outbreak of swine flu. Newspapers began to write about it, and on April 22, the news appeared on the front page of *Reforma*. Even so, the government waited until the final hours of the 23rd to inform the public about the epidemic and close schools.

The announcement was typical of a president who could do little, whose major trait was ambivalence. He spoke at eleven p.m., when many Mexicans were fast asleep. Perhaps he chose that moment so that the general alarm would be lessened since that hour has no rating. "I'm telling you this so you don't hear it," that seemed to be the motto of a president who seemed a true heir of Cantinflas.

The reaction was late and confused. Even so, on Wednesday the 29th, the citizens of the capital, so apt to run a red light, acted with extraordinary discipline. Dinner parties and meetings were canceled; people stopped going to the movies (theaters later closed), Masses were suspended, and only a few restaurants remained open. Soccer matches took place in empty stadiums, almost a cruel metaphor for the low quality of our teams. The army distributed millions of face masks, giving the city an unusual blue look. Above us, the sky was a mix of dust and pollution. The seasonal rains had yet to come. By day, the air burned, scorching the skin; by night, a filthy dew condensed, announcing storms that never managed to arrive.

In our flimsy society, conspiracy theories abound. Some spoke about "state terrorism" to refer to measures taken by the government. Although the dead were real, although the World Health Organization kept Mexico at a level four alert, and although the doctors confirmed the gravity of the epidemic, certain people, opposed to the regime, suggested there be marathon kissing sessions to combat "treacherous official propaganda." We'd moved into a situation worthy of George Orwell's dark utopia *1984*. Words changed meaning depending on who was using them. The proven inability of the president even led people to be suspicious of the president's method of "sneezing into the crook of your elbow," and some saw the act as some kind of new reactionary salute. The flu had become politicized.

According to official information, the sick reacted well to antiviruses, and there were more than a million doses available (by April 29, there were some two thousand infected). In this phase, the population disciplined its fears. There were no riots in the emergency rooms, the General Hospital had ten patients admitted for flu, and clinics were operating at normal levels.

To break the virus's transmission chain, avoiding contacts for ten days was recommended, a torture for one of the most gregarious nations on the planet, people who only enjoy whatever is happening in company. In Mexico, the first circle of hell is isolation.

The Aztecs were in the habit of adjusting their calendar with five unlucky days, dead times when it was forbidden to act: days without anything, an earthly limbo. The parenthesis imposed on us duplicated that Aztec severity.

Fear and anxiety were the best allies of this sequestration. Even so, not everyone respected the sanitary treaty. On the night of Sunday the 26th, in my neighborhood, the firecrackers of a local fiesta exploded and people were dancing to cumbia rhythms. The unstable life of Mexicans usually alternates between carnival and drama, and sometimes partying combines with catastrophe. In this sentimental appropriation of tragedy, we move from apocalypse to *apocalipstick,* to use the neologism coined by Carlos Monsiváis. The first Sunday of the epidemic the cumbia trumpets resounded in a dance hall near my house, advocating a deeply rooted Mexican tradition: workplaces make you sick, and fun places liven you up.

Since our best remedy for disasters is jokes, the next day my sister called to say "I'm suffering porcine *influence*—which explains why I'm so fat."

On Monday the 27th, I accompanied my daughter to the cleaner for the urgent chore of having a stuffed animal cleaned. We walked home. Opposite the front door of the house, we found the street sweeper's cart. It was carrying two huge drums filled to overflowing, with black plastic bags hanging over each side. Pushing it must have been very difficult. Nevertheless, the cart was moving on its own. "There's a tremor in progress," said the sweeper.

It was not an earthquake like the one of 1985 but it was a sudden and worrying shake, a sign that the earth hadn't forgotten the appointment that sooner or later we'd have with it.

The Confusion Virus

"I'm afraid," said a friend who returned to the city on the 27th after being away for a few days. "I thought the situation was under control, but no one knows anything."

The ten days allotted for breaking the transmission chain had begun. The patience and discipline of the first hours were challenged by uncertainty. "We need more information." This sentence was repeated by epidemiologists, journalists, tourists, neighbors, and family members.

Absent certainties, rumors gained ground. On Tuesday the 28th, there was panic buying of canned tuna, rice, and other products people gather for hurricane victims. People said Walmart was going to close. It's curious how rumors spread. We'll never know why people spoke specifically about Walmart. The fact is that it was empty information.

Starting on April 24, the federal government had closed places where crowds could gather. On the 28th, the government of the Federal District extended the measure to restaurants. Which made more people go to supermarkets.

The nation was governed by the conservative National Action Party (Partido Acción Nacional, or PAN) and the Federal District by the left-wing Democratic Revolution Party (Partido de la Revolución Democrática, or PRD). After an unusual unity in the face of the crisis, discrepancies appeared. Politics reached the level of pork rinds in green sauce. Business people criticized the closing of restaurants, and the minister of labor deemed the measure unnecessary.

Every single day, more than five million passengers pile into the subway. It was a source of contagion at the level of Dante's *Inferno* with such a severe virus. Closing down the subway system would have paralyzed the nation's economy, which was already suffering. The result was restrictions on "recreational spaces" but not on transit.

Monday the 27th marked my last visit to a taco restaurant. The waiter came over with the tray of desserts. As he offered them, he touched each one with his ballpoint pen. Had he succumbed to the very human habit of sucking on his pen?

While the city government was being accused of acting with excessive zeal, the federal government was fighting against statistics. In his evening press conference on Tuesday the 28th, the minister of health, José Ángel Córdova Villalobos, modified what had been said up until that point: of the one hundred and fifty-nine deaths associated with swine flu, very few had been caused directly by the virus. The autopsy of the case files was slower than the autopsy of the bodies. Until that moment, it was only possible to talk about seven proven cases.

If the deaths brought about by some unprecedented virus added up to seven, why had so many measures been taken? And what about the other deaths?

Let's imagine a science fiction story in which some aliens envious of our water land here armed with a lethal virus. There are one hundred and fifty-nine dead. The planet goes into shock, and the World Health Organization announces: "Only seven of the dead were infected with the virus." Does that announcement calm us down? Of course not.

There remain one hundred and fifty-two dead of unknown causes. To be beaten by an adversary you can't find causes even greater anguish.

The information flowed in slow, thick drops. The minister of health said that one of the dead weighed two hundred and twenty-eight kilos, suggesting that the person in question died from "complications," not influenza. That same night he insisted that the cases of pneumonia in La Gloria, Veracruz, had nothing to do with the influenza.

Was the federal government reducing the drama while the city government exaggerated it? The contradictions were more contagious than the illness itself.

Aztec Parable

By April 29, the Federal District had no meeting places except subway platforms.

The city was deserted as well on April 14, but for a different reason: the security zone set up for the visit of Barack Obama. That night, the president of the United States dined with Felipe Calderón in the patio of the National Museum of Anthropology. Their host was Felipe Solís, director of the museum.

I had the good fortune to meet Solís as a working archaeologist who in 1978 helped in the discovery of an essential item in Aztec culture: the effigy of the goddess Coyolxauhqui, murdered and mutilated by her mother, the implacable Coatlicue.

After carrying out explorations, Solís specialized in archaeological conservation. For years, he led the principal museum of pre-Hispanic art in Mexico. Perhaps the stress of Obama's visit weakened this man of incombustible enthusiasm. He died on April 23 of a heart attack. He was sixty-four years old and had a history of diabetes. Was he a victim of influenza?

Official reports indicated that was not the case, but since Mexicans are suspicious of everything, rumors were not lacking: "It would be extremely serious if Obama and his people thought their host died of influenza, so they're hiding the fact," said a friend who works in Foreign Relations.

A few months earlier, the Mexican government had protested against the "Texican Burger" created by Burger King. In the publicity posters, a tiny Mexican wearing a wrestling mask and wrapped in the national flag appeared next to a tall Texan. Even though the gringo was not in stupendous shape, Mexican diplomats judged that the advertising was discriminatory. Obviously, a nation worried about how it is represented in hamburgers cannot be very sure of itself. Were the alarms about influenza minimized so that Obama's visit would not be affected?

After the 1985 earthquake, the government was slow to ask for aid because it did not want Mexico to be seen as a dangerous place on the eve of the World Cup of 1986. Again and again, fear about how others see us restrained information, as if the earth shook or the virus mutated in order to bring down the head of state. Without having to read T. S. Eliot, the government discovered that "April is the cruelest month" and concluded the sickness was working against it. Sneezing became a dissident act.

By the 29th, there were more doubts about germs floating in the air. Meanwhile, chance was writing parables. Felipe Solís, the archaeologist who'd dug up a victimized goddess, died at the moment when a virus was threatening the new Aztecs with delivering them back to earth.

Mexican by Adoption

Scenes of contemporary Mexico: on Tuesday the 28th of April, the body of a victim of drug traffickers is found at the side of a highway. He was wearing a mask to protect himself from the swine flu. The next day, sicarios from the Gulf Cartel were arrested and what amounted to an arsenal taken away from them. They too were wearing masks. The epidemic did not represent a truce for organized crime.

For their part, souvenir makers adapted to the times by bringing out a stuffed animal. It came in from the cold with a name like a sneeze: Achufy. It looked like a flan with eyes made in China for some other purpose and could only be sold in Mexico.

A major question began to be heard in social gatherings: Just how Mexican was the virus? I chatted with two German journalists who came to Mexico to cover the epidemic, and they informed me that in their country people were talking about the "Mexican virus." They also told me that passengers coming from Mexico were received at the Frankfurt airport as if they were highly toxic mutants.

Is it true that a virus can have an "appellation of origin" like cognac, champagne, or tequila? To avoid having Mexico associated with such terrible news, the minister of health, José Ángel Córdova Villalobos, reminded us of the germ's pedigree: his genomic map included a Eurasian component. He clarified: "I'm not the one saying this. It comes from the Canadian and American laboratories, which are the ones who named it." This led to yet another important question: Couldn't that kind of work be carried out in Mexican laboratories? The samples were sent far away, slowing the formulation of a strategy, something more worrying than the national origin of the virus. Does Spain suffer a loss of prestige when we talk about "Spanish flu"?

Everything suggested that the virus had distant relatives, but it chose us to cause damage and offered an X-ray of a nation where medical care is deficient. There we find the Mexican element of the matter. People didn't die in the same way in other places. By June 3, it would be possible to make statistical comparisons. Mexico by then would have five thousand twenty-nine cases and ninety-seven deaths. The United States would have twice as many infected people (ten thousand fifty-four) but would only register seventeen deaths. The problem in Mexico was not getting sick but being taken care of.

On April 16, an acquaintance entered a private hospital with pneumonia symptoms. They didn't help him because his insurance did not cover those expenses. He was moved to a public hospital, where he died within a few hours. This was not some homeless person but a high-level functionary.

A nation with fifty million poor people was facing two epidemics: the virus and poverty. On the high-alert days, the beggars did not stop walking the streets. None of them wore masks.

Eyes as Novelty Items

No one noticed Lorena's eyes until she put on a mask. That's an exaggeration: no one had noticed them to such a degree.

The swine flu virus epidemic changed habits in the capital. The most obvious transformations were the cloth rectangles on the faces of the population. Men who weren't handsome became at least mysterious.

We faced the catastrophe unified by an item of clothing. It isn't always easy to say *we*. What does the word represent? What sort of identity does it convoke? A tribe addicted to company was threading its way through the labyrinth of solitude. Who were we? People who covered their faces with a patch of blue cloth.

Aside from that, we knew little. Why did an unknown virus spring up in Mexico? Why did the government wait so long to declare a state of emergency? The minister of health stated that he was disbursing information as he got it from the hospitals. That drop-by-drop technique couldn't be very accurate. We lived in a land where a patient could come down with pneumonia because he was forgotten in an icy cold room and had to wait shirtless for hours to get a chest X-ray.

Negligence was also reflected in patient histories. Whenever there's any doubt, a Mexican dies of "multiple congestion," which is to say more or less of a tamal.

Shortly before the crisis, my father decided to donate his library to the University of Michoacán. Neither of his children objected to the decision, which maintained the unity of the books that had shaped him. Making a sentimental gesture, a rarity in his case, my father asked each of us to take a few volumes "as a souvenir." Among the ones I picked was a first edition of Albert Camus's *The Plague (La Peste)*. In 1947, my father underlined a passage: "It might be said that the first effect of the sickness' brutal invasion was to force our fellow citizens to act as if they did not have individual feelings."

Who were we? People who wore masks. An item of clothing unified us and suggested new ideas: actually, Lorena's eyes were more beautiful. And, when the mask was resting on the throat, we recovered the forgotten miracle of seeing a face. Would we be able to see in that way when normalcy returned? In his allegory, Camus finds positive links that only arise as exceptions, in the face of having to overcome a tragedy. Would we retain the invisible thread the epidemic used to tie us together?

In Search of Patient Zero

Who was the first person to be infected with the virus? From being concerned with the influenza, we passed, as Harold Bloom might have said, to the "anxiety of influenza."

Until Wednesday the 29th, the ministry of health insisted that the four hundred cases of pneumonia in La Gloria had nothing to do with the swine flu. Nevertheless, laboratories in the United States and Canada confirmed on the same day that the first outbreak of Virus AH1N1 took place in that very spot. The sample came from Edgar Hernández, a five-year-old boy, and it was taken on April 3, twenty days before the emergency was declared.

Obviously, it's impossible to know if the boy was the first person infected. That community is in contact with migrants who work in the United States, and the virus may well have come from there. Things usually have an origin prior to the one we ascribe to them.

More important than finding Patient Zero was the managing of information. On April 28, when Córdova Villalobos said there were seven deaths that were definitely caused by the influenza, a female colleague asked him where that had happened. With the scrupulous attention to detail of a person who has no wish to make a mistake, the minister searched through his papers and read the report about six people who had died in the Tlalpan neighborhood. He added nothing to that. Which generated the sensation that the focal point of the epidemic was in the southern part of the city. That's the zone where the hospitals specializing in cardiology, nutrition, and respiratory illnesses are located, high-level centers that could certainly detect the virus. Unfortunately, many people were ignorant of that fact and thought the deceased had caught the virus because they lived in Tlalpan. The minister waited twenty-four hours before clarifying the matter.

Dr. Córdova Villalobos had become the overworked copilot of a ship with no captain. In the week that ran from April 23 to the 30th, President Felipe Calderón left his house three times, twice to attend meetings with his cabinet and once to receive medical assistance from China (a nation that one day after its donation arrested seventy-one Mexicans for medical reasons). Finally, on May 1, he visited the Naval Hospital.

A great deal has been said about the security measures taken in the president's office, from the disinfectant gel applied to every object to the sanitary checking of all the visitors he received. Although a responsible national leader should guarantee his health, it was obvious to all that he did not go anywhere near the viral region where the people live.

Calderón did not supervise medical attention and did not participate in any visible fashion in the communication strategy. According to a poll taken by the newspaper *Reforma,* fifty-four percent of all Mexicans believed information was being withheld.

The high-level administrations of international organizations were lavish with their praise of the efforts Mexicans were making. Even so, a week after the declaration of a state of emergency, there appeared contradictions in the lower-level administrators of those same institutions. Michael Ryan, director of Global Alert and Response of the World Health Organization, revealed that on April 11 he'd warned Mexico about the influenza outbreak (nine days after the biovigilance company Veratec had done so). That warning came about because of the pneumonia cases in the La Gloria community. Five days later, when there was news of a possible flu victim in Oaxaca, Ryan repeated his alert. While Barack Obama was visiting the Federal District and apologizing for the U.S. diplomats who defined Mexico as a "failed state," the World Health Organization warning was ignored.

The influenza found the government with its defenses down. The sources of prosperity in the nation were elsewhere. In its issue dedicated to the one hundred most influential people on earth, *Time* included a Mexican: Chapo Guzmán, a prosperous narcotrafficker.

Chlorine and Mayonnaise

"The city is a cadaver," Dr. Arnoldo Kraus, internist at the ABC Hospital, told me when I asked him about the idea of abandoning the Federal District.

Dr. Kraus was not referring to the idea that the capital was devastated but that it was deserted. Many people left town, taking advantage of the fact that offices and schools would be closed until May 6 (and even then, the return to class of younger children would be extended until the 11th). The World Health Organization designated Mexico on a level five alert, which meant that the epidemic by then was following a planetary course. Even if closing borders and isolating the nation was not recommended, China, Cuba, Peru, Argentina, and Ecuador canceled their flights to Mexico.

On Thursday, April 30th, President Calderón recommended quarantine. He requested we imitate him in his self-sequestration. Naturally, we packed bags to go to Acapulco, where only the waiters wore masks.

After a few days, we returned to a city that was recovering its normal rhythm even though that was not a relief. One of the first to be infected with the AH1N1 virus was Manuel Camacho, former head of government of the Federal District. He was given good treatment in the ABC Hospital and was able to go home. Those who hadn't governed the city did not have the same luck.

This does not mean that private hospitals function impeccably. I had some tests done at Médica Sur, one of our principal health centers. When I went to pick up the reports, the laboratory was closed. Since getting there meant fighting through an hour of traffic, I requested the reports be sent by email or fax. The answer was a jewel of Mexican surrealism: "We can't do that because the pages of the report are stapled." If something like that can happen in a place that claims to run like a Swiss watch, it's easy to imagine what goes on in state-run clinics.

On May 10, Mother's Day was celebrated in freshly opened restaurants. At the entrance to each one was a bottle of disinfectant gel that gave off a barbershop smell. The waiters wore hairnets and masks. By then forty-five people had died of influenza. Those were the confirmed cases. The complete number could only be determined in rumors, legends, and memories. The number of people infected in the United States soon surpassed that of Mexico, perhaps because detection methods there were more efficient. They had more people infected but fewer deaths.

On May 11, children returned to primary schools. The Ministry of Health requested that sanitary measures be at the highest level. This revealed another lack: fifty thousand schools did not have water.

The crisis was very different from what we went through with the 1985 earthquakes. In this case, we ourselves were the threat. Nothing was riskier than contact with a neighbor. The only solidarity we could show was that of a disciplined obedience to official regulations. The response, in that sense, was admirable. A city that lives so that things that involve multitudes accepted the torture of isolation.

But there was no lack of shocks, and panic buying created an opportunity to note two obsessions of the Mexican consumer: cleanliness and condiments. The products sold most widely were chlorine and mayonnaise.

Our lives went on in sequestration and in slow motion. Under those conditions we faced something as serious as the epidemic itself: being unable to do anything but wash our hands. Unlike what happened after the earthquake, it was impossible to go out on the street with a shopping cart to pick up chunks of the city. Helping implied being absent, putting up with impotence and frustration.

We behaved as we should, but others created a deficit. "What bothers me the most is the lack of solidarity in private medicine," said Ricardo Cayuela Gally, at the time managing editor of *Letras Libres*. He was right. For a week there was not a single gesture of support from the large health businesses. The hospitals where the sick person is seen as a customer who has to pay for the thread in his sutures, the box of Kleenex he didn't ask for, and long hours in the parking lot, which is a "separate business" and not a courtesy for clients, could have offered advice, consultations, or free analyses. If one of the large private hospitals had offered ten beds in a gesture of solidarity, it would have shown that not everything depends on the cash nexus.

Businesses too could have done small but significant things, like giving away masks. Telmex set up an orientation service about the influenza. It might have been more generous if the telephonic monopoly had set up a call station for free long-distance calls. Banks, so inventive when it comes to charging fees, did not open lines of credit in solidarity with the sick. The stores that awaken us on Saturday at eight to tell us that they have bargains did not donate beds to public hospitals. The trademark of those businesses was egoism.

Once upon a time there was a precarious country where people survived on chlorine and mayonnaise.

About the death of J. G. Ballard, Rodrigo Fresán wrote: "When reality begins to look too much like your fantasies, the time to leave has come." The English visionary left behind a world very close to ours in his stories. On the night of April 23, as I was writing my obituary note about Ballard, the president declared a state of emergency. What we lived through after that resembles the poetics of disaster of the author of *Crash*.

Little by little, we returned to a strange common life. From our initial hysteria, we moved on to habit and began to see the influenza as an exaggerated kind of cold against which you have to be vaccinated.

Beyond fear and epidemic, something curious was awaiting us: a reality that, in effect, resembled our fantasies too closely. Argentine novelist Rodrigo Fresán suggests that's the time to leave. For a Mexican novelist, it's the time to stay.

City Characters

The Quack

The charlatanism of our politicians, able to separate, with pleasure, words from deeds, obliges us to review the etymology of a word that in Mexico is the equivalent of something more than a pitch man and something less than a shaman: *merolico*.

Thanks to the fact that the Los Reyes publishing company brought out a facsimile edition of *Merolico's Memoirs (Memorias de Merolico)* with an attractive prologue by Jesús Guzmán Urióstegui, we can reconstruct the career of the character who came to Mexico like a hurricane of non-sense: Rafael Juan de Meraulyock, who would be known among his regular clients as Merolico.

Even though he only spent a year in the capital (1879–1880), not a day went by without his making life complicated or spouting rhetoric to sell the pearly waters of his cure-all. His influence in the nation came to be so great that congress had to debate a new law about professions. Was there any way in which this dentist, magician, physician, and actor could legally exercise his multiplicity?

The plazas of Mexico City listened to him, totally absorbed, women fell at his feet, reporters sought him out in the El Globo cantina. Dressed like a comic-opera character (blue frock coat adorned with eleven medals and lettuce-green tie), he would announce on his posters that he would stab a knife through his neck, as a martyr to some undefined oriental torture. But every time he appeared in public he wiggled out of that promise because he had more than enough vocabulary to deny the facts. Consummate con artist that he was, the only risk he took with his throat was an excess of words and the wine he loved so much.

According to Guzmán Urióstegui's calculations, while in Mexico, this medicine man extracted "around four thousand five hundred teeth, at the rate of three hundred a day." What could be more logical for someone whose eloquence left the public with its mouth hanging open than to take advantage of the situation and pull teeth? Actually, the statistic of three hundred extractions per day seems more appropriate for a wizard than an express dentist.

In his memoirs, Merolico tells how his life began in a Switzerland of "patient cows." Before he reached Mexico, he'd visited enough Spanish-speaking countries to perfect his adjectives. He wrote his autobiography with help of two journalists and published it as a foretaste of a work that promised to be as long and agitated as Casanova's. In the style of the great libertines of the Enlightenment, he transformed the confession of his excesses into a morality: a cynic details his vices in order to bring enlightenment through his defects. An enemy of tedium, he repudiated proper behavior with an aphorism: "Innocence is an essentially monotonous thing."

Merolico's star revolved around money. "For me, all metallic value is equal to the stars, themselves coins worth eight *duros* that God counts in order to amuse himself at night leaning over a blue and ebony counter, things we see but cannot touch, imponderable bodies, as scientific vocabularies call them." He sought gold like a gold miner guided by astral precepts. In other words, the esoteric arts enabled him to earn a very terrestrial fortune.

The last part of his *Memoirs* is dedicated to Mexico. One trait defines his literary style: a competitive spirit for comparing one thing unfavorably with another. Himself a disguise artist, he laments that Mexican ladies dress to be seen by others, like actresses in a theater, and try to change the color of their hair. He is even harder on his verbal colleagues: the journalists he meets in "third-rate restaurants, where the meat smokes first as beefsteak and after a week rises to the rank of croquettes." In editorial offices he confirms the venality of the medium: "sell-out newspapers and newspapers for sale."

Not to be trusted, "intent on leading public opinion astray," journalists are, despite everything, the nicest people he meets. On the other hand, he despises congressmen, maximum usurpers of language. Merolico owes his life to his public, unlike the paid counterfeiters who nap in comfort on their thrones. The man who sells potions for eternal life considers himself closer to the truth than the legislators:

> I've listened to three speeches, and none was as good, let it be said with no modesty, of the folk eloquence, which in its motley form made my fortune out in the public plaza from the height of my portable podium. It's true that the good people expect much more from my enchanted flask than from the poisonous pills fabricated in that laboratory from which come laws based on bribes along with the suspension of legal rights.

The polemicist is incapable of describing reality without challenging it to a duel. The congressmen provided him with the best targets possible: he considers them traitors who should wear a sign on their chests saying "FOR RENT!"

Like all keepers of hermetic knowledge, Merolico distrusts rivals to his wisdom. He discovers that in Mexico's social fog, appearances are worth more than realities. "At a gathering of fifty people, I was able to count forty-five national glories." The principal trick of the Mexican wise man consists in living without having to justify his profession. They're all called "doctor" (including carpenters), but none has a specific specialty. "I've noticed that the wise men of Mexico have never pursued a career. They are free-ranging wise men." Their talents are cultivated in secret, and they never lower themselves to the vulgarity of telling anyone what they are. Some combine filth with patriotism: "I know one who only washes himself with his own tears. He weeps every September 16."

Sharp-edged Merolico could not remain for long in a country where lying is a form of courtesy, where insults begin with the phrase "with all due respect." One year was enough for him to depart with his tricks for greener pastures. His fleeting visit left a lasting vision in a country which has not changed very much.

Ever since, in Mexican Spanish, a *merolico* is someone who tries to convince using a torrent of words: "Don't let anyone tell you, let no one tell you a tale; step inside and see it, the greatest elixir"; "Oaxaca tacos, piping hot"; "Bring home this rubber loaf of bread to play a trick on your cousin, your sister, your mother in law"; "they're marvelous, only a peso, they can remove any number of calluses"; "Just look here: a CD of orphic quality and the best romantic music."

This rhetorical impulse is so deeply rooted that it's used in circumstances where there is no need to convince. The security guards at Mexican airports are uniformed *merolicos:* "Place your electronic devices, your belt, your keys, your glasses, your loose change in the tray. Have you taken out your cell phone?"

Curiously enough, all this is said to a person who has already placed all those things on a tray—right before the guard's eyes. In our superstitious way of life, words are conjuring devices: only what is said aloud exists.

Beyond the security gate, in the airport duty-free shop, the traveler confirms yet another of Merolico's legacies: in Mexico, merchandise is not sold on its own. At the entrance to each section, an employee recites "Perfumes for the lady" or "Sir, we have your brand of whiskey." The only offer never proffered in those places is silence. Merolico convinced us that what is not spoken is not sold.

In honor of the foreigner who one afternoon took his place in the Plaza del Seminario, shook his sky-blue frock coat, and offered Mexicans the opportunity to free themselves forever from their terrible toothaches, we've come to use a word unknown in other Spanish-speaking nations.

The unforgettable Rafael Juan de Meraulyock did more than merely carrying out his fraud: he had the bravery to incriminate himself and to compare his intrepid truths with the simulation going on all around him. The frankness of the con man works through contrast: when he confesses his trickery, he calls into question all those who pretend to live in a state of purity. Unfortunately, nowadays, his legacy exclusively refers to public street cries or commercial soliloquies, not to the self-criticism he also practiced.

Words are shadows of disappeared bodies. Merolico's name now only defines those who abuse language to offer snake oil, the full-time charlatan, the seller with no substance.

Rafael Juan de Meraulyock would be surprised to see that his name is linked to this demagoguery, which to him always seemed the property of congressmen.

Places

Santo Domingo

Four monks live in the Convent of Santo Domingo, which in its days of glory housed up to one hundred and fifty friars and which today could hold, with room to spare, at least fifteen. The site is about to receive the designation *house* from the authorities of the Dominican Order in Rome, because it has lost relevance in the Mexican community. The lack of vocations and the scarcity of the faithful has caused one of the most beautiful Baroque temples of the eighteenth century to lose importance in the eyes of those who founded it.

The church presides over my favorite plaza in the city, which in the style of the books and characters of the Uruguayan author Juan Carlos Onetti seems to pass through brief moments of glory and long periods of oblivion.

In 1977, Manuel Capetillo published his phantasmagoric novel *Plaza de Santo Domingo* and re-created a location alien to tourism and favorable to ghosts, who seek refuge among the ruins. That same year, Fernando del Paso released his encyclopedic novel *Palinuro de México*. The protagonist is a member of Galen's hosts and studies in the Medical School located in the former Palace of the Inquisition, also created by the Dominicans. One chapter reconstructs the neighborhood where Palinuro investigates the mysteries of the body to the rhythm of the bells that court the spirit.

The literary revival of the plaza did little to change its fate. Even though it's only a few blocks from the Zócalo, Santo Domingo has something of "a place apart" to it. Not that it lacks interesting features. The Ministry of Public Education is located there (with titanic examples of Mexican mural painting), the Evangelist passages, the hostel, which houses the oldest restaurant in the capital, the dazzling Dominican church, and the ancient tribunal of the Inquisition, transformed into a university museum. Despite all that, this is one of those places travelers discover a bit by accident, only if they venture beyond the obligatory routes.

When I published an article in *Reforma* about the surprising philosophic homilies produced in Santo Domingo by Brother Carlos Mendoza, I thought it was enough simply to write the name of the church, the first seat of the order, for some interested party to go to listen to him. To my surprise, several readers went to Mixoac, where another church has the same name. As you see, this was not an obvious reference point in our urban life.

Perhaps my interest derived from the gossip that enchants every writer. A few key episodes in my family history took place there. It was there my father agreed to meet a girl who'd promised to run away with him and who stood him up (it's to that failed meeting I owe my existence). Also, my daughter's baptism took place in the oratory of the church, the same place where I attended the solemn Mass to honor the memory of Carlos Fuentes Lemus. It was also in that place that I tried to dissolve the family curse by making a date to meet a girl who knew the most diverse variations of artistic transgression, but who was unaware that radical things can also take place in the Masses of Brother Carlos, to whom, to further perfect coincidence, she was distantly related. Unlike my father's reluctant girlfriend, this woman did show up for the meeting, which sanctioned the reactivation of the eternal question: Do we suffer more from the anxieties of lost love or requited love?

I'll close the curtain on the intimate woes of my family. In any case, they offer no justification for the importance of Santo Domingo. Suffice it to say that constitutes one of those emblematic sites where the members of our small tribe not only peruse statues, heraldic emblems, and bell towers: we know that "things happened there."

That private impulse stimulates my interest in the place. Building the temple began in the sixteenth century, but its current configuration dates from the eighteenth century. Because of the Reform campaigns and the confiscation of clerical property, the convent lost a substantial part of its property, which became Leandro Valle Street.

In the plaza passageways, the "Evangelists" are to be found, scribes who for years wrote out letters for boyfriends with a surplus of love and a deficit of writing ability. Over time, they became part of the vast industry of pirated documents. In 1926, these writers of the people formed the Union of Public Typists and Typographers of the Federal District. On those keys, theses have been written and published, apocryphal credentials confabulated, inventories invented, wills and other testaments whipped up. Writing culture prospers in Santo Domingo with an underground economy that does not seem to upset the *Corregidora* Josefa Ortiz de Domínguez, whose effigy presides over the plaza. The work of Jesús Contreras, the exalted sculptor of *Malgré Tout*. The statue, dedicated to the memory of the pioneer independence figure who lived in the neighborhood for a few years, provides the inevitable institutional touch to the urban setting.

Founded by clerics who constructed a church, a convent, and an Inquisitorial jail, the zone had many uses. While there is no lack of cafés or cantinas, the spirit of the plaza is set by a successful mixture of things official with things illicit. In Mexico, there is no greater proof of economic dynamism than the combination of things authorized with things improvised. The "Evangelists" print "official documents" just opposite the Ministry of Public Education, while vendors of Chinese trinkets also have one of their bastions there. A few steps from the Ministry and on the same side of the street stands the National Coordination of Literature of the National Institute of Fine Arts. The writer Silvia Molina directed that office for some time and found out that to make things work she had to be on the good side of Martita, secretary to the leader of the ambulatory vendors of the zone, who ran the block where the National Coordination stands. In this land of paradoxes, underground commerce is highly organized.

Every day, hundreds of vendors crisscross the plaza with dollies loaded with merchandise destined for the local streets. Santo Domingo is more a passage than a market. It also serves as a forum for the protests of the passersby. The eyes of Josefa Ortiz de Domínguez fearlessly contemplate independent Mexico, where some demand more Chinese toys and others demand fewer Chinese toys.

By day, it's filled with people. By night, the place forces you to remember that only five Dominican friars live there. What is the future of the founders of the plaza? No one has defended that project more energetically than Brother Julián Pablo, who was the prior of Santo Domingo for many long years, a protean artist who became friend and confessor to the Spanish film director Luis Buñuel (nothing better than a good priest to keep a heretic on guard). Educated as a painter and architect, Julián took charge of the restoration of the neoclassical altar designed by Manuel Tolsá, the architect who designed the cathedral and the sculptor of the equestrian statue of Carlos IV, known as *The Little Horse*. To moderate the excessively white tone of the columns and the frontispiece, the Dominican artist adorned the altar with an attractive and illusory air of marble veins.

Julián Pablo lived in a room within the building, beyond the sacristy, where hangs perhaps the best and the most disturbing painting made in New Spain: *The Lactation of Saint Dominic* by Cristóbal de Villalpando. The immense oil has as its principal figures the three theological virtues—faith, hope, and charity—represented by three voluptuous women. These three are followed by a tumultuous army of women. An indisputable eroticism flows from the painting.

In that context of the empowering of women, the founder of the order receives a gush of milk from the breast of the Virgin Mary. The escorting army enhances the simultaneously erotic, maternal, and military sense of the gesture. The squirt of milk in the saint's mouth constitutes the "action" of the painting. The multitude of powerfully sensual women explains the effort and the desires necessary for that fragile moment to occur.

Once, Julián Pablo told me that he was responsible for Luis Buñuel's ashes. Villalpando's picture—rebellious exaltation of the faith—would seem to be the ideal accompaniment for the creator of *Un Chien Andalou*. Besides, it wouldn't be odd that the monk who revealed the works of Fellini, Visconti, Godard, Truffaut, Rosi, and so many others in the film series he organized in the University Cultural Center, which the Dominicans manage and which is located to one side of the National University, was the executor in charge of Buñuel's mortal remains.

The director's children have denied the veracity of that story, and Brother Julián preferred to evade a response, avoiding the subject with the sinuous eloquence that led him to compare religion with bullfighting and the priest with the nimble bullfighter who gambles his fate in the face of an inscrutable deity.

A friend of Carlos Fuentes, José Luis Cuevas, Octavio Paz, Ramón Xirau, and a good number of Mexican artists, Julián transformed spirituality into something so open and suggestive that it stimulated a heretic like Buñuel. Nothing like a good adversary to make you reconsider your own convictions.

In 2008, at the age of eighty-three, Brother Julián died after being the best religious witness of Mexican bohemian life during the second half of the twentieth century. One of his most outstanding disciples is Carlos Mendoza. With a doctorate in philosophy from the University of Freiburg and now professor at the Iberoamerican University, Mendoza represents, at the age of fifty-six, an example of renovation in theology and in social vocation within the Church.

Among Brother Julián's sermons, I remember two on the same subject: the difficulty of consolation when someone we love dies. The premature death of Carlos Fuentes Lemus, poet, painter, and photographer, called into question the superstition that says life has laws. His parents, the novelist Carlos Fuentes and the journalist Silvia Lemus, attended the Mass with unusual fortitude. The setting alluded to the huge efforts that the species has made for centuries to endure the inevitable outrage of death. The beauty of the temple, Bach's music, a song by Elvis Presley, young Carlos's favorite singer, did not alleviate the pain. In that situation, Julián said something similar to what he would say at the side of the coffin of the poet and philosopher Ramón Xirau: "Can pain erase the joys attained by the one who dies? There is no reason to be ungrateful toward God," he commented, an invitation to make memory another form of good fortune.

With regard to Mendoza: I'm putting together tatters of the words he spoke in March 2015 about Lent. Following Hannah Arendt, Simone Weil, and Giorgio Agamben, he spoke about Jesus' empty tomb ("this is the house of one who has disappeared"), similar to those of so many family members who searched for their children in the common graves that have transformed Mexico into a cemetery.

That Sunday, Mendoza reflected on the heaviness of the real in a violent and corrupt world and about the challenges we face to reach lightness under such precarious conditions. He recalled the challenging attitude of Jesus when he was judged, a yoke that imposes an end but does not supply the means to carry it through, and the rebellious words of Saint Augustine that legitimize the heterodox paths of passion, whenever that is carried out in love of one's fellow man. In an appropriate way, he chose the biblical passage where Jesus expels the money changers from the temple in order to criticize those who pay their respects at the altar of consumption. That day, the church of Santo Domingo became a lecture hall where the value of ethics in a time of discrimination and inequality was discussed. The words spoken by Mendoza were rigorously ancient and modern: a living tradition.

Understood as an obligatory ritual, the liturgy is a kind of tedium. Going to Mass is almost always disillusioning. Nevertheless, something repeated so often can still be an instrument for reflection, rebelliousness, and discomfiture. You do not have to be a Christian or even a person of faith to appreciate these sermon-lectures by Brother Carlos or Brother Julián.

What fate is the Santo Domingo clock counting out? For Carlos Mendoza, the logical destiny of the convent would be to become a museum which could still function as a church. That would allow Villalpando's painting to leave the dark sacristy and be shown in the church's main nave, and for the New Spain–style chasubles of the Dominicans—whose very weave reflects the cultural crossings of that era (silk brought here on the China fleet, Mexican gold thread), and which Brother Julián wore with the elegance of a leading man—to be exhibited in a gallery.

The painting with the armed women would inaugurate a pictorial tour of the plaza, which would go from the lactation of the saint to the murals of Jean Charlot, Amado de la Cueva, Diego Rivera, and David Alfaro Siqueiros, and to the sculpture of Ignacio Asúnsolo in the patios of the Ministry of Public Education, as well as to the paintings of Roberto Montenegro in the minister's office.

Originally, the building that houses the ministry was the Convent of the Incarnation, which caused consternation among the Dominicans because of the excessive proximity of so many women to the members of the order (in this sentence the pun is operative). Years later, Diego Rivera would make the building disturbing for another reason. In 1925, the Russian poet Vladimir Mayakovski traveled to Mexico to learn about the effects of a revolution that preceded that of the Soviets and contemplated the almost two hundred panels the painter was creating on the ministry walls. He wrote: "This first Communist mural in the world is now the object of the most furious attacks by the most outstanding members of President Calles' government."

The pictorial tour could conclude in Mexico's oldest restaurant, the Hostel of Santo Domingo, which preserves its sixteenth-century shape. The property, supposedly, was sold off by the Dominicans when they couldn't pay the debts they'd run up in consuming wax. Too many candles had burned without receiving in exchange sufficient tithes.

That is the mythical origin of the contemporary cathedral of chicken breast in cream and burnt milk fudge. The stained glass window of the restaurant is a reproduction of the cover of the menu designed by José Gómez Rosas, the Hotentot, and the mural that decorates the far end of the restaurant—a view of the Santo Domingo plaza in colonial days, a picture that in the 1980s adorned the one thousand peso note—was painted in 1956 by Antonio Albanés.

Nowadays, the most accessible works for visitors are those in the Hostel. Villalpando's painting occupies a secluded place in the sacristy of the temple, and you have to get permission from the ministry to see their murals. The future of the plaza will depend on making visible a fascinating mass of work, which hasn't become clandestine, but it deals all too excessively with discretion.

Most of the churches and convents in Italy have been saved by becoming museum spaces. For now, Santo Domingo seems to be going in the opposite direction and is moving toward being considered, with the modesty conferred by abandonment, as the simple dwelling place of five monks, a "house."

Death of a Poet

About fellow-poet Jaime Torres Bodet, José Emilio Pacheco wrote that he lived the life of a functionary and died the death of a poet. He occupied the office decorated with the signs of the zodiac that José Vasconcelos had designed when he was the first secretary of public education. He committed suicide in his own office, which was later bought by the literary historian José Luis Martínez.

Santo Domingo Plaza was the setting for Torres Bodet's bureaucratic chores and the place where yet another poet, Manuel Acuña, killed himself. "Whom the gods love, die young," as the saying puts it, one that goes all the way back to classical Greece and took on dramatic modernity with the 27 Club in rock music (Jimi Hendrix, Brian Jones, Kurt Cobain, Jim Morrison, Amy Winehouse, Janis Joplin). In *The Myth of Sisyphus*, Albert Camus points out that the only truly serious philosophical problem is suicide. Is there any way to explain those who make the decision to accelerate their fate with their own hand? Let's make the question more precise: Is there any way to explain those cases when there are no explanatory factors like an incurable sickness or the possibility of dying under enemy fire? I remember the poet Álvaro Mutis at the sessions held at the Citlaltépetl Refuge House speaking about the importance of welcoming to Mexico City writers persecuted for their ideas. Little by little, the subject shifted to poets persecuted by themselves, capable of burning in the excess of their great light: "People think being romantic consists in giving someone chocolates," warned Mutis in the epic voice he used to dub the voice of the narrator in the television series *The Untouchables*. "Nothing like that: the true romantic drinks arsenic, old boy!" he exclaimed, gesturing like an orchestra director concluding a symphony.

Those who make the pilgrimage to the graves of the youthful dead don't always do so out of morbidity or necrophilia. They visit the fatal site more frequently because they're moved by the incomprehensible mystery those willful annihilations represent and which affect the work of the artist like some unfathomable echo chamber.

On December 5, 1873, Acuña returned to room 13, the one he occupied at the Medical School. From 1571 until 1820, the building, constructed by the Dominicans, had been the seat of the court of the Holy

Office and for years a state prison. It was there Brother Servando Teresa de Mier, the Dominican who tried to show that the cult of the Virgin of Guadalupe had pre-Hispanic origins, was imprisoned. After housing the congress and the lottery, the building was handed over to the Medical School. Acuña was studying medicine and lived in a room the few visitors he had described as somber. In this case, the superstitions the number 13 arouse seem validated by the fate of a previous resident, who left that room to join the liberal forces of Santos Degollado and was shot dead in the streets of Tacubaya.

The final hours of the person preparing his own death seem infinite. Manuel Acuña said goodbye to the woman he loved in vain and the next day set his affairs in order. On his desk he left five letters with black ribbons explaining his fate and a glass containing traces of cyanide. A century later, José Emilio Pacheco wrote that this was "his real masterpiece." At the age of twenty-five, the poet calculated the effects of his drama to perfection. On December 5, he met in the Alameda with his friend, the poet Juan de Dios Peza. Seeing the wind tear a leaf off a tree branch, he observed, in the exalted tone of someone who wants his words remembered: "Look, a frozen blast ripped it from the tree prematurely."

He too was preparing a premature exit. He made a date with his friend for the next day, at exactly one o'clock, and he admonished him to be punctual. If he came late, he wouldn't be able to say goodbye before the trip he wanted to take.

They made their farewells in the house of Rosario de la Peña, the woman Acuña loved, the one to whom he dedicated his most famous poem, the "Nocturne to Rosario," fated to become, along with "The Bohemian's Toast" a favorite among professional reciters of poetry:

> Well then! I must
> Tell you that I adore you,
> Tell you that I love you
> with all my heart;
> that all I do is suffer,
> that all I do is weep,
> that I can stand it no more.
> and when I shout that I implore you

I implore you and speak to you in the name
of my last illusion.

Curiously enough, both "The Bohemian's Toast" and "Nocturne for
Rosario" are intensely Oedipal poems. In the first, Guillermo Aguirre
y Fierro has six bohemians drink a toast to the most valuable thing in
their existence. The champion, of course, is the last one: Arturo. After
listening to the eloquent but ultimately empty glories of his friends,
Arturo raises his glass to the only praiseworthy thing in this world: "To
my mother, bohemians!" This hyperbolic phrase of self-referential passion would engender the celebrated newspaper column in which Carlos
Monsiváis would quote the nonsense spoken by politicians.

The rejection Acuña suffered may be explained by two verses from
the same poem in which he announced that his love would arrive with
absolutely essential complement:

> And between the two of us
> my mother, like a God.

We know that after visiting Rosario, the poet returned to his room
in the Medical School. The next day he woke up late, as if he had no
other problem than preparing his death. He arranged the five letters he'd
written the previous evening, wrote a note to exonerate anyone else, and
drank the dose of cyanide, which left an aroma of bitter almonds in the
room.

Juan de Dios Peza was the first to breathe in the fragrant air in which
his friend had died. Thus, the legend of the suffering poet and his dis-
dainful muse was consolidated. On December 2, 1973, Pacheco, in one
of the first appearances of his column *Inventory*, which he would publish
until his death in 2016, wrote that "Rosario was a romantic dime-novel
character":

> Her fiancé, Colonel Juan Espinosa de los Monteros y Gorostiza, hero
> of the liberal wars, died in a sword duel in Mixcoac, in December of
> 1868. Espinosa de los Monteros fought his friend Arancivia because
> Arancivia made a joke to Rosario about one of the colonel's suppos-
> edly cowardly acts.

The ghost of the lover who died in a duel hovered in some way over the gatherings that brought together the two generations of liberals every Wednesday and Saturday in Rosario's salon, first in the entry to San Diego and later in Santa Isabel. It was there that the men of the Reform and the struggle against Intervention—Altamirano, Ignacio Ramírez, Guillermo Prieto—met with the younger men, the heirs of the promise.

All of them fell in love with Rosario, all left verses in an album that Ramírez described as an altar placed "at the feet of the goddess." Neither José Martí nor the young Luis G. Urbina, who met her twenty years after that December, escaped her enchantment. Rosario only responded to one poet, Manuel M. Flores, and with exemplary fidelity remained at his side until he died in 1885, syphilitic and blind.

Marco Antonio Campos, in his essay "Manuel Acuña in Mexico City," brings revealing facts to this case of, in the tradition of the Spanish Baroque poet Francisco de Quevedo, "love constant beyond death." One is the sarcasm with which fate deals with its victims. Acuña had been baptized by a priest named, of all things, Manuel Flores, the name of the friend who would arouse the love of his beloved.

Both Acuña and Flores appear in various engravings wearing the mustaches in Three Musketeers style that distinguished Romantic poets. Perhaps because of the disparity in their respective fates, Acuña is represented with sunken cheeks and Flores with the haughty face of a captain who defies storms.

Campos describes the room where Acuña died with the exactitude of someone who'd been there: "There was a cot with a tattered mattress covered by a Saltillo sarape, a bureau at the head of the bed, a rickety table painted light blue, three broken-down armchairs, and a book case made from boxes with three long shelves." With the same proximity, he describes the romance between Acuña and Laura Méndez, a poet of great intelligence and unequaled literary production with whom he had a child who died almost at birth, one month and eleven days after its father. The eternal courting of Rosario barely lasted from May to December of 1873. In the meanwhile, the poet carried on a more tangible and less impassioned relationship with Laura.

Sunken in poverty, disillusioned with medicine, incapable of contenting himself with his early literary glories, Acuña swung back and forth between his possible love for the woman poet and his impossible love for the muse of the poets. Two texts describe the extremes of this pendular swing: "To Laura" and "Nocturne for Rosario." The relevance of both is asymmetrical: the poet wouldn't be remembered for the words of requited love but for those of unrequited love. In a curious way, these poems sanction a reading in which they argue with each other and prolong in their verses the poet's vacillations.

Posterity invents posthumous duels in which the struggle persists in interpretations. Rosario de la Peña y Llerena was conquered in life by Manuel M. Flores, but was never able to marry him, just as she was never able to marry Espinosa de los Monteros, the fiancé who died in a duel trying to reestablish his reputation in her eyes. He was the man Acuña viewed as a posthumous rival. Rosario's tragic aura—she was rather more than a muse and rather less than a widow—would transform her into a legend and into the magnetic inspiration of other poets. Quite properly, she hated the idea of being linked to those deaths. As Campos tells it, for decades she contradicted herself in numerous interviews, vainly trying to modify the image Mexican culture had made of her.

Posterity insists in creating its own duels. Espinosa de los Monteros and Acuña fought in the next world. Both died, not because of her but because they used her as a pretext. But the colonel did not write poems that could ignite the popular imagination, so Acuña beat the soldier in that territory.

In another posthumous skirmish, he also overcame his colleague and namesake Manuel M. Flores. The "Nocturne" ultimately simplified the fame of an exceptional woman. As Marco Antonio Campos puts it, "Contradicting every biographical and historical truth, she would end up not as the Rosario of Flores but the Rosario of Acuña."

The story of what happened to the poet who lived virtually on loans in the Medical School would become an urban legend to which people from time to time would try to add truculent details. In one of the more scabrous versions, the poet meets Laura when she's just lost her father, takes advantage of her suffering, possesses her next to the coffin, she becomes pregnant, and he is left to repent about a passion that borders on crime.

The fact is that Manuel Acuña's brief life had an infinite denouement. One of his most celebrated poems anticipates those transfigurations. The medical school student writes: "Standing Before a Cadaver" and understands the body to be a "sovereign laboratory" where decomposition does not lead to nothingness but to the transformation of matter:

> And amid these interior changes
> your skull filled with a new life
> will yield flowers instead of thoughts.

Time has a curious way of measuring cities. Works conceived for eternity crumble, and fugitive instants return to us. On December 6, 1873, Manuel Acuña was found dead in his modest room on Santo Domingo Plaza.

That moment has never stopped taking place.

Shocks

The Disappearance of the Sky

hat distinguishes the city from other oceans? Nothing defines it better than an idea Carlos Monsiváis suggested but never completely developed: the post-apocalypse.

Even though danger signs abound in the environment, we believe that no harm can come to us. Our best method for combating drama is to think it already happened. "It was hard going, but we pulled through." This strange collective delusion allows us to think that we're beyond the apocalypse: we're the result, not the cause of the evils. It would be impossible to trace the nuclear radiation, the Richter scale 10 tremor, or the epidemic that left us this way. The decisive factor is that we feel we're on the other side of the disaster. Deferring tragedy toward a vague past is our habitual therapy. That explains the vitality of a threatened site that challenges both reason and ecology.

Seen from the present moment, the laudatory comments of the conquistador Bernal Díaz del Castillo (Tenochtitlán as a new Venice) seem like bitter jokes (not to mention the exaltation of Bernardo de Balbuena in his *Mexican Grandeur [La grandeza Mexicana]* ["From the regal nature of its sober streets, / very comparable to a chessboard"]).

The third-millennium citizen of the capital knows his city is a disaster. The yellow helicopters of Radio Red report that once again there are three hundred points of ozone in the air, and specialists mention the catastrophic processes that may leave us their visiting card. In *The Surface of the Earth (La superficie de la Tierra)*, José Lugo Hubp catalogues the threats that hang over the capital: floods, earthquakes, torrents of mud, eruptions, and the melting of the volcanoes.

We chilangos are not misinformed. We inventory calamities as if some fantastic algebra would nullify the total number of negative values. We're experts in signs of deterioration, we compare our rashes, we talk about babies with lead in their blood, and pregnant women with placenta previa. It isn't ignorance that keeps us here. We like the city more than we like the truth. Like the Don Juan in Stravinsky's opera *The Rake's Progress,* we've fallen in love with the bearded lady in the circus.

We love a terrible scenario whose defects we attribute to some past time: we live disasters as flashbacks, the mythical wound that we were fortunately able to survive. The result can be monstrous, but it is always ours. One of Monsiváis's aphorisms summarizes this tense way of loving the city: "There is no worse nightmare than the one that excludes us." We have to stay right here.

Although all metropolises arise against nature, few have had the destructive fury of Mexico City, where the annihilation of the ecosystem has been carried out with fanatical literalism.

In its origin, Tenochtitlán had two skies: the clouds were reflected in a lagoon. The history of the city narrates a double annihilation, that of the air and that of the water.

The floating empire of the Aztecs, which Renaissance cartographers compared to Utopia and its circles of water, was reduced to the dying canals of Xochimilco.

Built on a lake, México-Tenochtitlán lived to fight floods until the entire valley became desiccated. In the seventeenth century, the city was flooded for five years, and later, Sor Juana Inés de la Cruz wrote her poem "Castalian Flood," referring to the fountain touched by the hoof of Pegasus. If the hybrid animal represented creole New Spain, the floodwaters could be linked to that mythological spring. All of which allows us to think that the capital, far from sinking in the waves, received a providential baptism.

The German Heinrich Martin, who Hispanified his name as Enrico

Martínez, was a cosmographer, an interpreter for the Holy Inquisition, typographer, and hydraulic engineer. In 1607, he took charge of the project to drain the water that threatened to cover the streets. Little by little, the lake dried, until it was buried. Today, next to the cathedral, a statue commemorates Enrico Martínez. In a way consistent with the person who dedicated himself to fighting the work of water, the pedestal of his statue is used to measure the sinking of Mexico City.

Once the lake had disappeared, the work of destruction shifted to the air. Industrial smoke, the dust from the lacustrine valley, and the bellowing of automobiles set about blurring the sky. Chilangopolis looks more and more like the primeval grotto: Chicomoztoc, the dark chamber.

Our landscape is marked by those fundamental losses: stoplights burn over a buried lake, and planes disappear in a foggy cream, a nonexistent sky. A few years ago, when I went to see a show of children's drawings, I confirmed the fact that no child used blue to represent the sky; their crayons chose another shade for reality: "coffee-blue."

It's no accident, then, that Mexican literature documents the destruction of the air. In 1869, Ignacio Manuel Altamirano visited the Candelaria de los Patos neighborhood and talked about the "deleterious atmosphere" threatening the city; in 1904, Amado Nervo exclaimed "Our blue sky has been stolen!" In 1940, Alfonso Reyes asked "Is this the most transparent region of the air? What have you done to my high, metaphysical valley?" Three decades later, Octavio Paz would answer him:

> the sun did not drink the lake
> the earth did not swallow it
> the water did not return to the air
> men were the executors of dust

The subject also comes up in fiction. In 1958, Carlos Fuentes used Alfonso Reyes's expression, which by then could only be ironic, as the title of the first novel where the city is the main character: *Where the Air Is Clear*.

This impulse could not be absent from the work of the greatest critic of progress in twentieth-century Mexican literature: José Emilio Pacheco. The poetry of the author of *I Look at the Earth (Miro la tierra)* comprehends the world as a besmirched Garden of Eden and animals as mistreated species, all of them in danger of extinction. Even when he isn't dealing directly with ecocide, Pacheco hears an alarm ringing. His longest novel, *You Shall Die Far from Here (Morirás lejos)*, takes place in a Mexico City plaza and deals with the tense relationship between a fugitive and someone who is possibly spying on him. Even though the plot focuses on anti-Semitic persecution, you'll find there a solitary description of the urban landscape marked by the fall of the sky: "The air is polluted. Little by little, its poison corrodes and wastes away everything. Toxic substances float over the city, the mountains keep them from dissipating, the forests were chopped down, and in the valley, there no longer exists a vegetation that can destroy carbonic anhydride."

That image was composed in 1986, a time that now seems idyllic. Like Altamirano, Nervo, and Reyes before him, Pacheco contemplates the city as a site where the sky escapes.

In 1967, the year of one of our most severe tremors, Jaime Torres Bodet wrote "Statute," a poem he ultimately excluded from his book *No Truce (Sin truega)*:

> City: you were. You are no longer. You were flattened
> by streetcars, automobiles, magnesium lit nights.
> To see the landscape
> now, I need a precise,
> slow X-ray machine.
> What a sickness, your trees! What a ruin
> your sky.

Literature has been exactly the device Torres Bodet demands to check the city submerged under its many transfigurations. In that seismic year of 1967, the Angel of Independence fell to earth in Paseo de la Reforma. It was a symbolic moment in the life of the city: the sky stopped being above; that was the message the Angel was offering in its disorientation, but we were slow to understand it.

"The only problem with going to the Heavens," writes Augusto Monterroso, "is that you can see the heavens from there." We live in the imperfect paradise that can't see itself.

At night, the city lights up like a surprising sky come to earth. An episode from Italo Calvino's *Invisible Cities* enables us to conjecture about how this landscape came about and about what hidden intention it obeys. In that book, Marco Polo tells stories about his journey to the emperor of the Tartars in order to kill his boredom and inquire into the secret logic that animates urban spaces. One of the places that intrigues him most has grown in the style of a galaxy in the celestial dome. What justifies that design? Allow me to retell the story, taking some liberties.

For decades, legions of bricklayers construct walls and terrepleins that seem to follow the caprices of a demented god. The city is a delirium of construction. A day comes when, fed up with their aimless work, the men reject the sand and cement. Construction has become madness. Can there be a purpose to that effort?

Suddenly, among the hordes of workers appears someone who is the equivalent of an architect, a figure capable of fathoming a clear drawing in the chaos. The discordant workers interrogate him. Is there a plan that explains their labors, a meaning to the streets and buildings that endlessly multiply?

"Wait until dark and turn out all the lights," says the architect.

When the last lamp is turned off, the workers contemplate the celestial dome. Then they understand the project.

Up above, the map of the city shines.

When you land at night in Mexico City, you see lights that stretch out like a mantle of stars. It's certainly an exaggeration to suppose that the blue of the sky disappeared so the city could become its reflection, but those are the compensations the post-apocalyptic mind seeks, indispensable for living here.

Crossings

The City Is the Sky of the Metro

People who land by night in the city feel they've reached a galaxy. Following the dynamics of all macropoli, that luminous mantle should go on growing. What might its end point be? The arrows point down; the subsoil is our final frontier.

Construction in the center of Mexico City means practicing accidental archaeology. Setting foundations, laying telephone or sewer lines, all have to feel their way through the submerged Aztec city. This not only implies the possible discovery of a pyramid but contact with a cosmogony. In "Pre-Hispanic Myths," Enrique Florescano writes, "The idea that the interior of the earth contained a cave where essential foods were stored and where life was regenerated is the dominating concept of Mesoamerican creation myths." The dead and the origin are under the earth. It is no accident that the principal legends of the Indigenous world (the sagas of Quetzalcóatl or the prodigious twins of the *Popol Vuh*) narrate journeys to the underworld.

In 2017, we, descendants of the tribe that in emblematic form came from Chicomoztoc, "the place of the seven caves," live in a landscape marked by displacements and the search for new routes in the subsoil.

According to Paul Virilio, the pulse of a postmodern city is measured by the way in which time destroys space. There the greatest challenge is not building but speed. In a site like México-Tenochtitlán, born against water and sky, whose governing mechanisms are growth and movement, and which assigns a strong symbolic value to the underworld, there is no greater zone of definition than the metro.

In "Underground as Utopia," the Russo-German philosopher Boris Groys reflects on the Moscow subway, which in the Soviet imagination had a role similar to that of the Collective Transportation System in Mexico. Unable to construct an egalitarian utopia, Stalinism established an extensive simulation industry. One of its most efficacious compensatory mechanisms was the Moscow metro, the palace of the poor: the revolutionary aura was electric and remained underground.

In Alfonso Reyes's translation, *utopia* means "there is no such place." It's a nonexistent territory. Those who wish to approach it must seek solutions through compromise, intermediate zones, heterotopias. "The appropriate strategy for constructing utopias," Groys comments, "consists in finding an uninhabited place, preferably uninhabitable, within an inhabited environment." The projects of the early-twentieth-century Russian "desurbantists," who sought to break down the city-country dichotomy, failed because of their radical unreality. In opposition to the city as a cement forest, they offered an impossible city of exterior space, with mobile houses and pools that moved to the rhythm of the swimming.

On the other hand, the metro does bring to fruition numerous utopian requirements: its advance is unlimited, depending completely on orders from above, and it takes place in a regulated space where the traveler sees fragments of reality while the bulk of the scene remains in darkness. Groys writes, "Although the metro belongs to the reality of the metropolis, it remains fantastic; its totality can be conceived but never experienced."

These traits are shared by all subway systems: what set the Moscow subway apart was its ability to mix diverse eras in order to simulate a subterranean paradise. In its stations, the pictures in Socialist-Realist style and the austere Futurism of the trains shared space with the palace-like splendor of the lamps, a sumptuous architecture from no known place, with Islamic, Romanesque, or Renaissance façades.

Cinematic utopias usually conceive time as a linear progression. Their landscapes are not always convincing because they look too new. True utopia escapes known time. That is one of the insights of the film *Brazil,* whose settings suggest an aged future: the typewriters and the clothes are older than ours, and that confers on them a strange verisimilitude. The future is more credible if it's already used.

By mixing eras and styles, the Moscow metro reinforced its utopian condition. Even so, it was closer to George Orwell's fantasy than Saint Thomas More's. Its efficient spatial-temporal alterity was repressive. Once again, Groys: "The masses do not seem to enjoy the luxury offered up by the metro. They neither want nor can enjoy the art, cannot properly appreciate the fine materials or decipher the ideological symbols. Deaf, blind, and indifferent, they pass through the myriad treasure rooms. The metro is not the paradise of quiet contemplation but the inferno of perpetual motion."

There are curious similarities between the Mexico City and Moscow metros. They are dotted with symbols of failed revolutions; they confuse historical periods, and they take on the substitutional function of "subterranean heaven." Perhaps it's no accident that both were inaugurated one year after critical movements were eradicated. In 1934, the organizations of artists and intellectuals in the Soviet Union were dissolved in order to be brought together under a single, state-controlled organism; the Moscow metro opened in 1935. With regard to Mexico: the Collective Transportation System was the most important public work after the repression of the student movement in 1968.

But what unifies the two metros most strongly is the manipulation of the past. The Mexican metro stands out for its system of signals, a system that seeks to condense tradition visually. In 1969, each station on the line was represented by a pictogram to help illiterates and to allude to pre-Hispanic culture. The color assigned to this first route could not be more emblematic: Mexican Pink *(rosa mexicano).* This was not a map but a codex of orientations that branched out in the lines that followed, all following the same symbolic principle.

This appropriation of the past was accentuated with Aztec motifs in friezes and low reliefs, the presence of pre-Hispanic objects (including a pyramid in the Pino Suárez station), and the names of the stations (Tacuba, Mixcoac, Tezozómoc, Coyoacán, Mixiuhca, Iztapalapa). In

Panteones, next to an Aztec sculpture, a plaque reminds us that the earth is birthplace and grave, "the moist cave of origins," and Mictlán, the realm of the dead.

Bastion of the gray market, seat of exhibitions, concerts, book fairs, territory of suicide or birth, the metro is a city that moves. As in the movie *Brazil,* or in the tunnels of Moscow, the place offers up an extravagant temporal crossword puzzle. The trains are a fine example of French technology, and the design of some stations is so futuristic that they've been used as settings for science fiction apocalypses. The movie *Total Recall,* based on a tale by Philip K. Dick, was filmed in 1989 in the Insurgentes and Chabacano stations. The next year, I visited Chabacano to attend the debut of a composition for string quartet, *Metro Chabacano,* by the composer Javier Álvarez. I was surprised to see that on a high corner of the ceiling there were red stains. I asked an employee what that was: "It's the 'blood' the movie spattered," he answered.

For years, the station managers refused to clean up that "memory of the future."

The cement fretwork, the names of the stations, and the pictographic writing guarantee that the metro makes contact with the past. In that same setting, the cars move frenetically and open their doors for seventeen seconds. We find ourselves in an inconceivable pre-Hispanic modernity.

But the definitive effect of the place does not come from the architecture but from the people with inexpressive faces who ride the metro, as if they'd been bribed to travel. Every day, the Collective Transportation System moves more than five million riders. Even though there are many, they have been chosen. Riding the escalator down means being a witness to a precise racial segregation. The citizens of the underground city—here you may choose your favorite racial slur—are dark-skinned, trash, Indians, Mexicans . . . The gloomy masses that fill the cars seem to look toward the crypts the course of their lives leads them to.

On November 2, 2008, the Day of the Dead, I was one of the four million curious people who went to see the big show in the Zócalo. That November 2, Constitution Plaza was dominated by an immense Mictlantecuhtli, the god of the underworld. As usually happens on our feasts for the dead, almost all the motifs were pre-Hispanic. A triangular Mayan arch decorated with the god Chaac's toy top grabbed attention on one side of the plaza. Colonial Mexico, practically speaking, was barely represented, or only appeared because of the presence of the Metropolitan Cathedral and the National Palace. In eloquent fashion, the only installation related to modernity was a subway car filled with skeletons. The route it was taking could not be more logical: Panteones (cemetery).

Denizen of the entrails of the earth, the metro is the new thing circulating in the grotto of origins. Underground, there is a "no-place" where time bites its tail. The trips may be swift, but the path is subject to the logic of myth—it has neither beginning nor end, and is the place where, symbolically, a pyramid, a cross, and an electric vehicle are strictly contemporaneous.

Octavio Paz tried to reflect this incessant evolving in his writing. His longest poem, *Sunstone,* follows the circular meaning of the "ties connecting Aztec years." "Entire Wind" begins with the verse "the present is perpetual" and *Rappaccini's Daughter (La hija de Rappaccini)* ends with this certainty: "What happened is still happening." The metro circulates like a metaphor imagined by Paz, refutation of times and confirmation of a single, immovable time.

In the festival of the dead, the display metro car was of normal size and could be entered, and a long line of curiosity seekers formed outside. Origin and prophecy, the transportation of skeletons offered contact with pre-Hispanic cosmogony and a mirror of our future. Nearby stood the Mictlantecuhtli display. A sign reminded us that the god of death did not announce the end of things: the underworld is the place of perpetual recycling, where everything begins again. A few meters from there, in the Museum of the Great Temple it was possible to visit the effigy of Tlaltecuhtli, the goddess who devours cadavers and gives birth to new life. The biographies of Aztec deities resemble the routes of Mexican subways.

From a political perspective, we can say beneath the earth two axes of Mexican life intersect: the rhetorical importance of the past and functional racism. In accordance with that discourse, we should be proud of what we were and be selective in our present: "We respect the fact that we aren't equal," says the strangest Mexican "civic" refrain.

On ancient maps, an inscription signaled the dangers of the unknown:

Hic sunt leones (there are lions here). Beyond territory that has been explored live beasts, monsters, and the others. Curiously, a station in our metro bears the name Ethiopia and is decorated with lion effigies. That subterranean Africa suggests that our lions travel on the subway.

Following Jorge Luis Borges, the only thing we know about the future is that it differs from the present. Where do times go on the metro? Where are its half-asleep, robotic, and silent masses going? Perhaps the true lesson of the tunnels consists in imagining the surface from down there in order to give another value to streets, to demonstrate, secretly, that the city is the sky of the metro.

"Take heaven by storm!" shouted a hyperbolic individual who'd just made a landing coming from utopias.

The hordes move forward in the false day of the cars. Outside, virtual and powerful, the city awaits them.

City Characters

The Zombie

I'll call him Rodrigo Woods. We became friends in high school. He'd just moved to the capital, knew no one, and sat down next to me in class. He was a descendant of the legendary Englishmen who'd brought soccer and whiskey to Pachuca. His freckled face with its rectangular jaw proved it. I seemed interesting to him because I wanted to study medicine, but was having difficulty choosing between science and short story writing. For him, there was only one possible career: he wanted to take the Hippocratic oath; life was worthwhile because of illnesses. The surprising thing is that he was more interested in living with them than in curing them. He wasn't a hypochondriac but someone in love with symptoms, a theoretical sick man.

Every week, he would choose some malady and imagine how he'd behave if he had it. With such conviction that he would take on the illness.

"A hypersensitive person cannot run any longer," he said when I criticized him on the basketball court.

With the same conviction, he asked me to finish a history report for him because he was focused on the possibility of suffering from bladder stones.

He didn't enjoy pain or annoyances but did take pleasure in the facts revealed to him by the unforeseeable reactions of the body. He chose himself as the model for an illness in order to study it intensely. When I majored in sociology, he was hard put to forgive me. Even so, his friendship remained constant.

He did in fact enter medical school. His heavy study load made it difficult for our friendship to go on as it had, but we were never out of touch. One day we agreed to meet at the Medical School, outside an auditorium. I arrived before the lecture was over, peeked in at the door, and contemplated a strange scene: Rodrigo stretched out on a pallet, naked from the waist up. The professor was using him to explain how to remove a rib. I entered the hall and sat down in the last row. One of his classmates explained that whenever a volunteer was needed to pose as a patient, my friend would raise his hand.

As the years went by, his ability to introject sufferings led him to psychiatry, the field he currently works in with great success and another name (you will soon see why I talk about him using a pseudonym). A few months ago, he said: "The person myself is has no name."

He talked that way because he was studying Cotard's syndrome. I was familiar with the subject because of the *Brief Clinical Dictionary of the Soul* by the physician and writer Jesús Ramírez-Bermúdez, but even so I couldn't impress him. Instead of celebrating our common interest, Rodrigo Woods looked at me sadly. For him, I will always be someone who wasted his life by not becoming a doctor.

I managed to get him to talk to me about his new favorite malady. At the end of the nineteenth century, the French psychiatrist Jules Cotard diagnosed this "negation delirium," a special variation of melancholy in which the sick person takes on an absolute and defensive negation. Isolated from all responsibility, the patient defends himself from the outside and dynamites his language, trying to express himself through the strange path of verbal impoverishment. In this way, he protects himself. Transformed into nothing, he cannot be affected: he lacks lack. The apocalypse has already occurred, and he survives without hope.

Hearing that, I thought that it was the ideal suffering for the citizens of Mexico City. I mentioned that to Rodrigo, but he went on with his tale without paying me any attention. He reported what a patient told him. "When the world collapsed, I thought I was fifty years old. But there is no time any more. No more years." That person had saved himself not only from temporal events but from the very possibility that anything could happen.

As he explained to me, in a strange way, total negation leads to a delirium of grandeur. Surrounded by the impenetrable void, the patient believes himself immune. He lacks a fate, and nothing touches him. Thus, he achieves an empty immortality.

"That's the ideal Mexican!" I repeated, and this time he paid attention to me. Another patient, seeing an avocado, said to him: "That is not a fruit. The thing has no plant and fell from beyond. If it has no time, it won't rot." For my friend, this cosmic resignation—the tranquilizing melancholy of being exempt from intervention—seemed to represent the national soul.

In 2010, I stopped seeing him for a few months because I was abroad teaching. I came back for a short time, taking advantage of the fact that in my university they were celebrating Thanksgiving Day. On Saturday, November 26, 2011, a date I'll never forget, a man accosted me on Avenida Revolución. That long street is a disaster of horrible shops and stores devoid of charm that seem to reproduce the imperfections of El Paso, Texas. But in this case, the most alarming thing was not the setting. The man facing me had eyes like saucers. From his right cheek dripped a bloody mass.

His physical devastation wasn't the worst part. The monster knew me: "What's happening, Johnny?" Seeing my stupefied face, a voice from beyond the grave tried to calm me down: "The person myself is has no name."

Rodrigo Woods had disguised himself to take part in the Zombie Walk. His idea of the national soul tested its own theory in that activity: on that November 26, Mexico could break the world record in the proliferation of intermediate beings who renounce human life without reaching the great beyond and wander in a timeless void.

Until that moment, the largest concentration of zombies had taken place in Australia. It seemed odd to me that a country that already possesses the koala bear, the kangaroo, the dingo, and the platypus would want to be filled with zombies.

"We are going to win," said Dr. Woods.

As some curiosity seekers photographed him, Rodrigo observed that the melancholy immortality typical of Cotard's syndrome and so appropriate for Mexicans incarnated the idea of the zombie to perfection: "Since we cannot cure ourselves of our capacity for negation, we can at least make it active."

Since he's known me for so many years, he did not try to recruit me for his cause: "A person with doubts cannot be a zombie," he said in parting, reminding me of my Hamlet days in high school, when I didn't know whether to be a doctor or a writer. The zombie has a half-life, but he doesn't vacillate.

That night, the news shows showed the multitude disguised with terrifying perfection, the participants in the Zombie Walk. The capital had broken the Guinness record for souls in torment.

On Sunday, November 27, I read in *Reforma* significant opinions about the pilgrim zombies. Antonio Marín, who wore a necklace of reproduction baby feet around his neck along with a bloody umbilical cord, explained that in his life without makeup he worked as a general physician in the Institute of Security and Social Services for State Workers (I was surprised he had the same profession as my friend: does a break from work of someone dedicated to saving lives consist in imagining himself a zombie?). For his part, Pablo Guisa, organizer of the successful march, made this identifying declaration: "Zombies are democratic because they are equal-opportunity biters. They do not distinguish between left and right but attack everyone."

That same Sunday, when UNESCO recognized with routine appreciation that the mariachi is the patrimony of all humanity, the zombies showed that they find themselves quite at home in Chilangopolis.

We have the largest reserve of the living dead. Besides, our ghosts are altruists and make donations to those most in need: the parade was organized with philanthropic goals and gathered two tons of rigorously zombie food, by which I mean imperishable food.

Shocks

The New Meat

The protagonist of this episode is real but has no name. On November 11, *Reforma* included a note about her on the front page, keeping her name a secret in order to protect her from potential reprisals, because the intrepid young lady worked undercover in a network involved in the theft and sale of cell phones. Besides, she was disguised as a zombie, so it is more appropriate to recognize her for her alarming jaws than for her credentials from the National Electoral Institute.

At the time of Juan Rulfo's centennial in 2017, Mexico was a bastion for the living dead. The Zombie Walk that broke participation records in 2011 never stopped bringing together thousands of people willing to walk through the capital showing the scabrous possibilities of radical makeup. Like José Guadalupe Posada's skeletons, the marchers, with extraordinary sense of humor, reveal that passage to the beyond does represent a passage to a "better life."

In the 2017 edition of the march, a girl decorated with devouring jaws passed by next to bald zombies whose eyes hung out of their sockets until she discovered that they'd stolen her cell phone. She was on Calle Madero, which honors the apostle of democracy but also the more informal variations of the economy. She spoke with street vendors and immediately got information, either because she was very convincing or because her terrifying disguise helped in making people answer her questions quickly. The fact is that she was sent to Plaza Monroe, where some pieces of merchandise return to the market as pirated goods.

She checked several shops and saw a phone that looked like hers but with a golden case. She asked if they might have one with a silver case. "One like that just arrived," said the seller. He went to the storage room and brought it back for her to check. She touched it with her index finger: her fingerprint made contact with the soul of the apparatus and the operating system unblocked. That magic touch proved it was hers. Should she resign herself to buying her own cell phone or simply ask for a discount by proving it was her property? Neither. There came a great zombie moment. The girl with the jaws shouted against the abuse, alerting the other clients about the theft. She knew she was in the midst of a mafia of thieves. "A sensation of being not only in the wolf's mouth but on his very teeth," she said eloquently to the journalist who interviewed her later. But she did not allow herself to be possessed by fear.

The uproar reached the ears of the plaza administrator, who spoke to the owner of the shop and with the salesperson who then returned the cell phone free. Zombie justice!

To avoid reprisals, the girl and her friends were escorted to the San Juan de Letrán metro station, one that alludes to the oldest church in Christianity, dedicated to Christ the Savior. The episode ended outside that urban sign of religiosity, closer to the telephone than to its owner, that is, the gizmo that made its way through the numinous cycle of death and resurrection.

The story told by *Reforma* summarized essential traits of our urban life: cultural syncretism, criminality, pirating, the bravery of a woman, the solidarity of the witnesses, the sudden or obligatory honesty of people who usually support abuses.

In a more profound way, this street tale also alluded to the new relationship we all have with technology and to the disconcerting future of the species. The girl who paraded through the streets tricked out in an attractive bloody outfit had provisionally assumed the posthumous condition of the zombies. But an identifying remnant remained with her body: her fingerprint. The revealing thing is that this unmistakable trait was not used to identify her but to find her device. Coming into contact with her index finger, the cell phone came back to life. In these times, our skin activates the artificial flesh of a mechanism.

Will the day come when our bodies will be used fundamentally to keep machines awake? Fingerprints and the iris of our eyes have become tools to animate robots, the new flesh we depend on.

The notion of the individual dilutes to the degree that technology takes control of our acts. The operating systems of computers and telephones are neurological extensions of our brains, prosthetic devices we activate more and more and control less and less.

When we're asked for identification, the decisive proof is not that the photo looks like us but that we look like the photo. In an equivalent form, our bodies are beginning to be a pretext for the functioning of machines.

The zombie girl of this episode has no name. Foreshadowing of a strange future, her means of identification wasn't used to individualize her but to turn on a device.

City Living

The Political Illusion

Heberto Castillo: Blank Strips of Paper

In September of 1974, I turned eighteen and joined the Mexican Workers Party (Partido Mexicano de los Trabajadores), which at the time had fewer than a thousand members and no official recognition.

Indifferent to the dogmas of orthodox Marxism, the PMT sought a Mexican path to social democracy. Our most visible leaders were the engineer Heberto Castillo, the daring creator of structures that formed part of the Coalition of Teachers during the student movement of 1968, and Demetrio Vallejo, a railroad leader. The two had met in the Lecumberri Prison. What another inmate, the novelist José Revueltas, said about the prison—that it was the nation's principal center for political education—was no joke.

Contrary to what was happening (or what we imagined was happening) in the Communist Party of Mexico, we in the PMT did not talk about "theoretical Marxism." Nor did we recite the slogans of Marxist orthodoxy which I'd heard in sociology classes at the Universidad Autónoma Metropolitana–Iztapalapa ("It isn't conscience that determines being but social being that determines conscience"; "Religion is the opium of the people"; "From each according to his ability, to each according to his needs"; etc.). There was no clear chain of command, and we didn't try to form political cadres but instead to take advantage of each member's heterodox energies. Our Saturday assemblies were absolutely democratic, which means they competed with eternity (it was to no purpose that Heberto reminded us again and again that "the only worthwhile meetings are those of belly buttons"). Anyone could take the floor to suggest that way in which we should reinvent the nation.

We launched our struggle in a rather small space, a second or third floor in a building near the Monument to the Revolution, and we continued it in a broken-down and enormous apartment on Avenida Bucareli, near the principal newspapers of the time. The "new" offices seemed to have belonged to a union convinced that the struggle depended on beating the doors until the hinges burst and on not painting the walls.

Our official organ was *Popular Insurgency (Insurgencia popular)*. Rogelio Naranjo and Eduardo del Río *(Rius)* contributed marvelous caricatures, and Heberto spent long hours trying to get articles from Carlos Monsiváis and Pablo González Casanova. While the party's future was doubtful, its publication was not a place for novices. Those of us who'd just joined had to find a different forum.

Along with friends, I founded another newspaper. We didn't have the money to print large editions, so we decided it would be a *dazibao,* or wall poster, a mural newspaper destined to decorate the walls of the central committees. The Spanish initials of the party, PMT, inclined us to call the paper *PiMienTo* and that its motto would be "The hot sauce for all committees." The basic idea was to combine militancy with cultural education. The articles were very short—after all, they had to be read by people standing up. In one of our first issues, we wrote about Ray Bradbury's *Martian Chronicles*. Demetrio Vallejo took me aside and in his high, nasal voice asked, "Comrade, can you explain what extraterrestrials have to do with the struggle of the workers?"

PiMienTo's lifespan was even shorter than that of *The Wild Bunch,* a newspaper I published using a mimeograph machine in high school and where I wrote the gossip column. I had more of an impact with the gossip than I did in my first adventure with militant journalism.

Heberto Castillo found other jobs for me, asking that I accompany him to the print shop where *Popular Insurgency* was printed. As always,

I was surprised by our leader's curiosity, which transformed any matter into an encyclopedic passion. He asked how the shop was organized, at what speed it worked, on what days demand was highest. You'd think he was planning to set up a similar business. But his questions corresponded to a different spirit; he wanted to know things that might become useful in an unexpected way.

Heberto had the strange mind of an inventor. Practical life interested him for the possibilities it had which he'd yet to discover. Seeing the rotary press, he noticed that one machine cut blocks of paper, wasting good-sized strips. "Does all that go into the garbage?" he asked. The answer was yes. Heberto ran his hand along one of the strips: "Would you give me this waste?" From that moment on, the PMT had an arsenal of thin strips of paper. I asked Heberto how he planned to use them: "I don't know yet," was his emblematic answer.

We youngsters in the party followed Heberto around with an idolatry to which he was not indifferent. Sometimes he fought it, other times he stimulated it. He detested the cult of personality and asked us to vote in deciding even the most trivial matters, but he also enjoyed the attention with which we listened to his anecdotes or how we laughed at his outbursts of humor. Irony was one of his principal traits. At meetings it worked as a double-edged sword. We weren't Marxists or Maoists or socialists or communists. Our desire was a democratic, pluralistic left still to be defined. We fought against social inequality and in favor of freedoms. Our main challenge was to exist as an organization.

Hostile to all forms of authoritarianism, Heberto would listen to proposals and counterproposals until a smile crossed his face and he would emit a sarcastic remark as a rapid spur. The effect was usually instantaneous and not always popular: the leader did not win the debate proselytizing but using his rapid way of ridiculing his opponent. With the same skill he exercised to make abstruse mathematical calculations about the resistance of materials, he would demolish the twisted rhetorical structures of his adversaries.

With a rather sectlike air, we would refer to Heberto as the Engineer. We read his clear articles in *Excelsior,* edited at that time by Julio Scherer García. After 1967, we began to read him in *Proceso.* But he didn't like to debate about his articles or hear any praise of them. His journalistic activity was only one of the many secondary activities he practiced in his peculiar political life. If he'd concentrated on being an engineer and on the structures he patented with enormous success (he invented the three-dimensional steel and cement assemblage called tridilosa used to build the World Trade Center and the Siglo XXI Hospital—among many other buildings in the city), he could have founded a corporation. He did not venture into politics for lack of ability to do other things, out of a thirst for power, or a vocation for intrigue, but out of a desire to change reality, a desire as precise as the calculations he'd made in his first profession.

Like the Argentine author Roberto Arlt's backroom geniuses, who set up laboratories in the Buenos Aires slums, Heberto, in his office devoid of curtains, faced the multiple problems that materialized as if they were exciting technical challenges. When the PMT organized an Oscar Chávez concert in the Arena Coliseo in order to raise funds, the Engineer pondered the sale of tickets as if he had no other mission than to be a show promoter.

In a party as yet unendorsed by the masses, the task of getting a carpenter to repair the bandstand for nothing fell on the leadership. Heberto took on those annoying chores with focused consideration. When our illusions were superior to reality, he would, every single day, discover a new, practical solution for changing the world.

One day, he decided we needed new seals to receive still future militants. I went with him to a downtown store, and once again saw him ponder the different aspects of an issue. He tested the consistency of the inkpads, then picked up a wooden seal and a plastic seal. The man behind the counter did not know which was preferable. It was Heberto who figured out, beyond the shadow of a doubt, which seal the PMT deserved.

"I became humanized in 1968, but especially in jail," he told me once. "Before, I was an ogre."

In *The Newspapermen (Los periodistas),* Vicente Leñero left an impeccable record of Heberto's severity as an engineering professor. Even though he was an amateur painter and a passionate novel reader, Heberto scolded Leñero for reading literature during class.

Strict with others but especially strict with himself, the leader of the PMT opened himself to emotions thanks to the heartrending lesson of the student movement and his companions in the Lecumberri Prison. I never heard him complain about being locked up or the beatings he'd suffered, the repression that certified his exemplary character.

Once the novelist Jorge Ibargüengoitia ran into him at the entrance to the newspaper *Excelsior* to which both were contributors and said, with his usual irony: "I want to walk a bit with you to see if I get beaten up too."

Heberto never stopped living under rigorous scrutiny. For him, prison was a painful summary of the nation but also an accidental seminary where he found the stimulus to change his life. There he held extremely long discussions about science, literature, chess, religion, regional food dishes, the many things he would incorporate in the most heterodox way into social struggle.

Once I walked him to his house, in the Romero de Terreros neighborhood. I was surprised to see there was no lock on the door. All you had to do was turn the knob to enter. "It's better if they arrest me without problems," Heberto smiled.

Accustomed to threats, he concluded that nothing protects you like acting in a natural way. In the living room, he showed me an oil painting in vibrant colors. "I painted it in jail," he said. "I also wrote some stories. I'll show them to you if you promise to be merciless." I promised to be honest, something not very simple for those born under the sign of Libra, always eager to find balance. But Heberto found many things to do before trusting me with a manuscript.

Everyone was surprised by the relationship between Heberto and Vallejo, and more than a few compared them to Don Quixote and Sancho Panza. The mad idealism of the Engineer found balance in the solid pragmatism of the railroad man. Hardened in union battles, Demetrio distrusted intellectuals-turned-militants and had memorized hundreds of jokes starring Pepito in order to squelch any sign of seriousness in conversation. He loved to eat goat, and from time to time some of us militants had the privilege of sharing it with him.

For two hours straight and with no break, he would tell jokes that in that prudish era were called "off-color." I often thought about the hours when Heberto and Demetrio would be together on long journeys throughout the country, the one making calculations about propellers like insane windmills capable of dispelling smog, the other talking about smutty puns. Our leaders had the credentials of honesty and vocation. They'd both suffered imprisonment and torture; they were not members of the PRI or the dogmatic and fratricidal variations of left-wing parties. But their magnetism always had some eccentricity to it; we followed them in search of a nation that didn't exist and would perhaps never exist.

Our principal task was to recruit people so we could request formal recognition as a party. At every meeting, we would invite sympathizers to sign a document and give us their information. Then we'd visit them so they would give us the number on their census card—a document which, at the time, no one carried around with them. Most repudiated the enthusiastic temerity they'd shown at the meeting: if we could get to their homes, so could the police.

Fear is contagious, and when we visited fearful people, we suspected that something could happen to us. Even though we lower-level militants lacked any importance, we knew that someone could be following us. I recall a desolate walk through the Granjas de Guadalupe neighborhood, near the Tecoco marsh. We were walking along dirt roads searching for elusive addresses scribbled on paper. The sky was crisscrossed by cables used to steal electric power and looked like a map of the area: a labyrinth that turned back in on itself.

In addition to signing up members, we used the opportunity to proselytize, putting up posters to raise the consciousness of the city. The safest bet was to tape them to the fences around vacant lots, but in that abandoned neighborhood there were only abandoned places. Every deteriorated space was a house. We resigned ourselves to put up the posters even if we risked being caught. A worker who accompanied us showed he was much wiser than we were: "Hang them straight, or people will think we were afraid," he said. No one caught us, but we didn't raise any consciousness either.

During those years, I entered hundreds of dwellings belonging to frightened people, who for us represented hope.

People would give us donations, buy a book by Rius or Naranjo cheaply printed by the PMT, and sometimes they would even give us their address, but they were afraid to corroborate their good intentions with a membership that could cost them their freedom, or their jobs. Would we, someday, manage to gather the signatures that would allow us to exist? Was there a way to bring our desires back to earth?

The democratic left was a conjecture for which Heberto invented stimuli every day. His certainties could not overlook a title that came from one of our greatest caricaturists: *The Belly Comes First (La panza es primero)*, by Rius. Sooner or later, in Mexico, social events become a stupendous pretext to sell snacks. Things can turn out for the better or for the worst, but they always end up at the steam rising from a highly seasoned pot. Hungry himself for ideas and food, Heberto decided to incorporate gastronomy into the social struggle. There could be nothing more logical in his omnivorous concept of politics than to turn our convictions into sauces.

Among the many people he'd met in prison were some mythical taco makers. My father wanted to contribute to the renovation of the country with some money he couldn't figure out how to get rid of. A few years earlier, in 1969, he'd received an inheritance that worried him a good deal. I remember the afternoon when he brought me and my sister together in one of those after-dinner sessions in which he would say profound things we didn't really understand but with which we fabulously agreed with. That time he emitted this opinion: "We've received some money and we've done nothing to deserve it. We have to give it to the poor."

He talked about the properties left by his mother, about the annoying social inequality in our nation, about the immorality of inheriting something in a world of pain and sacrifice. Carmen and I listened to him with the intrigued silence usually reserved for a submarine captain. We did not raise our fists in a sign of approval because at the ages of eleven and thirteen we had yet to perfect our left-wing gestures. But we did applaud the stupendous idea of lacking properties.

When he told Heberto that he had some money, the leader of the PMT spoke with a prophetic spirit: that sum would be enough to set up a taco stand, the most profitable business in the nation. The earnings would go to the many needs of the party.

There was a dinner in a garden in which Heberto introduced his friends and where we tried their famous tacos.

For something to belong to the left, it must produce polemics. The tacos were a subject of debate. The repertory was exquisite, but not ordinary. The most conflictive point was this: all the tacos were made from stewed meat (pork rind in green sauce, beef stew, nopalitos with eggs, stuffed chiles, and other marvels not always to be found on the menu). Missing were the traditional tacos of meat cooked over charcoal or grilled.

"These taco makers are different," explained Heberto.

Couldn't they make the other kinds of tacos: shepherd style or charcoal broiled? They neither could nor wanted to. They would be heterodox, or they wouldn't be anything.

That's how a taco stand, La Casita, on the corner of Pilares and Coyoacán Avenue came into being. At the time, I was working in Radio Educación, which was nearby, so I tried my best to bring in customers.

Our struggle was never as iconoclastic as it was on that menu. To the many breakings with standard codes we were proposing, we added a taco stand exempt from the workings of charcoal or the vertical spit of tacos al pastor. Heberto prophesied a success that would transcend normal limits, with the same enthusiasm he marshalled to oppose things that were merely real. For his part, my father would interrupt his philosophy classes to speculate on the commercial possibilities of tinga and, by then converted to Heberto's menu, decided the tacos were splendid.

Many years later, I attended a breakfast at the Lebanese Club in support of Heberto Castillo's candidacy for president. It was the least proselytizing event I ever attended. As far as his being an engineer was concerned, the founder of the PMT was not only interested in structures but in a great variety of inventions. I've already mentioned his idea of creating cyclopean propellers to dispel the city's smog. Another of his proposals was to bombard the clouds with ions in order to produce rainfall in desert areas.

During that breakfast, a reporter asked him about his ideas for changing the climate. He answered that the method was already being used at the Moscow airport, where the clouds were dissolved in order to enhance the pilots' visibility. An exemplary scientist, he gave a master class on the earth's atmosphere and completely forgot the tasks of persuasion, flattery, insult, and lies that usually define politicians during campaigns.

While other candidates made deals, public and secret pacts, and offered seductive promises, Heberto talked about clouds with expert enthusiasm. His honesty, his intelligence, and his courage were vastly greater than that of his adversaries, but reality is realistic. Magnificent ideas do not always displace conventional tastes.

All this to say that it wasn't only his campaigns that fail. La Casita too was a disaster. Heberto and my father had to abandon their crusade to join snacks to the social struggle. Today, on that same corner, an orthodox taco stand is doing very well.

The closing of La Casita affected me with the same seriousness that every other thing affected me at that time. From my eighteenth to my twentieth birthdays, I did not live a single moment when I wasn't worried. During those years, I read a lot of Dostoyevsky. It didn't alleviate my problems, but it did make me feel that having those problems was Dostoyevskian.

My principal argument in the PMT had to do with the actual condition of militancy. In broad terms, the members of the party fell into two groups: full-time and part-time. Obviously, the full-timers were the important ones because they dedicated their lives to the cause. I wrote the scripts for the rock program *The Dark Side of the Moon,* studied sociology, attended the short story workshop led by Miguel Donoso Pareja, but I was too scattered to transform the nation.

The acid test for the militant was to participate in a tour outside the city. Once, I went to an organizing committee meeting in Ciudad Nezahualcóyotl. We got to a brick house where a militant had been killed. A man asked me, out of genuine curiosity, if I drank milk every day. I felt shame, an intense repentance, and understood that I would never be a model social fighter. I turned down invitations to accompany the Engineer and Demetrio on their tours, but the matter never stopped tormenting me.

Once, Heberto heard me arguing with a comrade about the dilemma of dedicating one's life to militancy. "Come with me," he asked me to follow him to his office, as precarious as the other rooms of party headquarters. "Don't stop studying. There are lots of militants (the phrase couldn't be more ironic in a party with only eight hundred members). We're fighting for a society without classes, not without courses. "Don't be a slacker," he added affectionately.

A short while later, he summoned me again to his office, where he handed me some typewritten sheets of paper. "I warned you to be implacable," he reminded me. These were the two stories inspired in his journeys as an engineer. The themes were too allegorical to produce good literature, but the plots were worthwhile.

Forty years later, I remember one of the stories. When he was working as an engineer, Heberto visited a town covered with dust, where he was going to direct a project. A woman came out of a shack and asked him if he wanted to wash his hands or if he'd rather have her make him tea. "I'd like both things," said the Engineer. "But I only have one cup of water," answered the woman.

The most moving element in the anecdote was not just the woman's poverty but the fact that while she only had one cup of water, she'd decided to give it to a stranger. The anecdote justified Heberto Castillo's political life.

"What did you think of the stories?" he asked a couple of weeks after giving them to me. "Truth is always revolutionary," Antonio Gramsci said. Sure, but it also helps you lose friends. I remained silent, and Heberto looked at me from behind his glasses as if he were asking: "Have you learned anything here? Don't we want a different world?" I spoke the truth. "The only thing worth more than criticism is self-criticism," said Heberto, patting me on the back with his big hand.

The founder of the PMT was fully aware of his value. He could be proud and sometimes pretentious, but his big decisions benefited others. His enemies accused him of fomenting the cult of personality and called his followers "hebertists," not only for blindly believing him but for believing in the "democratic opening" the PMT proposed. Heberto's preference for dialogue and his rejection of suicidal radicalism caused him to be criticized as an altogether too docile accomplice of bourgeois democracy.

Nevertheless, he passed into history because of a generous gesture: he gave up his personal objectives in favor of a broader project. In 1988, he stepped away from his campaign for the presidency in favor of another engineer willing to change the nation, Cuauhtémoc Cárdenas.

There are political parties that fight to exist only to discover that their greatest achievement is to disappear. Ours was one of them. The PMT disappeared in order to blend in with the other left parties. Heberto aspired to be the candidate for that new entity, but he understood that Cárdenas's possibilities were greater than his.

I read the announcement at a newspaper stand in Tizimín Plaza, opposite the Sanctuary of the Holy Kings. I saw a pile of newspapers, the *Diario de Yucatán,* and took the top one. The sun made it red hot. Heberto was stepping aside. "Only self-criticism is better than criticism," I remembered.

I saw the Engineer for the last time in 1996, a year before his death. We were on the same plane to Chiapas. He was going to a meeting of the Concord and Pacification Commission, where he functioned as a mediator between the government and the Zapatista Army. He was wearing the same poncho he wore walking around San Cristóbal. He looked like the Mexican version of one of Tolstoy's mujiks.

Heberto Castillo could be stubborn and isolate himself from people who were not at his level of personal merit, a difficult mark to meet. He paid the price for betting on rectitude in a profession that consisted in simulation. His articles in *Proceso* summarize a clear, congruent political vision. The anecdotes about his life reflect his morality.

I never found out how he used those strips of paper the printer gave him, but they stayed with me as a metaphor of what we should be doing. Nothing is superfluous, no matter how trivial it seems. Those pieces of paper were waste and were of an uncomfortable size, but they were blank. We could have written our hope on them.

From Regent to President

I'll deal with the 1985 earthquake in another chapter. For purposes of argument, I'll simply say that President Miguel de la Madrid was unable to deal with the tragedy. To the contrary, it was civil society that acquired naturalization papers, took to the streets, and accomplished much, much more than the government. The capital acquired an independent face; it could take care of itself.

Two years later, a left-wing front led by Cuauhtémoc Cárdenas won the elections in the capital and quite possibly in the entire nation. We'll never know because the PRI went on to perpetrate the most spectacular fraud in our sullied electoral history. Manuel Bartlett, secretary of government, announced the crash of the computer system, and shortly after, Diego Fernández de Cevallos, of the PAN party, allowed the destruction of the manual registry of that operation. A wave of discontent swelled because of this mockery of the popular will.

In 1994, the Zapatista Army of National Liberation took up arms, and Manuel Camacho was designated to negotiate with the rebels. A short while later, Luis Donaldo Colosio, the PRI presidential candidate, was assassinated. Carlos Monsiváis wrote with bitter irony, saying that "was the year we never got bored."

In June of 1994, there were elections, better organized than those of 1988. One of the lessons of democracy is that the worst candidate can win cleanly. I voted for the first time in 1976, when there was only one candidate for president, José López Portillo, from the PRI. Tired of the electoral farce, the other parties refused to present candidates. Jorge Ibargüengoitia wrote a humorous piece in *Excelsior:* "This Sunday is election day. How exciting! Who will win?" My disillusioning debut as a citizen led me to think, along with millions of other disillusioned citizens, that all we needed was a really democratic process to have better candidates. Nothing could be further from reality. Over the course of time, the old and new political parties reached the conclusion that in Mexico democracy is a business where problems are administered but not solved.

The case is that in the summer of 1994, with an authentic possibility to decide, the electorate was shockingly faithful to custom: the PRI won again. Many people attributed the fact to a fear of change and to the so-called "fear vote."

I published an article in the Mexican edition of the Spanish newspaper *El País* titled "People We Don't Know Have Their Reasons." Everyone you know criticizes the government, but the people you don't know make up the majority.

In any case, the ferment for a transformation was under way. In 1997, the first elections for president of the Federal District were held, and Cuauhtémoc Cárdenas was the principal actor in a disconcerting surprise. Those of us who had advanced degrees in lost causes discovered to our shock that even we could win.

At that moment, I was working on the newspaper *La Jornada,* on the left, where I was in charge of the culture supplement. It seemed obvious to me that on Sunday, election day, no one would be interested in anything but the mayoral race.

The Federal Electoral Institute was led by José Woldenberg, an academic veteran of left-wing adventures. His enemies, from the hard-line
sectors of the left, declared that he was faking a democratic operation in
order to favor the PRI. Those prophecies of disaster mixed dogmatism,
suspicion, and doubt with correct thinking. Despite the fact that the
voting card had become the least counterfeited document in the nation,
despite the fact that an enormous and costly operation held the votes,
and that the computer system promised almost instantaneous results, it
was difficult to accept beforehand that for once the game was fair.

I felt affection and admiration for José Woldenberg, but as a reporter,
I felt obligated to recall the epigraph from Joseph Conrad that Graham
Greene uses to open his novel *The Human Factor* (1978): "I only know that
he who forms a tie is lost, the germ of corruption has entered into his
soul." Sentiments liquidate objectivity.

Many friends on the left wanted Woldenberg to fail at his task in
order to show that any attempt to renovate the system from within cannot work. Others of us could sin in the opposite direction, having too
much confidence in his sympathy and in the tolerance and patience with
which he listened to the interminable and abstruse proposals of the various political parties. Protected by the smoke from his cigar, Woldenberg stayed calm without stepping away from his role as arbiter. He may
well have been the only Mexican who smoked for the public good (it's
no accident that he gave up his diet of seven cigars a day when he left
the Instituto Federal Electoral, or IFE). Would he be the civic hero we
needed or the traitor others prophesied?

We decided to put his picture on the front page of *La Jornada Semanal*
under the only title that could make any sense on Sunday, July 6, 1997:
"Democratic Culture." Fabrizio Mejía Madrid and I interviewed him at
his offices in the IFE. "I'm very tense," he apologized before the conversation, "I have to be very careful."

Even though we were not looking for some sensationalist remark and
only wanted a sketch of what could happen, the moment acquired the
aura of a historic moment. "From six a.m. until eight p.m., we shall have
a virtual country which will be in the hands of the electors," we wrote
in the introduction.

Woldenberg spoke cautiously about what might happen that night: "By their very nature, elections cannot crystallize definitive facts. The electoral formula presupposes both coexistence and competition. Any authoritarian scheme that thinks there exists only one truth, only one contingent entrusted with it, only one party which is the derivation of the book and that believes others are nothing more than classes, ideologies, and demonized interests, puts us in a dynamic infused with intransigence."

On Sunday morning my telephone rang several times to offer up "a dynamic infused with intransigence." Various friends were disappointed with me: *La Jornada Semanal* had been turned over to the "system." We'd justified the official version of a farce. Those critics did not argue about the statistics that revealed the enormous effort to construct a reliable and scrutinized platform or the sensible opinions of those who directed the process. For them, the turbulent waters of politics presaged a conspiracy: the ship would sink.

That night, when we learned that Cuauhtémoc Cárdenas would be the first democratically elected head of government in the city, those same friends congratulated us for interviewing Woldenberg. Obviously, the celebration was biased because it was concerned only with the results and not the importance of the electoral process itself.

On July 6, the Zócalo was witness to the night of the suns. Flags bearing the Aztec sun designed by Rafael López Castro filled the plaza. The left had won. That artificial light amid the darkness would not last long, and the party of the sun would, little by little, be eclipsed.

In 1997, Chauhtémoc Cárdenas initiated the series of governments under the PRD—the Party of the Democratic Revolution. During the two decades of PRD governments, there were also changes in electoral management. The IFE became the National Electoral Institute and went from being an independent institution to being an enclave controlled by parties. The capital offered liberal guarantees and social advances superior to those of other regions in the nation, but it also became the hostage of drug dealers, tribes of vendors, distributers of pirated goods, the most speculative real estate interests, and an economy that privileged international franchises and augmented social inequality.

In reality, the most important factor in Mexican politics since 1994 has been the Zapatista movement. But this book is not about Chiapas but Mexico City. Cárdenas has not stopped being a significant figure in public life. He's called the "moral leader" of the left to show he has influence even if he holds no position. The expression has become more and more literal: he's an ethical model, something difficult to equal in our tempestuous national politics, taking into account that we're talking about someone who has been a sub-secretary, a governor, a head of government, and, three times, a presidential candidate.

From his early childhood, Cárdenas seemed destined for the nation's history: he was the first baby to live in Los Pinos, the official residence of Mexico's presidents. A short time later, in the Brígida Alfaro kindergarten, he met Porfirio Muñoz Ledo, his comrade in political adventures, the man with whom he would found, many years later, the Democratic Current of the PRI.

Respectful of institutions to a degree that sometimes drove his followers to despair, Cárdenas has also been able to disagree. He made a call for renovation from within the official party, but his summons fell into silence, as if he'd made it in no-man's-land, so he decided to abandon the only political institution that at the time was winning elections. That was not his only separation. On November 25, 2014, after the kidnapping of the forty-three Ayotzinapa students in a state governed by the PRD, he abandoned the party he himself had founded.

Son of the most decisive Mexican leader in the twentieth century, he did not live in the general's shadow. As sub-secretary of agriculture in the state of Michoacán, he aimed to be an efficient man within the system. Although his exit from the PRI changed that equation, it also aroused suspicion. Those of us who were militants in the PMT thought his protest would have little resonance.

But Muñoz Ledo's rhetorical windstorm and Cárdenas's charisma (the tranquil strength of a man who knows how to listen and never gives in to passion) brought about the creation of the Democratic National Front, a totally new opportunity for the left, only stopped by the 1988 fraud.

Debates have not been the strong suit of a politician who prefers the extended reasoning of speeches and who rarely speaks of things about which he is ignorant ("I don't know; I'll find out," he says sincerely, shocking reporters). In his third presidential campaign, he was confronted by a right-wing populist of undeniable charisma, who wore cowboy boots to kick coffins bearing the emblem of the PRI. The impetuous rancher who promised to purge the budget of the vermin, the black snakes, and other plagues seemed more radical than the engineer. But Vicente Fox's bull-riding ended when he moved into Los Pinos, where he left his cowboy hat and his rebelliousness hanging on a hook.

Cuauhtémoc never stopped fighting for the change that did not come with the National Action Party (PAN). He was over eighty years old when he received a peculiar invitation to start all over again along with his old kindergarten school friend, Porfirio Muñoz Ledo: to write the constitution of Mexico City.

The Book of Books of the City

In January of 2016, the Federal District ceased to exist, and Mexico City became the thirty-second state in the republic. Once the handmaiden of power, the city metamorphosed into a center of power. But now the city would need its own constitution.

One hundred constitutional deputies made up the assembly that would decide the content of the capital's magna carta. The composition of that group was subject to deals made in the highest reaches of government and produced a traditionally unjust result: the PRI, which had received just seven percent of the votes in the last election held in the capital, would have the same number of deputies as the Movement for National Regeneration (MRN), which had received more than thirty percent.

The constitutional deputies would need a draft constitution to use as a point of departure. Twenty-eight citizens, me among them, were summoned to compose that draft. We all accepted without knowing who the other participants might be. "Why did I get myself into this labyrinth?" The question would echo in my mind, beginning on February 16, 2016, the first Tuesday in our work session. At 5:45 p.m., I walked across the Zócalo, where the flag was being saluted, entered the Palace of the Government, guarded by police carrying shields, passed through security (less rigorous than at any airport), took the unbelievably slow elevator to the third floor, stopped at the men's room, where a few days later my umbrella would be stolen, and entered the Oval Chamber only to see that it was round (that geometric mystery announced another: we were supposed to square the circle).

For years I'd been writing articles in favor of turning politics over to the citizens, and here we were with an opportunity to put forth, starting from zero, issues unrelated to party agendas. At the same time, nothing could be more problematic than leaving laws exclusively in the hands of the constitutionalist deputies who have kept jurisprudence from being a tool that would help the people know their rights and instead turned it into a pretext for lawyers to litigate. From the outset, I assumed that I could only do what I was best at in that collective project, that is, be a reader. I would make it my business to keep the complications of the text to a minimum.

At the swearing in, a friend said: "You're the only man here not wearing a tie." That seemed a good sign to me, a sign that I could fight for plain wording, closer to the language of ordinary citizens and similar to the wording of other constitutions I was reading at the moment. I called them "Plan B" because of the names of the cities: Barcelona, Berlin, Bogotá, and Buenos Aires.

There were few politicians among the twenty-eight present. Alejandro Encinas, Cuauhtémoc Cárdenas, and Porfirio Muñoz Ledo helped to create an atmosphere of agreeable concord and contributed their vast experience. I must make special reference to Porfirio, who came to the meetings after a gourmet meal in which he'd redesigned the world, lighting a cigarette which he only stopped smoking in order to light another, and could quote from memory Articles 41 and 47 of the Lisbon Convention, which defined good administration and accountability. Porfirio functioned as a master of ceremonies, making jokes that soothed discord and sharp observations that improved arbitrarily truncated arguments.

From the beginning, a tension made me recall that the undecipherable intrigues of politics have been described as "the darkness." Senator Miguel Barbosa, at the time of the PRD and later of Morena, torpedoed every initiative.

"We've got to use our pencils," said Cárdenas, meaning that we should start writing straightaway. Barbosa interjected: "I already did, many years ago. Whenever you like, I'll bring you three constitutional projects."

When Porfirio presented a list of subjects to develop, the senator cut him short: "That's not a constitution. That's a press release. Any one of my advisers could bring you a document that's really worthwhile."

He addressed other proposals with the same haughtiness. After he attacked Loretta Ortiz, I made a commentary about our work style: we could not design the civility of the city if we were not civil in our meetings. Luckily, the senator soon abandoned our group to dedicate himself to his intrigues. But that wasn't the only annoying situation. One of the big problems in gathering together people the media describe as "notable" is that they often believe they are. A few specialists on specific subjects limited their participation to giving lectures on the greatness of their subjects, forgetting that we were involved in a team effort.

Other people were exemplary. Mauricio Merino was brilliant in leading us through the issue of anticorruption. Loretta Ortiz dealt with international issues, and Father Miguel Concha took up human rights (and at a critical moment he reminded us that we should protect the secular character of the state). Lol Kin Castañeda and Marta Lamas dealt with matters of gender in an inclusive and generous way. Carlos Cruz and Clara Jusidman took charge, to the point of fatigue, of the detailed compilation of all the proposals.

I worked less than any of them. I took part in the matter of cultural rights, written out with the help of Eduardo Vázquez Martín, Alejandro Salafranca, and Bolfy Cottom. I participated in composing the anticorruption system designed by Mauricio Merino and his team from Center of Economic Research and Teaching, and I proposed an article about the constitution's being the force of law, that the will of the people should be respected, even if that will were stained with blood.

It was important to guarantee the sense of legality, even if a dictatorship were to come to power. Since that idea represented a symbolic extension of democratic life, it became Article 71, that is, the last article in the constitution. This is what it says:

Constitutional Inviolability

This Constitution cannot be altered by force and remains the law of the land even if institutional order is broken. It can only be modified democratically.

I read it to a personal acquaintance who knows me, who said, "It doesn't sound like something you wrote." Inevitably, our ideas translated themselves into bureaucratic Spanish, which confers a legal appearance on words. I did not triumph as a reader of the magna carta, and it's saying very little to note that the baroque clauses of legal claptrap would have been worse without my help and that of the other members of the constitutional committee.

Our work did not draw the kind of attention aroused by the naming of the national soccer team, but many citizens of the capital wanted their voices to be expressed through us. By April 12, we'd received more than thirty thousand messages from chilangos; by May 17, eighty-three thousand, and by May 31, two hundred and seventy thousand.

I emerged from the process feeling that I'd taken—involuntarily—a master's level course in law and failed it. Around that time, I visited the common graves in Tetecingo, Morelos, along with Javier Sicilia, and I returned to the Palace of the Government to face the legal documents as if they were yet another common grave. One hundred years of manipulative jurisprudence could not be erased by a small group of citizens. Certain words have legal value, others do not, it's that simple. The dictionary has been perverted, so that terms in common usage acquire the mystical prestige of "technical" terms.

Porfirio would toss out decisive reflections: "I don't want to overreact, but corruption is the nation's fundamental problem. The autonomous offices have been sequestered by the very interests they're supposed to control. Corruption should be defined as the sale of an act of authority." Unfortunately, these ideas did not manifest themselves in such an eloquent style in the document. Whenever he saw signs of anxiety or disillusionment, Porfirio would remind us of how important our task was.

"We are writing a requiem for the Count of Montesquieu. There will no longer be any powers beyond those already established. Now the autonomous offices will exist. We're in rough seas inventing a new law."

The disorder in the crew and the possibility our ship would sink made our venture seem intrepid. These epic outpourings could last long enough for someone who'd asked to speak to remember they had to go to another meeting. When Porfirio finally got back to the list of those who should take part and noticed that an eminent lady lawyer had departed during his fiery speech, he simply said: "I frightened Miss Muffet away!"

With the fervor of a Roman tribune, Porfirio insisted on the need to write a preamble in epic style, the equivalent of the UNESCO constitution, so he recited: "Since wars are conceived in the minds of men, it is in the minds of men that the bulwarks of peace should be erected." Our proposed constitution would begin with that breath of prosodic grandeur. Among other things, the preamble says: "Let us remain loyal to the echo of the ancient word, let us care for our common house, let us restore through the laborious work and conduct of solidarity of its daughters and sons, the transparence of this place that emanated from water."

To my way of thinking, the most important result of the sessions was the definition of a *person of the capital:* any person by the simple fact of being in the city qualifies as such. A civilizing space, the city confers instantaneous citizenship.

How bad was the end result of the project? If we compare it to the nation's magna carta, which has received more than six hundred emendations since 1917, we can say we succeeded in producing a rather coherent project, especially if we take into account the fact that we had to comply with the requirements of Article 122 of the federal constitution, itself designed to maintain control over Mexico City. Even though there were formal restrictions, we worked without interference from the local government and with no other salary than the desire to prefigure a space where we could all live together with our differences. We did not write a definitive text, just a proposal. Therefore, we chose to be closer to hopes than to limitations: a constitution should not reflect what we are through inevitability but what we reasonably can be.

In some cases, we invade the minute territory of regulation for a simple reason: what doesn't exist should be explained. A good example is the struggle against corruption. In a nation where there are no autonomous offices to watch over the government, it's worthwhile spelling out a possible system of control so such an initiative may be understood.

Writing a constitution after the fall of a dictatorship or at the end of a revolution is easier than writing one in a civil environment itself the result of a century of normalizing activities. It's not the same as starting from zero to give new meaning to the arithmetic which has been badly used. Even if it wasn't perfect and even if it fell into abstruse juridical jargon—a territory where the verb "to aid" is conjugated—the result was innovation. The best proof of that is the resistance the document aroused. Some commentators discarded the project as a hippie utopia, and later the government of Enrique Peña Nieto pushed the alarm button.

We must clarify some misunderstandings that arose from misinterpretations. One of the most dramatic referred to the possible disappearance of private property. "A phantom stalks Mexico City . . . the phantom of Communism." Nothing could be falser. Article 9 of the project recognizes the rights established in the federal constitution, which guarantees the extant system of property.

Another accusation was that in creating new rights for people, we exceeded the limits of the constitution. That too was incorrect. The Supreme Court of Justice determined that local constitutions can indeed augment the gamut of rights.

It was also said that we invited people to smoke marijuana. Our proposal established that the consumption of cannabis would not be illegal and that we favored its medical and scientific use, *when and if* the General Health Law were reformed in that area.

We were also criticized because we created rights for strolling vendors and informal workers. In a city where half of the economy is unofficial!

Our document did eliminate political privilege (something important in the Mexico of criminal governors like Javier Duarte and Guillermo Padrés) and offered the possibility of revoking injunctions, giving greater power to the citizens.

Were these goals unattainable? We composed the proposal knowing that we would be turning it over to reality, that is, to the congressmen who would have to turn it into law.

Our document had to be faithful to a capital that, since 1997, has supported a social-democrat political option. The PRD has implemented every possibility to degrade itself, but its twenty years leading Mexico City have left conquests superior to the current reality of that party. Those of us who composed the proposal took into account the guarantees citizens of the capital already enjoy and that are yet to be put into practical effect. Gender equality, abortion rights, euthanasia, common-law marriage, and plebiscites are activities with which parties may have their differences but which if voted on one at a time would be approved by the majority of the people in the city.

For four extenuating months, the one hundred constitutional deputies worked without pay to evaluate our proposal. Even if the makeup of the congress gave an exaggerated representation to the PRI, the final document supported a high percentage of the original text (almost eighty percent).

Neither the final version of the proposal nor the constitution was perfect. Even so, the exercise advanced the rights of citizens of the capital.

As you might suppose, the populace did not flock to the *Official Newspaper* to read the new magna carta of the capital as if it were an exciting serial novel. The document ran the risk of being relegated to the remote desks of juridical seminaries until the General Procuratory of the Nation, the Senate, dominated by the PRI, and the Federal Executive contested it, proving its unheard-of vitality.

When the Church hierarchy opposed the showing of the film *The Crime of Padre Amaro,* based on the novel by the Portuguese author Eça de Queirós, the producers launched a publicity campaign with the question "Why don't they want you to see it?" Rejection based on dogma stimulated the curiosity of the public.

Something similar happened with the request that the Supreme Court of Justice review the new laws. If we'd been able to have the support of publicity agents to support the constitution, the slogan would have been "Why don't they want you to have these rights?"

Ceremonies

The Security Book

We live in a dangerous world, where nations protect themselves according to their degree of paranoia and level of technology. The guiding principle of security consists in detecting the things that can get worse and in anticipating what the enemy might do.

The most common form of protection in Mexico City is a book where people note their arrival at an office. Is it logical that a nation which offered the world inviting flavors like vanilla and chocolate is so suspicious of those who visit its offices? From what does this local custom protect us?

It's well known that not everything that reassures us derives from a rational principle. Leopold Bloom, in Joyce's *Ulysses,* carries a potato in his pocket because he thinks it relieves his rheumatic pains. This suggestion helps him walk through Dublin for more than six hundred pages.

Trickery and faith combine with reasoning and sometimes acquire the appearance of logic. Even so, I still do not understand our most widespread contribution to the planet's security, the book you have to sign in at the entrance to a building. We are facing something even less read than the constitution, but something more important.

Let's analyze the matter closely. The book itself has a unique size. It's too big for any task that isn't obligatory. Its hard covers discourage carrying it anywhere. No one would use such an uncomfortable volume for notes. Derived from another age, it makes you think about the diligent labors of a bookkeeper in the nineteenth century who would have used it to jot down accounts receivable and accounts payable, the variable balance sheet of his profession.

The book rarely stands alone. If there isn't a guard next to it, one stands in front, without anything happening. In order for the book to have meaning, the guard should say: "Care to sign in?" Tied to the book is a ballpoint pen. This means that if you want to steal the pen you have also to steal the book, which weighs about four kilos. The string that ties up the pen indicates that security matters are serious here.

It's happened to me more than once that these books have pencils tied to them. In those cases, the facts can be erased or falsified. Even so, no one seems to judge the book less secure for all that.

If the guard noted down the identification details on his own, he would be able to verify them. But he leaves that job in the hands of the unknown visitor: he doesn't document or compare the name. He doesn't even understand it because he's reading it upside down. You can check yourself in as Joseph Stalin, Osama bin Laden, Marta Sahagún, or Rabina Gran Tagora.

As far as I can see, no criminological study has revealed that the crime index would increase if sign-in books in office vestibules were eliminated. Nevertheless, in this age of computers, sign-in books exist and are multiplying. A complete mystery.

Let's move forward with the analysis. Sometimes, the security reinforces itself in the following way: in addition to signing in, you have to hand over some form of identification. In exchange for it, you get a name badge. Would that change the plans of any terrorist? It's an annoyance, of course, because you can hand over a fake document and kill someone while wearing a name badge.

In point of fact, identification papers are not requested in order to check who is entering but to show suspicion. Which leads to another subject. Rigorously guarded places do not accept identification documents that say you're a member of a health club or a driving school. We live in an original nation, which says you need a voting card to enter certain buildings. Despite that, the most reliable of our documents is never carefully checked.

Suppose the visitor hands over his legitimate accreditation from the National Electoral Institute, does that mean he will behave properly? His identity has been temporarily sequestered; something important has stayed behind at the reception desk. Which does not necessarily force you to behave in exemplary fashion. To the contrary, losing an identification document can provoke you into acting like the unknown person you hadn't dared until that moment to be.

It's obvious that identification documents could supply reliable facts if they were photocopied, but that's too much trouble. Besides, from time to time the lights go out.

A land of syncretism, Mexico mixes modernity with atavistic traditions. There are corporate buildings with machines that read irises and fingerprints gathered in archives worthy of a science fiction movie. Even so, the hardbound book with its blue lines does not disappear. Once I went to a bulwark that had television cameras in the vestibule, the corridors, the elevators, and other places I failed to notice. I walked down the stairs: on each landing, a sign pointed out that the closed-circuit system was active. The reception area had two security islands (one counter with about ten screens on it and another next to the entrance, where I'd written my name). The place was guarded day and night by the unsleeping eye of the cameras. But there was no way anyone would stop using the book.

Is there someone who reads the numerous names of the visitors? Or how much time they spend on their visit? Is there a general archive of security books? Is there anyone interested in knowing that on January 20, 2006, Juan Hernández was in office number 303 for one hour and fifteen minutes?

The book makes things difficult and that generates a control fantasy. In our peculiar concept of efficacy, we think that making things difficult is a frontal and unquestionable way of intervening.

On the lined pages there is usually the expression "Reason for Visit." Ninety-nine percent of the visitors write in the same reason "personal." An alibi for anything. In a certain way, we confess our guilt beforehand. If something bad happens, it would be terrible if we'd written out our complete name and it would be even worse if we'd alleged a "personal" motivation.

The pages of suspicion await you at the entrance to a building. Nothing has happened yet, but all we have to do is wait. The book doesn't anticipate crimes: it anticipates the guilty.

City Characters

The Sewer Cleaner

S ince poverty creates more jobs than technology, strange jobs abound in the city. I've always been intrigued by the unverifiable work of those who unplug drains. On any afternoon, your doorbell rings and a total stranger asks for money for having relieved the lower intestines of the city. To prove to you that he unblocked your drain, he drags along a cart loaded with mud and junk. Although other municipal jobs are more complicated (installing a high-tension cable, trimming the tops of trees), this is the only one that demands an obligatory tip. The unfathomable social contract guarantees the begging rights of the drain man.

Unlike the street sweepers or the employees of the Federal Electricity Commission, drain men have no official uniform: they possess no other identification than their filth-covered hands. Is there a union that backs them up? Do they follow a master plan of drainage or is this a matter of volunteers impelled by scatological despair?

One of the great mysteries of this job is that it's impossible to know if it really took place. The drain men work in complete secrecy. They only turn up at your door once their job is done and they can ask for the relevant cash. To justify themselves, they point to their cart. Did they pull all that out of your drain or do they carry around a generic sample they use to trick people in all the entryways in the city?

The truth is that this disquiet is useless. We are faced with a custom that is not only deeply rooted but indestructible as well. The drain men have a secret agreement with human generosity in a nation where tips are more important than salaries and where begging has all sorts of manifestations, some easy to see, others dissimulated.

It turns out to be hard to live in a territory of dearth without a proper donation strategy. That the city doesn't explode is owed, to a good degree, to the network of coins that pass from hand to hand like the illusion that a shared life is possible. The vast social fabric in which chance doles out the pennies demands we give something to the drain men. If they leave empty-handed, the cycle of urban life may suffer permanent damage.

Besides, in a city that once was a lake, no one is unaware of how important the subsoil is. The drains regurgitate news from other times. In a grand episode from *Les Misérables,* Jean Valjean is chased through the sewers of Paris. Victor Hugo reveals the hidden city that justifies the orderly city of the surface. The dream in Paris stone depends on a nightmare animated by rats. To understand the parks and boulevards thoroughly, you have to understand their other side, the only place where nothing is hidden, the underworld of drainage. "A sewer is a cynic," writes Victor Hugo: "It says everything."

In Mexico City the drains say even more because the soft subsoil is not stable and floods abound. For that very reason, we attempt to hide what happens down there. Sergio González Rodríguez observes in his documentary *The Lower Depths (Los bajos fondos)*:

In its cosmological plans, Christian theology always marks a difference between heaven and hell, the High and the Low. Its symbolic derivations established the poles of virtue (beauty and the harmonious), the perfect life, sanctity, and the mystic versus vice, deviant or perverted behavior, the ugly, the prosaic and trivial. This topographic principle extended to the ordinary World in order to judge the merits and actions of men. Rectitude would be the infallible path; the meaning of orthodoxy, a foretaste of paradise. The opposite could only hold the stigma of a diabolical outcome, "that worm which pierces the world." This form of spatializing and ordering has replicated itself in cities and bodies, something embedded in the normative nature of the West and that reappears in another structural opposition: the public and the private, generic knot of the subject's identity.

The sinful is associated with the inferior, in an ethical sense, but also in a spatial sense: the "lower depths" are the irregular places where transgression has its opportunity, and the hidden basement of the city houses the ordure we don't want to see.

During the colonial era, filth was tossed into the street. Drainage mitigated our undesirable cohabitation with our fecal matter, but, every once in a while, it returns to center stage.

It hasn't been easy to tame a landscape where rivers have been channeled into tunnels. Filth simply cannot be avoided. The drain man belongs to the zone we don't want to see, the filled-in latrine that threatens to take over the surface and never stops sending signals: the first odor you breathe when you land at Mexico City is shit, a sign that the landing strips are resting on a subsoil in the process of decomposition.

What kind of contract do we make with the man who assures us he's cleared the intestines of our street? How much you should pay for work whose utility cannot be proven depends on your sense of charity. By way of comparison, we can consider an emotionally complex case, that of the hurdy-gurdy players who manipulate their instruments in public plazas. They play traditional music which is almost never agreeable. The out-of-tune sound that emanates from the device reminds us of the state of the nation. It's there we see the key to its success. Is there any way for us to reject something uncomfortable when we recognize it as "our own"? Although very few people actually like listening to the sickly melody of the organ grinder, those favoring their eradication are even fewer in number. The organ grinders belong to our sentimental archaeology and comply with all the requirements to be official: they have a union, professional identification cards, and a uniform as sad as their music: the pale color of barren soil. We love them on the far edge of taste or need. They are as impossible to renounce as our baby teeth, which, if we keep them in a plastic bag until we're adults, can never be thrown out.

Let's go back to the main character in this chapter. Among the pious-labor relationships, none is more unbreakable than the one we establish with drain clearers. To my way of thinking, the transaction is possible because it has a symbolic content, one difficult to express but just as sharp as the high notes of the hurdy-gurdy that make our hair stand on end. Can there be anything more disagreeable than sinking one's body into a drain pipe? The drain men announce that they've submerged themselves in public refuse, and, something even more precise, they clean out the part that corresponds to you, your unfindable filth.

Terminal issues are beyond names or questions. Staring into that face from the underworld, no one asks for proof and certainly does not want to hear details.

What secrets do they discover in their passage through the depths? We have no idea. All you have to know or suspect is that those men (I've never seen a woman among them) have entered the other side of urban life, which should function without being explained, its inconceivable digestion.

Last December, the black gang returned to my house. I opened the door to a man about sixty years old, covered to the eyebrows with mud: "We've unplugged the drains for the New Year," he said in a voice rarefied perhaps by the lack of air underground. He was followed by three young men who seemed to have used their hair either to clean or to dirty objects.

The man waited while I dug into my pockets. He breathed through his mouth, producing a raspy sound. He reminded me of the image of Xipe Totec, Our Lord the Flayed, the god of renovation who waits with his mouth open to spout a prophecy.

I was tempted to break the code and ask what he'd found in the drain on my street, but he could have said just about anything or, even worse, he could have detailed my refuse.

I dropped the coins into his filth-covered hands.

"Happy New Year, sir," said the drain man.

I saw the street strangely deserted. The future seemed as inscrutable as what was taking place under the house.

Who was this person to whom I had to give money for cleaning out the invisible entrails of life?

He was time, which presents its bills in its own way.

Shocks

The Earthquake:
"Stones of This Land Are Not Native to It"

On September 19, 1985, a violent shove yanked me out of my dreams. I was on a ground floor in the Tlalpan neighborhood, on the southern extreme of the city, where the soil, made of volcanic rock, is more solid and the tremors provoke less alarm.

The house had been built by Andrés Casillas, a follower of Luis Barragán. Its walls were as solid as those of a convent. I felt protected by the place I was in and by the relationship I'd had with earthquakes up until that moment. I was born in 1956, a year before the Angel of Independence came down after a tremor. My family took that quake as a sign that life could be complicated. In 1957, my mother was twenty-two years old and was facing several challenges. The main challenge was a baby howling in a time before disposable diapers. When the Angel came down, the earth entered into a concordance with her anxieties and allowed her to conceive the personal myth of having given birth to a child of earthquakes. Years later, that legend would seem magnificent to me: instead of thinking that the subsoil was protesting my arrival in the world, I concluded it was welcoming me "Mexican style," with rattles that echoed in the heart of the earth.

As a boy, I enjoyed the sudden swaying of the house, so similar to my father's footfalls, which shook the hallway when he came to say good night to me. When I was young, I associated the tremors with the temperament of the redhead I was in love with and, something more complex, I understood that the character of Mother Earth was very much like that of my own dear mom. Living in a city on the verge of a nervous breakdown made me love it with an Oedipal passion from which no therapy could rescue me. For four years, the manuscript of my first book, *Waterway Night (La noche navegable),* waited its turn to find a place in the coveted catalogue of the Joaquín Mortiz publishing house. On October 24, 1980, a tremor shook the city, and Joaquín Díez-Canedo, head of Mortiz, called to say: "Because of the earthquake, your book came out."

Origin of the world in pre-Hispanic cosmogonies, the earth seemed to support the painful birth of my book.

All this by way of saying that, as a matter of principle, I was not worried on September 19 that the earth moved more than it does usually. The house I was living in had no buzzer. To enter, you had to ring a bell. At 7:18 a.m., the bell rang on its own.

The Shock of Being Alive

"The peals of bells fell like pennies," López Velarde wrote. In this case, they fell like machine-gun fire. I got into a door frame. The floor above was where my friend José Enrique Fernández lived. In the madness of the moment it occurred to me I should shout to wake him up, as if someone could sleep with that crunching of matter, but all I did was wait in the doorway. Even if it was merely symbolic protection, I understood I was on the threshold between life and death.

When the bell stopped ringing, the silence acquired a curious unreality. The calm was suspicious. I picked up the telephone but there was no dial tone. No electricity either.

José Enrique met me in the dining room, with the black face of a ghost. His ex-wife lived in the Condesa neighborhood, in the Basurto Building famous for its Art Deco design and the fragility of its construction. There was no way to call her or anyone else. José Enrique worked for Melody Records on Avenida Arcos de Belén. He intended to go there, passing by the Basurto Building.

Did the city still exist? The possibility of a decisive erasure, a grand-scale and demented annihilation, took shape in our minds. What could have happened with the Torre Latinoamericana, the downtown neighborhoods, the many apartment buildings?

We went to the car to listen to the radio. Jacobo Zabludovsky was describing what was going on by means of satellite telephone. The journalist who after the Tlatelolco massacre of 1968 restricted himself to speaking about the weather, that morning recovered his primary vocation and gave a complete account of the situation. We started listening to his story at the moment his voice broke as he contemplated the ruins of the television studios where he'd spent the greater part of his life. Shortly after, he reported that the building on Arcos de Belén, the one José Enrique intended to get to, was rubble. The city was nothing but ruins, the scene of a war with no other enemy than fate.

José Enrique was one of the many omitted victims that day. In 1979, a tremor collapsed the Universidad Iberoamericana in the Campestre Churubusco neighborhood, just before classes were due to begin. My uncle Miguel, a Jesuit and a law professor at the Iberoamericana, interpreted the tragedy in this way: "It's a warning from God. He's giving us another chance: if the tremor had begun later, we'd all be dead." His theory was based on the fact that the fury had fallen on empty classrooms.

The 1985 earthquake also happened early in the day, but it was no warning from God. Some people escaped because they hadn't gotten to work yet; on the other hand, others died because they stayed home. The seismic shocks were too strong for them to choose their damage: they were of an 8.1 magnitude. In 2010, I would survive an 8.8 shock in Santiago de Chile. Both cataclysms put the quality of building construction to the test. Although the one in Chile was much more severe, it caused less damage. The Mexican version revealed the extent of real estate speculation: on September 19, the earth carried out the scrutiny the government would never conduct.

I listened to the radio until I learned that the National University mountain climbers were asking for volunteers to go to aid stations. The meeting place was the stadium of University City; the only requirement was that everyone bring a shovel.

In my failed bachelor days, calamity came bearing the name "daily life." Whenever I had a problem, I would visit neighbors. The last time it was to ask for one of the kittens the family cat had just given birth to (my house was infested with rats who climbed up the ivy as if they were squirrels). They weren't surprised when I asked for a shovel, and I wasn't surprised that they had one.

At the university stadium I discovered the new talisman of citizenship. The volunteers tied a bit of yellow cloth around one arm. That was all they needed to fight for the city.

Whose idea was that? Yellow is not a very popular fabric color, and all this took place before the Democratic Revolution Party (PRD) made it the color of their emblem. If they'd chosen green, there would have been more than enough flags to cut strips from. But historical contingencies make for capricious decisions. Was a hard-to-find color chosen to present us with a challenge? Was seeking elusive yellow fabric a cabalistic idea for conjuring danger? The fact is that México, the Federal District, transformed into a miraculous place where rags of an absurd color appeared everywhere, as if grandmothers of various generations had stored them away along with eternally single socks, only if by chance their descendants might need to show the rare heroism of being alive. If we could find thousands and thousands of yellow strips of cloth, we could be strong enough to save our city.

Meanwhile, Miguel de la Madrid decided that a natural disaster could project "a bad image" of Mexico. The president acted in a way consistent with a long tradition in the governments that defined the twentieth century in Mexico. He decided that the best way to fight a tragedy is to deny its existence. Against all logic, he rejected international cooperation in these terms: "We are prepared to deal with this situation, and we do not have to turn to external aid. Mexico has sufficient resources, and, together, people and government, we shall move forward. We are thankful for good intentions, but we are self-sufficient."

To what resources was he referring? The leader who three years later would orchestrate the most flagrant electoral fraud in our history had no idea what he was talking about. Without knowing the magnitude of the catastrophe, he refused to ask for help so as not to be seen as being vulnerable. In the megalomania of power, he declared: "We can do it on our own."

Meanwhile, in the corridors of the university stadium, one thing was clear: we'd have to fight tooth and nail to save the city.

Reports came in over the radio from the most damaged areas. Brigades were organized to go to Colonia Roma. The mountain climbers would scale buildings using ropes and the volunteers armed with shovels would work at the street level.

With that strategy in hand, we boarded a van. We didn't know one another; we had no idea what we were capable of doing. We were there, hours after an earthquake, in a city where urgency became collective. What united us? At a distance, it seems absurd to have relied on something so precarious, but in the sincerity of the moment, a talisman filled us with confidence; we had a yellow rag tied around our arms.

The Secret War in Mexico

On the way to Colonia Roma, we talked about omens and premonitions. When viceroys governed New Spain, eclipses and comets were seen as portents of tragedy. In 1985, Halley's Comet made its terrestrial visit. Its previous arrival, in 1910, announced the Revolution. My grandmother saw it in Yucatán when she was eleven years old. She also met Francisco I. Madero at a meeting. The apostle of democracy gave her a kiss that branded her like the blazing heat that galvanized the nights in those days.

What was the return of the comet announcing? To commemorate the seventy-fifth anniversary of the Revolution, celebrations and cultural displays were prepared. I wrote a cinematic adaptation of the historic episode known as "the Zimmermann telegram." During the First World War, Germany offered help to Mexico so it could recover the territory lost to the United States. The motive was not philanthropic: if the Americans were enmeshed in a struggle inside their own nation, they couldn't take part in the European war. The offer was made by the German minister of foreign affairs, Arthur Zimmermann, and became linked to his name. Venustiano Carranza's government rejected the "aid." The historians Barbara Tuchman and Friedrich Katz had done an exceptional job in retelling the events I was adapting to the screen. The production was to be paid by the Secretariat of Foreign Relations. Our intention was to present the hidden side of Mexican diplomacy during the Revolution, appropriating Katz's suggestive title: *The Secret War in Mexico*. The script opened with Halley's Comet in 1910, a harbinger of the revolt, and ended with its return in 1985, symbol of the unfinished business of an interrupted revolution.

Writing that script put me in touch with the madness and the ineffectiveness of governmental administration. It all began with the outlandish demagoguery Mexican functionaries use to appear grand: "Don't hold back, we have resources; if you need a scene shot from a helicopter, do it; we know that today's movies require money; there's cash to deal with any eventuality; if you have to stage a battle, do it." Like so many official projects, this monument to ambition was empty.

The earthquake of 1985 revealed the graft which had allowed schools, hospitals, and apartment buildings to be built using government money but without watching over the foundations. The most important part of a public building is the plaque that tells who inaugurated it. What you don't see (the structural materials) is consigned to oblivion.

Public buildings usually follow the method used to build castles out of playing cards. Our film was to be shown in November. By September, the functionaries had discovered that their grandeur did not measure up to the costly real world. Adapting history to the screen was less complicated than adapting it to the budget. A combat sequence was progressively pauperized. From a warlike fantasy in the style of *Lawrence of Arabia* we descended to a meeting of the General Staff in a palace, with generals who climbed out of period coaches. Then Foreign Relations discovered it really didn't have money for carriages or majestic locations, and the "battle" became a kind of roundtable discussion where the military men argued.

The real "secret war in Mexico" is about the management of public funds. The devastation of the city forced a reconsideration: the festivals of the seventy-fifth anniversary of the Revolution represented a squandering of money that had to be stopped. The production was canceled. They did manage to pay me for the "initial treatment" of the script, but—metaphor of metaphors—the check got lost in one of the Foreign Relations offices in Tlatelolco, which was damaged by the earthquake. Finding it was just as difficult as finding the birth certificate of Doroteo Arango—better known as Pancho Villa.

During the second half of the twentieth century, public works followed a process similar to that of our film: the promises were superior to the possibility of ever putting them into practice, and a class of instant millionaires deposited into their accounts the budget for railings.

In 1985, the Juárez Apartment Complex, the Tlatelolco Residential Building, the General Hospital, the offices of the Chancellery, the offices of Social Security next to the Monument to the Revolution, and other buildings inaugurated as symbols of public pride failed to conform to safety codes. That stone demagoguery was destined either to collapse or be abandoned.

La Calle del Oro

As we traveled north in the van, someone talked about Halley's Comet and the curious fact that the comet's tail was invisible. Since superstitions engender imaginative classifications, another volunteer said, with absolute conviction: "If the comet is there, but you can't see its tail, tragedy is a certainty." On that ride, with no other information than conjecture, we listened to him as if he were Nostradamus.

Little by little, the city confirmed his idea. We passed from a figurative landscape to another that was growing progressively abstract. On Avenida Insurgentes, at Colonia Roma, we found buildings that were still standing but which had lost their outer walls. So, from the street it was possible to see kitchens, clothing in closets, and furniture, as if we were looking a doll house. Other structures were reduced to rubble. Piles of debris blocked traffic. Among the houses there were impromptu vacant lots, amorphous holes, craters, cavities. The van was smashing glass as it went on. The air smelled of gas.

In his long poem "Red Earth," Francisco Segovia imagines the surprises of an expedition to Mars. Face-to-face with the undecipherable strangeness of the landscape, he exclaims:

> The stones of this land
> Are not native

There's no better way to describe what we felt when we reached the Calle del Oro, which links Avenida Insurgentes to the Miravalle roundabout. Scattered everywhere, broken, definitively alien, the stones *were not from there*.

I don't know why we were dropped off on that corner. The name couldn't be more ironic. What wealth could we find on the Calle del Oro ("the Street of Gold")? The climbers went on, making for Plaza Río de Janeiro, where they would scale buildings from which people couldn't escape. Our mission consisted of turning a chaotic mound of debris into orderly piles of debris, to transform improbable chunks into comprehensible chunks.

I climbed up a mound about three meters high. After a little digging, I found a bill with the building's address. I was on the remains of a sixth floor. The building had collapsed into three meters of rubble.

Not far from there, at the General Hospital, an international team of doctors was faced with a greater challenge without government support on another sixth floor. The Gynecological-Obstetrics Unit had fallen down, burying twenty-five doctors and one hundred patients. One female doctor was still alive, pinned down by a beam.

In *Nothing, Nobody: The Voices of the Earthquake,* Elena Poniatowska captured the scene, narrated by Marie-Pierre Toll. To free the young doctor from the beam would require an engineering team, and she was badly hurt. For twenty-eight hours, her colleagues kept her alive with transfusions, until they finally got her out. One of the volunteers who took part in the rescue said he stayed there for so long surrounded by ruins that could collapse at any moment because he knew that the other doctors who worked in the Gynecological-Obstetrics Unit were already dead. Among them, Xavier Cara, one of my best friends as a teenager, but at the time I didn't know that. While we were digging away on the Calle del Oro, a group of surgeons was trying to save a doctor in the name of all those who'd already died.

We worked for hours without producing major results. We moved pieces of cement, papers, the arm of a chair, the propeller from a fan, isolated forms, parts of something, useless fragments. We took them to a cart and piled them up on the street, where others tried to put them into some kind of order. We constructed ruins to save ourselves from ruin.

Did all that work matter? We rescued no one, and perhaps we only rescued ourselves by convincing ourselves that we could react, do something useful. Or maybe all that did not happen totally in vain.

Others plan and decide battles, but afterward someone has to pick up the pieces. Peace begins with street people who take charge of the debris, pick up shoes, buttons, broken combs, useless weapons, things that before had a meaning and a destiny. That was us, the garbage people, the people of filth, waste, detritus, people who carry bits and pieces from one place to another in an insistent litany of objects.

At what moment does serenity reclaim its rights? Suddenly, something definitive is revealed. Filth worked over so many times becomes a form of calm, and the fatigue of those who have no other answer than fatigue acquires another meaning and indicates that there is no longer any war and that peace is possible because we're breathing something different and blessed: the air smells of soup.

Goethe wrote a unique chronicle about the Franco-Prussian War in which he interviewed a German soldier who was convinced that his army would lose the war. What prophecy guided him? That soldier had had the opportunity to taste the soup of his enemies. Amid the labors and rigors of the campaign, he discovered to his shock that the man in charge of the enemy bivouac had seasoned the soup with exquisite care. It was impossible to conquer troops fed with such tasty soup.

In *War and Peace,* Tolstoy put into practice the technique of "infinitesimal proximity" to explain the details that secretly define history and which Goethe confirmed in his article. At about six p.m. a lady touched my shoulder: "Take this, blondie." She held out a plastic glass. It contained pastina, with the pasta in the shape of seeds. Nothing ever tasted better to me. The name of the street took on another meaning because of those seeds: the gold of the city was made up of its remains.

The Mole Man

The true heroes were elsewhere. My friend A., a high school classmate, dedicated himself to rescuing people in spaces he could only enter by risking either his life or one of his body parts. He wrote his name and telephone number on his extremities in case he lost one. On the many occasions when we talked about how he would lower himself into the spontaneous crypts formed by building collapses, I've been shocked by the neutral tone in which he narrates his daring feats. That apparently utter calm does not derive from an emotional deficit or some arrogant indifference in the face of danger but from his firm belief that survival is a technique, something that depends on practical decisions, never some sudden fury.

When he was an adolescent, A. was indifferent to his studies and faced life with a curious calm, but critical moments require a special temperament, and he demonstrated an unusual ability to make decisions under pressure. The rescuer is not someone who looks for dangers without emotion; he's an analyst in a hurry.

Astronauts leave the earth's surface with the same fortitude as the mole men when they submerge themselves in ruins. The difference is that in space and within the spaceship there are instructions for doing things that don't happen in the tunnels formed by debris. In such circumstances, moving a brick can either free a body or cause another collapse. A. got used to making decisions that never depended on hunches. He saved lives by putting his own at risk, and something changed for him under the earth.

One of the most surprising consequences of the earthquake was that it created a network of solidarity that doesn't exist on ordinary days. In *The Plague (La Peste)*, Albert Camus wonders why we need tragedy on a grand scale for collective goodness to appear.

When there was no more light in Colonia Roma—my body in agony because of muscles I'd never used until then—I tried to find some way to get home. I was covered with dust from head to toe and barely had the strength to hold my shovel. A taxi stopped even though I didn't hail it: "Where to, young fellow?" "I don't have any money." "It's free." "I'm going all the way to Tlalpan." "All trips are free." The collective generosity didn't last long, but it didn't have to exist at all. Over the course of those days, we acquired an emergency personality, superior to our own.

Those who faced major risks were tested in a more demanding way, one that took them to a kind of spiritual conversion. The astronauts return to earth with a mystical air that makes them seem out of place: aeronautical engineers who suddenly talk like prophets. Something similar happened with the mole men. A. was no longer the same. He took on danger using rational calculations and kept calm in overwhelming circumstances. But suppressing nervousness conferred on him not only the possibility of staying alive but a strange pleasure. Surrounded by wreckage and beams on the point of collapse, he survived with the controlled tension of a Formula 1 driver or a war correspondent. When he came back to the surface, he found a dark, indifferent world alien to adrenaline.

Post-traumatic stress has been studied a great deal—the anguish clamped down during the drama then bursts out when you're safe. Sometimes the survivor feels guilty for not having died with his comrades. Arthur Koestler wrote a beautiful essay about a British pilot who broke all records of heroism but did not accept the undeserved condemnation of being alive and wanted instead to identify himself with his dead colleagues in a final suicide mission. Sometimes, for someone who has taken risk to its final consequences, life without danger has no flavor to it. This leads him to seek out unusual compensations. Which was what happened with A. I'm certainly simplifying his story, but the fact is that after his time as a mole man he increased the fascination for wild animals and for dealing with them, which he'd always had. There could be nothing more logical for a mole who returns to the surface than to fraternize with beasts.

Later, those activities landed him in jail, where he again changed, now with no hope of salvation. A hero of survival became a fragile, diminished man. Able to enter and exit a tunnel that collapsed seconds after his adventure, he was done in by the humiliation of prison.

When he got out of jail, we went to a Rolling Stones concert in the Foro Sol. I was with my son, thirteen at the time. As we left, we began to go up the overpass to cross Circuito Interior. There were too many people, and everyone was pushing. I wrapped my arms around my son to protect him from being punched, but it was A. who was most affected. He suffered a breakdown on the stairs and we had to walk down. The overcrowding put him back in his prison cell: "For a year, I couldn't hold my arm out without touching someone else."

We waited until the crowd left. Little by little, A. caught his breath, but his eyes were seeing the ignominy of the prison. Saving people had brought about an addiction to risk that he tried out with high-risk animals. A tiger knocked out two of his teeth, and a crocodile bit his foot. He trafficked in animals for impresarios and politicians. He fell into the roulette game of favors and influences, and at a certain moment he lost important support. His wild animal business was investigated and he ended up in prison.

The hands that had pulled people out from under rocks now trembled at any contact with strangers. We were the last to leave Foro Sol.

Nowadays, A. sells dogs, and every once in a while I buy one. I ask him for a Labrador and he gives me something similar that then grows like a strangely hairy dachshund. People who watch our insane transactions think he's cheating me. They don't know that I'm paying a hero.

Aftershocks

On September 20, at 7:39 p.m., there was a 5.6 magnitude quake. Even though it was much milder than the previous tremor, its psychological impact was greater. I'd just returned from my labors at the Calle del Oro, where I'd seen buildings seconds away from collapse. The second tremor was the shove that would end the city. I walked out onto the street, fell to my knees, and prayed.

The historian Antonio Rubial points out that during the times of the viceroys, the duration of tremors was measured in credos. The aftershock in my case lasted two "Our Fathers."

The second tremor was more frightening than damage-causing. The real aftershock was psychological, but not all the consequences were negative. A couple, friends of mine, had been trying for years to have a child. They'd been examined by doctors and everything physical was fine, but one of those mysterious traumas that influence the body blocked the pregnancy. On the night of the aftershock they made love. The sensation of danger had been so great and the certainty of being alive was so deep that they forgot their intimate terrors and became finally what they'd wanted to be from the beginning: two bodies adrift that joined together. Nine months later they had a little girl. Those of us who were their closest friends suggested they name her Aftershock. They refused to use that absurd name no matter how hard we argued that during the days of the earthquake the truth was identical to the absurd.

There was another kind of social aftershock. The aid that arrived late and against the will of the president went into the dark dead end of corruption. While I was in a doctor's waiting room, someone offered me Canadian blankets intended for the victims.

Luckily, other reactions involved ethics, though not always in ways that would calm you down. The earthquake brought about an obligatory examination of conscience among many. No one survives without giving or demanding explanations. Survivors are speculative: You could have died and you didn't, does it make sense to go on living as you are if the roof can fall in? Is it really worthwhile being with this person or that job in this city? Certain aftershocks bore the label "divorce," "career crisis," or "move."

Toward the end of September, I had dinner at the house of the poet and novelist Alejandro Sandoval. His birthday is on the 23rd and mine is on the 24th. The dinner couldn't be festive, but we got together anyway and I spoke about what I'd seen as a volunteer. Then I said something that Alejandro would remind me of years later. I said that the most serious aspect of the earthquake was not what we'd already lived through but the damage we would go on feeling over time. Those postponed consequences would be in hiding like some slow poison.

How many people had died without our knowing for certain? Surviving was a fluke. All you had to do was think about the utterly destroyed buildings where we'd spent long hours: the bar in the Hotel del Prado, the Regis movie theater, the INBA gallery on Calle de Dinamarca, the Súper Leche Café. On some other day, at some other time, we'd have died there. Who in fact had died? Sooner or later, someone would ask, "Do you remember So-and-So?" The drama deferred its effects and its aftershocks.

One of my best high school friends, also a classmate of A., was Xavier Cara. We both discovered our passion for literature at the same time, we both attended Miguel Donoso Pareja's workshop at the university, we both published stories in the *Shared Zeppelin* anthology, and we both memorized tales by Julio Cortázar using the mnemotechnic of idolatry. Xavier gave me a copy of Cortázar's *Hopscotch* with a dedicatory note as long as one of Cortázar's "skippable chapters." In it, he describes my physical being as a skinny kid, the pimples on my face, my "bourgeois intellectual" complex, the possible failure of our literary vocation and our political militancy, and the "pseudo-concretion" in which all our acts ended. We were virgins, minors, people with no compass. We hesitated about whether we should dedicate ourselves to writing or to medicine. We lived in a different age than Chekhov, and it seemed impossible to do both things. We suspected we could fail at both. But we were friends at an age when only friendship matters. In his dedicatory note, Xavier described a complicity he thought eternal, something logical, because when you're young everything is eternal.

Leaving Colegio Madrid, in the Mixcoac neighborhood, we would walk along Félix Cuevas toward Avenida Coyoacán. There Xavier would take the bus to Colonia Cárcel de Mujeres and I would take another to Del Carmen. On important days, we would share a slice of cake from Don Polo. Since we were just kids, we'd talk about what didn't happen: women or our ultimate vocation.

Xavier studied medicine, and I dedicated myself to writing. Life separated us with differing schedules, differing troubles, and all sorts of changes. In 1992, I published *Argón's Shot,* which is set in a hospital. In a vicarious way, I became a doctor through writing. I thought this was a good opportunity to look up my friend. It was then I found out he died seven years earlier while on duty at the General Hospital. As I worked through the successive drafts of the novel, I'd mentally dialogued with him, thinking about how he would judge different scenes, not knowing I was talking with a dead man.

It seemed absurd not to have looked him up before, to have taken for granted that we'd get together again. My sadness was mitigated by anger: Xavier Cara died because of the Mexican government's corruption. The Gynecological-Obstetrics Unit, intended to receive life, was built by acolytes of death. Upset by the news, I spoke of nothing else for many days. I ran into Alejandro Sandoval, and he reminded me that I'd said that the earthquake would never happen and that we'd still be in touch over the years.

Whenever I move—either to a new house or new country—the first thing I pack is my copy of *Hopscotch.* Cortázar's novel has aged, but the dedication is my principal fetish, a black box with a final message "A friend is someone who feels for you," written in high school handwriting.

What I'm writing here tries to confirm that.

The Implicit Lake

Carlos Monsiváis used to say that in the Mexican cultural world a person with fewer than eight different jobs qualifies as unemployed. The screen adaptation of *The Secret War in Mexico* took up part of my time, but I was also working in a more formal way in the Notimex agency, coordinating, under the temperamental orders of Alejandro Rossi, the syndicated writers service. After the earthquake, we requested an article from the geophysicist Cinna Lomnitz. According to his studies, the 1985 tremor was especially damaging because the seismic waves traveled in the same way they would in the drainage area of a lake.

Built originally over water, Mexico City is sinking into a swampy subsoil. We know this, but we still live in the superstition that we are on solid ground. But geology has another memory and does not forget the lake bed. Our days flow by on an implicit lake.

On September 19, the lake did not return to the surface: its ghost returned. The seismic waves created the ebb and flow of a tide while our houses sank.

The majority of the world's capital cities grow up along a river, a lake, the sea, a shoreline. Does it make sense to build until we dry it all out? "The beach is under the cobble stones," was one of the sayings of the 1968 French student uprising. The phrase tried to return to the paradise destroyed by a sterile progress, a poetic gesture the equivalent of the epitaph the Chilean poet Vicente Huidobro created for himself:

> Open the grave:
> At the bottom of this grave
> > you can see the ocean.

Inventing oases is a rebellious gesture. Mexico City grew stimulated by the opposite principle. On our streets, the Parisian graffiti is painfully literal: the asphalt covers a lake.

Toward the end of *Nothing, Nobody: The Voices of the Earthquake,* Elena Poniatowska is gathering testimonies in a shelter. One of them contains a metaphor for building in the Federal District:

It's hard to convince that child over there in the corner to speak or eat. He lost his mother, his grandmother, and his four brothers. We think he lived in Colonia Roma. Yesterday, he began to play with some wooden blocks. He uses them to build a tower and then knocks it down. Fear and the absence of his family reduced the child to silence. Only his shaking hands could say something. The scattered blocks explained what being an orphan meant.

For years we were like that boy. We spoke little about the earthquake and wrote even less. Ignacio Padilla wrote a long essay about the absence of a literature about the 1985 tragedy, comparing it with the climate of negation that settled in postwar Germany and which W. G. Sebald described in *On the Natural History of Destruction*. The circumstances are very different. Conscious of their ignominious acts, Germans could not see themselves as victims of the annihilation. They couldn't even contemplate the ruined landscape. We chilangos don't suffer an equivalent shame. In any case, we could be proud to have responded when the government did not do so.

On May 31, 1986, Miguel de la Madrid opened the World Cup of Soccer at the Estadio Azteca. On that day the "earthquake party" made itself felt. Civil society subjected the president to a sudden plebiscite: those one hundred and ten thousand people gathered together in a celebration, and hearing the president's voice, burst out with a unanimous obscenity.

It wasn't shame that impeded an extensive earthquake literature. Perhaps it was modesty. In 1985, I finished my book *Time Past: Imaginary News,* which narrates eighteen Mexican years through imaginary news articles. The tragedy could have provided another conclusion, but I didn't want to modify the final story. In the prologue, I justified my decision: "I distrust those who in certain moments are more opinionated than fearful."

Yes, we were fearful, afraid of dying, afraid that others might have died, afraid to express our fear. Being weak requires courage. If the president wanted to hide his vulnerability, we should learn to be vulnerable.

We turned to folkloric techniques to detect earthquakes: we hung forks from the ceiling. If they started banging into one another, we'd have to run out of the house.

Sometimes we suffered imaginary tremors. We would place a glass of water on the dresser to measure our nervousness. If we felt some shock, we'd glance at the glass. If the water was still, the problem wasn't the earth but ourselves.

The person whose alarm system is some forks and a spoon hanging from the ceiling: what authority does he have to explain his survival? The earthquake revealed corruption plots and confirmed the ineffectiveness of the government. Many things could be criticized. Beyond that, there was something more profound, the sensation of being helpless, the essentially precarious nature of breathing every day. It's hard to talk about that. In a genuine, animal sort of way we knew we were impotent. The earthquake taught us a basic lesson, as old as the first human settlement: we are not the owners of the city. Sure, we can fight with the debris so the city can exist. It's our identification card as citizens: you belong to the place where you're prepared to clean away the shit.

Like Francisco Segovia on his imaginary trip to Mars, on September 19, 1985, we found out that the stones of this land are not native to it, but we are.

Ceremonies

The Aftershock, a Postscript to Fear

On September 19, 2017, Mexico City swayed in another tremor. Thirty-two years after the earthquake of 1985 we had yet another date with uncertainty. Once again, we turned out for rescue work, gathering food, calling for donations, and once again civil society was more efficient than official initiatives. This time, the government wasn't absent, as it was in the days of Miguel de la Madrid, but in no way was it the leader of the resistance. Strictly speaking, we showed the virtues of anarchism, a concept that because of ideological distortion is linked to chaos, when in fact it implies an order without authority.

Almost four decades after the first tragedy, we were still in the city. What explains this will to remain? The Lisbon earthquake led Rousseau to reflect on the risks of being part of an environment and assuming that the objects that surround us are more important than our lives:

> Without abandoning the theme of Lisbon, you will recognize, for example, that it was not nature that brought together in that place twenty thousand houses of six or seven floors and that, if the inhabitants of that city had been more scattered and more lightly housed, the damages would either have been lessened or non-existent. Everyone would have fled, and by the next day would have been seen twenty leagues from there and so happy.

But people must stay, must insist on poking about in the ruins, exposing themselves to fresh tremors, because what is left there is worth more than whatever anyone could carry away!

Rousseau criticizes the risky and capricious style of building in cities. It is not nature that piles one story on top of another. The 2017 earthquake again revealed that in Mexico, buildings are put up outside the norms (with tragic consequences, that is how many of our schools are built). The capital has been the victim of long-term real estate speculation. Every large piece of property that comes onto the market becomes an immense shopping mall. That's what happened with Parque Delta, the city's principal baseball stadium, and that's what will happen to Estadio Azul, the municipal baseball stadium. When the airport moves over to Texcoco, we'll see glittering logos of the transnational franchises pop up on the old runways. Along just two kilometers of Avenida Universidad there are at least six cathedrals of commerce, as if the city had no other meaning but sales.

By the same token, more buildings over twenty stories are being constructed on terrain softened by mud and subject to seismic shifts. Increased population density will make the traffic even more insufferable. The main motivating force behind this overwhelming expansion is the economic benefit urban developers reap and the resulting support they contribute to those who govern the city and hope to govern the nation.

The earthquake constituted a demolishing criticism of the absurd way construction is carried out. Rousseau is right again: it isn't nature that puts women and men at risk but the way in which they live together. Fond of the solitary life, the author of *Emile* gradually stepped away from worldly tasks and deplored the fact that people remain in cities, tied to their belongings. "How many unfortunate people perished in that disaster because they tried, this one to grab a suit, this other his papers, this other his money!" Greed clouds your eyes.

Nevertheless, even though Rousseau denounces the madness of running unnecessary risks, he also shows, contradicting his intentions, that a person is worth the same as his context. Saving your skin is important, but doing so is impoverishing if it means losing not only your property but something more profound: memories, personal histories, the collective chorus that makes us what we are. The will to remain can be the result of our greed in not wanting to lose what is ours but also, and this is the meaningful part, a peculiar altruism: accepting the fact that the city does not belong to us but, rather, that we belong to it.

September 19 was a Tuesday. Two days later, I was supposed to turn in my weekly column for the newspaper *Reforma*. The only subject I could think about was the earthquake. The editor, Ricardo Cayuela Gally, and his family had moved into my house after losing their apartment in Colonia Condesa. We improvised our daily routine as best we could. My daughter, Inés, insisted—quite properly—on helping people more in need. She found a shelter station for Jojutla in Morelos, to which we brought food and medicine and, through the painter Francisco Toledo and Almadía Editions, we channeled aid to victims in Oaxaca.

It was in that context that I had to turn in my article. I didn't feel able to make an analysis of what happened and telling my personal experiences seemed trivial to me, less important than the experiences of others. At the same time, I recalled another phrase that materialized in the days after the earthquake I suffered through in Chile in 2010 and which caused me to write my book *8.8: Fear in the Mirror (8.8: El miedo en el espejo)*: "No one survives in silence." After a tragedy, language is like the mixed-up alphabet of a typewriter: it first appears as disorder, but little by little it takes shape in order to give meaning to something devoid of meaning. We speak in order to understand something that challenges understanding. Exercising more superstition than certainty, we think that if we can say something, we can also overcome something. Words heal.

José Woldenberg, who publishes in *Reforma* one day before I do, confessed he could only think about the tragedy and that he had nothing to contribute at that moment. In order not to sidestep his responsibility as a weekly contributor, he quoted passages from Mario Haucuja's book *Earthquakes*.

I considered describing the primary gesture made during the rescue work. One volunteer would raise a fist, and the others would fall silent in order to listen for any signs of life. That gesture of solidarity was the determining factor in our common life: to open a space in order to hear someone else, the victim, the person most in need.

Nevertheless, instead of creating a narrative out of that scene, I chose to set it out in the style of a litany, disconnected phrases that would repeat a single theme. I did not intend to write a poem, though many people read it that way. If I had to choose a genre for that text, I wouldn't pick a literary genre but one that was seismological: it was an aftershock. I began with a phrase I'd written when I remembered the 1985 earthquake thirty years after the tragedy, and which appears on page 340 of this book: "you belong to the place where you're prepared to clean away the shit." In a more or less sleepwalking state, I wrote a heterodox column my colleagues at *Reforma* helped me fit to the page, requesting the necessary words to fill in the space.

It was a circumstantial text, like any other. The poet Pedro Serrando, who wrote a beautiful essay about "The Raised Fist," reminded me that, after all is said and done, all writing follows the peculiar contingency that provokes it.

No one can calculate either the resonance or the oblivion in which certain words fall. "The Raised Fist" ceased to belong to me the moment it was published. Those who made it their own showed that all language is collective, that there are no individual literatures, and that the ultimate meaning of a text depends not on the person who writes it but on the one who reads it.

It was hard for me to finish this book. Mexico City is an inexhaustible encyclopedia. Even though I proposed giving up a will to completeness, I yielded again and again to the temptation of adding more details to my portrait of the monster. But living in this valley surrounded by volcanoes means understanding that there are external limits. I didn't know how to write the last word to my work, but the earth itself did.

My farewell is this litany:

The Raised Fist

You are from the place where you gather garbage.
Where lightning strikes the same place twice.
Because you saw the first, you're waiting for the second.
And you're still here.
Where the earth splits open and where people join together.

Once again you arrive late:
You're alive because you're unpunctual, because you didn't make
    the meeting

that death set up for you at 1:14
thirty-two years after the other meeting which you also
didn't get to on time.
You are the omitted victim.
The building shook and you did not see your life flash before
    your eyes,
as happens in movies.
You felt pain in a part of your body you didn't know existed:
The skin of memory, which brought no scenes of
your life but only the crunch of matter.
The water also remembered what it was when it was the owner
of this place.
It shook in the rivers.
It shook in the houses we invented in the rivers.
You picked up the books from another time, the person you were
long before those pages.
It never rains but it pours
    after the national holidays,
      closer to revelry than grandeur.
    Is there space for the heroes in September?
    You are afraid.
    You are brave enough to be afraid.
    You don't know what to do but you do something.
    You neither founded the city nor did you defend it from
      invaders.

You are, if that, a beggar of history.
    The one who picks up the trash after the tragedy.
    The one who piles bricks,
    gathers stones,
    finds a comb,
    two shoes from different pairs,
    a wallet containing photos
    The one who puts scattered. parts in order,
    pieces of pieces,
    remains, only remains.
    Whatever your hands can hold.

You are the one who has no gloves.
    The one who distributes water.
    The one who gives away his medicine because his
horror is cured.
    The one who saw the moon and dreamed strange things but
didn't know how to interpret them.
    The one who heard his cat meow an hour before and only
understood it at the first shock, when the water
flowed out of the toilet.
    The one who prayed in a strange language because he'd forgotten
how to pray.
    The one who remembered who was in which place.
    The one who went to get his children at school.
    The one who thought about people who had children at school.
    The one who was left without batteries.
    The one who went out onto the street to lend his cell phone.
    The one who entered an abandoned shop to steal
and repented in a mall.
    The one who knew he was superfluous.
    The one who was awake so the others could sleep.

He who is from here.
    He who just arrived and is already from here.
    He who says "city" meaning you and I
and Pedro and Marta and Francisco and Guadalupe.
    He who's gone two days without light or water.
    He who's still breathing.
    He who raised a fist to ask for silence.
    Those who kept that silence.
    Those who raised their fists.
    Those who raised their fist to listen for someone living.
    Those who raised their fist to listen for someone living
and heard a whisper.
    Those who do not stop listening.

A NOTE ABOUT THE AUTHOR

Juan Villoro, born in Mexico City in 1956, is Mexico's preeminent novelist. Author of half a dozen prize-winning novels, Villoro is also a professional journalist. Trained as a sociologist, he has been well known among intellectual circles in Mexico, Latin America, and Spain for years, but his success among a wider readership has grown since receiving the Herralde Prize for his novel *El testigo* (The Witness).

A NOTE ON THE TYPE

This book was set in a version of the well-known Monotype face Bembo. This letter was cut for the celebrated Venetian printer Aldus Manutius by Francesco Griffo and first used in Pietro Cardinal Bembo's *De Aetna* of 1495. The companion italic is an adaptation of the chancery script type designed by the calligrapher and printer Lodovico degli Arrighi.

Composed by North Market Street Graphics,
Lancaster, Pennsylvania

Printed and bound by Friesens,
Altona, Manitoba

Designed by Cassandra J. Pappas

972 Villoro Juan
Villoro, Juan,
Horizontal vertigo :
22960002124138